LESTER DEKOSTER holds the B.A. degree from Calvin College and the M.A. degree both in philosophy and in library science from the University of Michigan. Before wartime duty as a Communications Officer in the Naval Air Transport, he taught several years in a large high school. Following the war he became Assistant Professor of Speech at Calvin College. In 1951 he was appointed Director of the Library at Calvin College and Seminary. He is one of the editors of *The Reformed Journal*, is an active Democrat, and frequently lectures on Communism as well as on Christian education. He resides with his wife and four children in Grand Rapids, Michigan.

Vocabulary of Communism

"We hold these truths to be self-evident: that all men are created equal, that they are endowed by their Creator with certain inalienable rights, that among these are life, liberty and the pursuit of happiness...."
—Declaration of Independence

"The socialist revolution marks the end of the history of exploiting class society that has lasted for thousands of years, the liberation of society from all forms of oppression, the beginning of an epoch of genuine brotherhood, of equality among peoples, the establishment of eternal peace on earth, the complete social regeneration of humanity."
—Fundamentals of Marxism-Leninism

"The aim of my writings and lectures is this: to turn men from theologians into anthropologists, from lovers of God into lovers of humanity, from candidates for the hereafter into students of the here and now, from lackeys of a heavenly and earthly monarchy and aristocracy into free, self-respecting citizens of the world."
—Feuerbach, Lectures on the Essence of Religion

VOCABULARY
OF COMMUNISM

Definitions of key terms, summaries of central ideas,
Short biographies of leading figures,
Descriptions of significant things and events

by

Lester DeKoster

Director of Calvin Library
Calvin College and Seminary

William B. Eerdmans Publishing Company
Grand Rapids, Michigan

*for Leslie, Paul, Mark, Stephen
and Ruth*

Preface

FROM ALL SIDES AMERICANS ARE URGED TO STUDY AND TO MASTER Communism and the Marxist theories which underlie it. When we do so, we find that Communism has a vocabulary of its own. Not only does it have its own technical terms and foreign names, but it takes words in common use and pours its own uncommon meanings into them. The study of Communism becomes, therefore, not only difficult but misleading.

The purpose of this handbook is to assist the student of Marxism-Leninism, as the Communist now calls the theories underlying the Communist movement, to a better understanding of the words, phrases, men, and movements he encounters in his reading. In Section I, it defines, often by quotations from the sources, the key terms used by Marxist writers as they use them; it summarizes the central ideas, from Marx to Khrushchev, in the development of the Communist system and its variations; it gives short biographies of the leading figures; and it describes the significant things and events of Communist history.

The handbook is not for the expert, but for the non-specialist student, especially one who is for the first time or nearly the first, making his way through Marxism. Such a Vocabulary as this could, of course, be expanded to the size of an encyclopedia. Wherever the line is drawn, some words, persons, and events fall on the farther side; but most of the definitions and identifications which the general student of Marxism is likely to need are, I trust, included.

Following the alphabetically arranged entries (Section I), the basic works of Marxism, which I call the classics of Marxism, are briefly annotated (Section II), as are those critical works which might be called anti-Marxist "classics" (Section III).

The student will remember that this is a handbook to the study of Marxism, *not* to its refutation. My criticisms of it have appeared in another volume, *Communism and Christian Faith,* which can be studied along with this by those who wish to do so. However, to set a perspective in which Marxism-Leninism may be engaged, I have introduced this volume with an essay comparing the basic document of American liberties with the basic document of Communism — the *Declaration of Independence* contrasted with the *Communist Manifesto.*

—LESTER DEKOSTER

Contents

Introduction

Two Documents in Conflict

THERE IS GOOD REASON WHY MR. J. EDGAR HOOVER AND MANY OTHER eminent Americans advise their fellow citizens to learn to know Communism well — an end to which this *Vocabulary* seeks to make its own modest contribution. Mastery *over* an enemy frequently depends upon mastery *of* him and what he believes. Moreover, today the world hangs poised over a choice between two ways of life, both of which Americans ought profoundly to understand — the democratic way of life and its Communist competitor.

In a real way, two historic documents vie today for the allegiance of men. One of these documents is the American *Declaration of Independence;* the other is the *Communist Manifesto*. The fateful choice between them will write the political history of the next quarter of this century. What we as Americans know of both documents will equip us the better for leadership at home and abroad, as the choices are being made.

There are some striking similarities between the *Declaration* and the *Manifesto*. Both are revolutionary documents. They possess, that is, the mysterious keys to men's hearts; they tap human will; they focus aspiration; they release vast quantities of men's energies. They are, I say, revolutionary, in intent and in effect. So it has been in history.

Again, both are futuristic documents. They point a way into tomorrow. If they look back, it is only for guideposts to what lies ahead. They have an eye for the horizon, and are restless with today.

Once more, both are humanistic documents. That is, they are concerned with man, and man's liberties and well-being. Both were struck off the hard anvil of oppression as instruments of liberty and justice.

Struck off, indeed. For both were written in the passion of haste,

11

and on commission, by relatively youthful men, impatient to right wrongs and better men's lot. The Continental Congress appointed a Committee of five to draft the *Declaration,* and one of these, Thomas Jefferson, age 33, produced the basic draft in forty-eight hours. The Young Communist League of London appointed a committee of two, Karl Marx and Frederick Engels, aged 29 and 27 respectively, to draft its *Manifesto,* which they did in a matter of days.

Thus it was that in 1776 and in 1848 two documents, of seemingly similar character and intent, were thrust into history. There were consequences, of immeasurable significance to mankind, to you and to me. These consequences are writ large in our times, and cannot be missed — though they can be misunderstood — even by him who runs. The political order founded upon the *Declaration,* while never perfect and often more than falling short of its own aspirations, has sanctioned a degree and an extent of liberty and justice among men hitherto unknown. The political order founded upon the *Manifesto,* though boasting substantial technical achievements, has crushed liberty and justice to a degree and an extent unparalleled. So it has been in history.

Why should this sharp contrast have arisen? Why is it that in so far as men have been *true* to the *Declaration,* liberty has flourished; while in so far as men have been *true* to the *Manifesto,* tyranny has triumphed?

Probably several answers could be adduced, but consider one fundamental distinction between these two apparently similar documents. It is this: the *Declaration* ascribes human rights to man's Creator. You know the language it uses:

> We hold these truths to be self-evident: that all men are created equal, that they are endowed by their Creator with certain inalienable rights. . . .

The *Manifesto,* on the other hand, challenges man to carve out his own rights, validate his own liberties. You may know the language it uses:

> The Communists disdain to conceal their views and aims. They openly declare that their ends can be attained only by the forcible overthrow of all existing social conditions. The proletarians have nothing to lose but their chains. They have a world to win. Working men of all countries, unite!

If history declares anything, it fairly screams that men who set upon carving out their own rights resort always to brutality, secret police, and firing squads to assist in the process; and the rights of the few — tenuous as they are — are won at the expense of the many. So Russia, China, Cuba teach us. Communist man climbs grimly toward his freedom on the backs, and over the bleaching bones, of his fellows. Rights resting solely on human validation are always of limited degree and extent — they rise, that is, only to the height that sheer force propels them, and they extend only to those who share in in controlling that force. So it is in history.

The rights envisioned by the *Declaration*, on the contrary, are of *unlimited* degree and extent "Inalienable" in degree — that is, no one may steal them, nor may the holder sell them. And universal in extent — "all men," *no less* than "all men"!

But why "inalienable" and why "all men"? Oddly enough — at first blush — the rights spoken of by the *Declaration* are universal, and inherent in man, just because the *Declaration* does not think of man as a *carver of* destiny, but as a *creature with* a destiny. A creature receives according to his Creator's pleasure; he is stuck with what he gets. But he is also inalienably in possession of what he gets. The potter, to use an ancient example, makes vessels out of clay. He fashions them to the shapes and uses of his choice. And, behold, precisely because the potter's vase is a creature, so it confronts every other vase with a character indelibly its own; no number, however large, of other vases can give this character, or rightfully take it away. Supposing we were gifted to hear one vase saying to another, as they stand on the shelf, "I have this shape, this function, this character as my own, because they were given me by the Potter!" And listen, then, as every other vase responds, exultantly, *"And so have I!"*

This is what the *Declaration* says in imperishable prose, and in so saying it rises to absolute first rank among the political documents of man. It says that because we are creatures, we possess rights which no other man, or combination of men, may transgress. We have rights which need not be carved out by the destruction of "existing social conditions," and cannot be invalidated by concentration camps. What the Creator has given, the creature *has*; and woe to those who conspire to take such rights away. So it is in fact.

And when men are *true,* therefore, to the spirit of the *Declaration,* what must inevitably happen? Human rights are honored, equality is respected, and liberty and justice flourish. So, we may humbly but proudly insist, it has been in much of American history, and is now.

True it is that some men quite deliberately, and all of us thoughtlessly from time to time, grossly belie our own *Declaration*. Seemingly, the "inalienable" rights *are* alienated, bruised, destroyed. It is an ancient and mysterious fact that the creature wills to play the Creator, leaving havoc in his wake. But the penalty is immediate, as well as eternal. Unhappy is the people where rights are without respect; uneasy rests the head which boasts the tyrant's crown.

And never more uneasy than when the boast is made in the language of the *Manifesto*. Was ever tyrant more suspicious than Stalin? Or ever did one commit progressively more appalling crimes to appease those done before? The creature who will, by destruction of society, master his own fate is mastered as no other man by his own engines of destruction. And thus it is, that when men are *true* to the *Manifesto*, death stalks the land and haunts their dreams.

Our challenge, then, this day is not one to carve out our destinies in defiance of our times; this method requires hangmen and torture chambers. Rather, our task is to realize, by profound respect, the rights inherent in all men, and thus, incidentally, to recognize these rights in ourselves. Only thus will we "sell" the *Declaration* to a waiting and watching world. So may it be in history!

Let us remember that the Communist leadership pays our *Declaration* the marked, though grudging, respect of never once taking the risk that their people have unfettered opportunity to choose between it and the *Manifesto* at the ballot box, propagandized and enslaved as their people are. Secure in this heritage, then, let us live out of it, cherish it, preserve it, enrich it. And resting upon it, let us master as best we can that Marxist, alien doctrine, to understand as profoundly as we may what it is in these two competitors that makes the *Declaration* a beacon to justice and freedom and the *Manifesto* "darkness at noon."

I have not thought it necessary to append to each Marxist definition in this vocabulary the disclaimer that it is, perhaps, a misuse of a term, or contrary to practice, or is likely to mislead. I have tried to give an honest representation of the meanings which Marxist terms have for the Marxist, not only to be helpful in the understanding of Marxism, but also to save the beginner from the serious mistake of pouring "our" meanings into "their" terminology. For between our way of life, and theirs, from which words, too, take on their meaning, there is a great gulf fixed, measured by our contrasting appreciations of God, nature, and man.

Student's Guide to Key Concepts

Some "little old lady" is supposed to have said that reading the dictionary is interesting but slightly disconnected. For the student who wishes a thread to guide him through a more "connected" survey of the basic Marxist terms discussed in this *Vocabulary,* the following lists are offered as suggestions.

COMMUNISM AS AN ECONOMIC SYSTEM

Read the following entries, in the order suggested:

MARXISM
SOCIALISM/COMMUNISM
LABOR THEORY OF VALUE
BOURGEOISIE
PROLETARIAT
WAGES
SURPLUS VALUE
EXPLOITATION
CLASS STRUGGLE
THEORY OF IMPOVERISHMENT
CAPITAL
CONSTANT CAPITAL
VARIABLE CAPITAL
PRIMITIVE ACCUMULATION
IMPERIALISM
CLASSLESS SOCIETY
COMMUNISM
UTOPIA

COMMUNISM AS A PHILOSOPHICAL SYSTEM

Read the following entries, in the order suggested:

MARXISM
MATERIALISM

15

MATERIALISM, HISTORICAL
DIALECTICS
METAPHYSICS
THESIS-ANTITHESIS-SYNTHESIS
NEGATION
NEGATION OF THE NEGATION
CONTRADICTION
PARTISANSHIP
OBJECTIVISM
LEAP
FEUERBACH
HEGEL
MAN
NEW MAN
MORALITY

COMMUNISM AS A POLITICAL SYSTEM

Read the following entries, in the order suggested:

PARTY
PARTY-LINE
REVOLUTION
REVOLUTIONARY DICTATORSHIP OF THE
    PROLETARIAT
PERMANENT REVOLUTION
SOCIALISM IN ONE COUNTRY
DEMOCRATIC CENTRALISM
STATE
FEBRUARY REVOLUTION
RUSSIAN REVOLUTION
SOVIET UNION
REVISIONISM
CHINESE-RUSSIAN SPLIT

Other appropriate entries will probably catch the eye as the reading progresses, and the asterisks in each entry can be followed through.

List of Abbreviations

NOTE: IF ONLY ONE WORK BY A GIVEN AUTHOR IS CITED, REFERENCE TO this work is made by author's name, volume number, and page number. If two or more works by a given author are cited, reference to these is made by author's name, title abbreviation, volume number, and page number.

Bochenski, J. M. and Blakely, T. J., eds.		*Studies in Soviet Thought.* Dordrech-Holland: Reidel, 1961.
Chernyshevsky, N. G.		*Selected Philosophical Essays.* Moscow: Foreign Languages Publishing House (F.L.P.H.), 1953.
Cole, G. H.		*History of Socialist Thought.* 4 vols. (in 6). London: Macmillan, 1953-58.
Crankshaw, E.		*The New Cold War, Moscow v. Peking.* London: Penguin, 1963.
Deutscher, I.		*Trotsky*: I. *The Prophet Armed.* New York: Oxford University Press, 1954. II. *The Prophet Unarmed.* New York: Oxford University Press, 1959.
Dutt, C., ed.		*Fundamentals of Marxism-Leninism.* Moscow: F.L.P.H., 1961.
Engels, F.	*A.-D.*	*Anti-Dühring.* Moscow: F.L.P.H., 1959.
	C.M.	*Communist Manifesto* with Marx). *Selected Works,* I, Moscow: F.L.P.H., 1958.
	D.N.	*Dialectics of Nature.* Moscow: F.L.P.H., 1954.

	G.I.	*German Ideology* (with Marx). New York: International, 1947.
	MEGA	*Marx-Engels Historisch-Kritische Gesamtausgabe.* Moscow: Marx-Lenin Institute, 1927–.
	Rem.	*Reminiscences of Marx and Engels.* Moscow: F.L.P.H., n.d.
	S.C.	*Selected Correspondence of Marx and Engels.* New York: International, 1942.
	S.W.	*Selected Works of Marx and Engels.* 2 vols. Moscow: F.L.P.H., 1958.
Gunther, J.		*Inside Russia Today.* New York: Harper, 1958.
Heilbroner, R.		*The Worldly Philosophers.* New York: Simon and Schuster, 1953.
Hook, S.		*Marx and the Marxists.* New York: Van Nostrand, 1954.
Kalinin, M. I.		*On Communist Education.* Moscow: F.L.P.H., 1952.
Kautsky, K.		*The Labour Revolution.* London: Allen & Unwin, 1925
Kennan, G.		*Russian and the West Under Lenin and Stalin.* Boston: Little, Brown, 1960.
Krupskaya, N. K.		*Lenin.* Moscow: F.L.P.H., 1959.
Lenin, V.	*A.R.*	*Against Revisionism.* Moscow: F.L.P.H., 1959.
	K.M.	*Karl Marx.* Moscow: F.L.P.H., n.d.
	L.-W.C.	*Left-wing Communism, an Infantile Disorder.* Moscow: F.L.P.H., n.d.
	M.E.-C.	*Materialism and Empirio-Criticism,* Moscow: F.L.P.H., n.d.
	P.N.	*Philosophical Notebooks. Collected Works,* 38. Moscow: F.L.P.H., 1961.
	P.R.	*Proletarian Revolution and the Renegade Kautsky.* Moscow: F.L.P.H., 1952.

	S.R.	*State and Revolution.* Moscow: F.L.P.H., n.d.
	Works	*Collected Works.* Moscow: F.L.P.H., in progress.
Marx, K.	*Cap.*	*Capital.* 3 vols. Moscow: F.L.P.H., 1957-61.
	C.G.P.	*Critique of the Gotha Program. Selected Works,* II.
	C.M.	*Communist Manifesto* (with Engels). *Selected Works,* I.
	G.I.	*German Ideology* (with Engels). New York: International, 1947.
	H.F.	*Holy Family* (with Engels). Moscow: F.L.P.H., 1956.
	P.P.	*Poverty of Philosophy.* Moscow: F.L.P.H., n.d.
	Rem.	*Reminiscences of Marx and Engels.* Moscow: F.L.P.H., n.d.
	S.C.	*Selected Correspondence of Marx and Engels.* New York: International, 1942.
	S.T.F.	*Second Thesis on Feuerbach. Selected Works,* I (*Theses on F.*).
	S.W.	*Selected Works of Marx and Engels.* 2 vols. Moscow: F.L.P.H., 1958.
Mehring, F.		*Karl Marx.* Ann Arbor Paperback, 1962.
Plekhanov, G.	*D.M.V.*	*Development of the Monist View of History.* Moscow: F.L.P.H., 1956.
	O.D.	*Our Differences. Selected Philosophical Works,* I. Moscow: F.L.P.H., n.d.
	R.I.H.	*Role of the Individual in History.* New York: International, 1940
Rostow, W. W.		*Dynamics of Soviet Society.* New York: New American Library, 1954.

Rothstein, G., ed.		*History of the Communist Party in the Soviet Union.* Moscow: F.L.P.H., 1960.
Stalin, J.	*D.H.M.*	*Dialectical and Historical Materialism. Works,* I. Moscow: F.L.P.H., 1952. New York, International, 1940.
	P.L.	*Problems of Leninism.* Moscow: F.L.P.H., 1945.
	S.W.	*Selected Works.* Moscow: F.L.P.H., n.d.
Strachey, J.		*Menace of Fascism.* New York: Covici-Fiede, 1933.
Trotsky, L.	*H.R.R.*	*History of the Russian Revolution.* 3 vols. New York: Simon and Schuster, 1932-34. (One vol. ed., Ann Arbor: University of Michigan Press, 1960).
	L.&R.	*Literature and Revolution.* New York: Russell, 1957.
	M.L.	*My Life.* New York: Grosset and Dunlap, 1960.
	T.I.L.	*Third International After Lenin.* New York: Pioneer, 1957.
Werth, A.		*Russia Under Khrushchev.* New York: Crest Books, 1962.
Wolfe, B.		*Three Who Made a Revolution.* Boston: Beacon, 1955.

Supplementary materials to this list, as well as to the volumes listed in Sections II and III of this volume, may be found in either or both of the following bibliographies:

R. N. Carew Hunt	*Books on Communism.* London: Ampersand, 1959.
Robert F. Delany	*The Literature of Communism in America.* Washington: Catholic University of America Press, 1962.

SECTION I

The Vocabulary

ABSOLUTE SURPLUS VALUE. "The *surplus-value produced by prolongation of the working-day, I call absolute surplus-value" (Marx, *Cap.*, I, 315). See *Relative Surplus Value; Surplus Value.*

ACCUMULATION. See *Primitive Accumulation; Primitive Socialist Accumulation.*

ADZHUBEI, ALEKSEI. Son-in-law of *Khrushchev and editor of the official Russian newspaper *Izvestia.* See *Press, Soviet.*

AESTHETICS, MARXIST. In this view beauty is objective; that is, it belongs to the object and not to the viewer's emotional response to his experience. Beauty also has a class basis, and what one class considers beautiful another class may think ugly, or common, as, for example, pale or ruddy cheeks, strong or delicate hands, etc. Judgments of beauty also vary as economic conditions change. Art comes under the "principle of *partisanship" in the sense that it, too, must advance the cause of the *proletariat, and "art for art's sake" is suspect.

AGITATION/PROPAGANDA. Agitation differs, in Marxist theory, from propaganda in the fact that the agitator presents one or a few ideas to many people, while the propagandist presents many ideas to one or a few persons. The agitator does not attempt to explain, *Lenin says, but only seeks to arouse emotions; the propagandist gives reasons and aims at developing understanding. A good propagandist, therefore, might not be a good agitator, and *vice versa.*

Proganda spreads ideas, while agitation aligns forces for action.

AGITPROP. The abbreviation for the Russian state bureau employed by the government for indoctrinating its own people with *Marxism-Leninism and the current *Party Line. Agitprop stands for *Agitation and Propaganda; it publishes a *Guide for the Propagandist and Agitator,* and keeps the *Guide* up to date with supplements which reflect the latest Party Line. Agitprop operates 6,000 or more schools to train its representatives, and has no less than 375,000 actively in the field. (See Gunther.)

ALIENATION (Estrangement). The philosophical doctrine, developed by the German thinker *Hegel, and used by *Marx in the form given it by the German theologian *Feuerbach, that spirit, or idea, alienates itself in matter. For example, the designer's idea of a table comes to expression in an actual table; the table is the opposite of the idea, for it is material. This is Hegel's use of the term. For Feuerbach, alienation means man's giving to the idea of God all of the attributes which really belong to man himself. Man's salvation depends upon his taking them back. Marx uses the term to indicate the worker's giving himself to his work. The thing he makes is, in fact, his alienated self; and thus *exploitation of the worker by taking from him unjustly any part of what he makes is really robbing the worker of his very self. Further, man finds out who and what kind of creature he is only by the self he finds alienated in the things he has made. "The object as being for man, as the objective being of man for other men, is at the same time the existence of man for other men, his human relation to other men, the social behavior of man in relation to man" (Marx, *H.F.*, 55).

ALL-RUSSIAN DEMOCRATIC CONFERENCE. See *Predparlament.*

ALL-RUSSIAN EXTRAORDINARY COMMISSION. Special Soviet police force organized in 1917 to combat counter-revolution and espionage, which became the dreaded *Cheka or secret police. Headed by F. E. *Dzerzhinsky.

ALL-UNION BUREAU OF RUSSIAN SOCIAL DEMOCRATIC LABOR PARTY. A counter-revolutionary group, once active in the Soviet State Planning Commission and other Soviet administrative agencies; exposed and wiped out in 1930-31.

ALL-UNION LENIST YOUNG COMMUNIST LEAGUE. See *Komsomol.*

ANARCHISM. The doctrine that the state is the source of all oppression, and must be overthrown by violence, and that no participation in any state function, even elections, is just. Between *Marxism and anarchism there has been constant struggle. See *First International.* *Lenin says: "We are distinguished from the anarchists by (1) the use of the state *now,* and (2) at the time of the *proletarian revolution." *Trotsky writes: "The

principles of liberalism can have a real existence only with a police system. Anarchism is an attempt to cleanse liberalism of the police. . . . Being a shadow-caricature of liberalism, anarchism as a whole has shared its fate" (*H.R.R.,* II, 179). In *M.L.* Trotsky adds: "Anarchism, a theory very sweeping in its verbal negations, is lifeless and cowardly in its practical consequences" (129). See *Bakunin; State.*

ANTHROPOLOGICAL PRINCIPLE. The term used to designate the basic philosophical theme found in the work of *Chernyshevsky — "a man must be regarded as a single being having one nature, arising out of the human body, which as material is primary" (132ff.).

ANTID OTO. Pen name used by Leon *Trotsky while writing from exile in Siberia in 1901. Articles over this signature were published in *The Eastern Review,* a liberal newspaper published in Irkutsk.

ANTITHESIS. See *Thesis-Antithesis-Synthesis.*

ANTI-PARTY GROUP. At the 21st *Congress of the Russian Communist Party, 1959, a group composed of *Malenkov, *Molotov, *Kaganovich, *Bulganin, and *Shepilov was singled out for *criticism as the Anti-Party Group. They were charged with having been critical of all achievements made after the death of *Stalin.

APRIL THESES. See *Theses of April 4.*

ARTICLE 58. That section of the Soviet Penal Code which provides for punishment of those engaged in counter-revolutionary activity against the Soviet State. See *Socialist Legality*.

ASSOCIATION OF ST. PETERSBURG WORKMEN. An early Marxist workers' group, founded in St. Petersburg in the fall of 1885 by P. V. Tochissky. Broken up by police in 1888, the remnant formed the Brusner Group in 1888-89, out of which sprang about twenty workers' circles, each containing six or seven members, including the first Russian Marxist circle of working women. The Brusner Group organized the first *May Day Celebration in 1891, when between 70 and 80 workers gathered for a secret out-of-town rally. Speeches given here were secretly printed and widely distributed. In 1892 this group was broken up by police, but Marxist circles continued to appear in the principal Russian industrial cities. In Kazan, a certain V. I. Ulyanov joined such a circle in 1888 — his name later, V. I. Lenin.

AUGUST BLOC. Union of *Mensheviks, *Left Bolsheviks, Jewish *Bundists, and *Trotskyites formed under the leadership of *Trotsky in Vienna, August 1912, to oppose the establishment of *Pravda (newspaper). Of short duration.

AVELING, Edward (1851-1898), English writer, active member of *Socialist League, and husband of Eleanor Marx, the second eldest daughter of Karl *Marx. Aveling was, with Samuel Moore, the translator into English of Marx's *Capital*, which Marx wrote in his native tongue, German.

AVENARIUS, Richard (1843-96), German philosopher of the school known as *Empirio-Criticism, also *Positivism. Avenarius held that in knowledge the knower and the thing known are mutually dependent, in fact, imply each other; that is, being or world implies thought or thinker, both existing in the medium or mode of consciousness. The world depends for its existence, then, on the knowing individual, and matter exists in the experience of being known. *Lenin called Empirio-Criticism "subjective *idealism," and pronounced it untenable. His *Materialism and Empirio-Criticism* is directed against the school of Avenarius and *Mach, and their Russian adherents. Avenarius's chief work: *Critique of Pure Experience*. See *Empirio-Criticism*.

AXELROD, Pavel-Borrissovich (1850-1925), South Ukranian by birth, Jewish by nationality. He started his political activity in the *South Russian Workers' Union as an adherent of *Bakunin and *anarchism. Influenced by *Lasalle toward *Marx, he joined *Plekhanov in founding the *Emancipation of Labor Group which was the direct ancestor of the *Bolshevik Party. With *Lenin and others he was on the editorial board of *Iskra. He participated in the Revolution of 1917 as leader in the Bolshevik Party.

BABOEUF, F. N. (1760-97), French revolutionary who wished to push the French Revolution of 1789 on to a communist society. He was executed during the Revolution.

BAKUNIN, Michael (1814-1870), one of the founders of *anarchism. Born in Russia, he was active in the German Revolution of 1848. At its collapse he was sent back home, where he was sentenced to Siberia. From there he escaped to go to Europe and eventually London (1861). There he joined the League of Peace and Freedom, a mildly revolutionary group. This he left in 1868 to form his own International Alliance of Socialist Democrats, which he took into the *First International in 1869. *Marx writes: "At the end of 1868 the Russian, Bakunin, entered the *International* with the aim of forming inside it a second *International* called the 'Alliance of Socialist-Democrats' *with himself as leader.* He — a man devoid of theoretical knowledge — put forward the pretension that this separate body was to represent the scientific part of the International . . ." (*S.C.*, 316), of which Marx would have no part. Marx secured Bakunin's expulsion from the International in 1872, but the bitter struggle wrecked the organization. *Plekhanov writes: "Bakuninism is not a system. It is a mixture of the socialist theories of the Latin countries with Russian peasant ideals" (*O.D.*). *Engels: "Bakunin has a peculiar theory of his own. He regards not *capital but the *state as the evil to be abolished, because the state has created capital and sustains it. Hence complete abstinence from politics; rather conduct *propaganda, win over the workers, abolish

the state, and substitute the International — social liquidation" (Ltr. to Cuno, Jan. 24, 1872, *S.C.* 319ff.). E. H. Carr has a biography of Bakunin; see also Cole, *H.S.T.*, II, ch. 9. See *Anarchism*.

BARRACKS (*Kazarma*). Name of the newspaper published in and for the Russian Army during World War I by the *Bolshevik Party.

BASE AND SUPERSTRUCTURE. See *Production, Mode of; Materialism, Dialectical*.

BASLE RESOLUTION (of 1912). A resolution against war adopted at Basle, Switzerland, by the Emergency International Socialist Congress, held November 24-25, 1912. It emphasized the *"imperialist" character of the threatening war, and called upon *socialists everywhere to "take advantage of the economic and political crises created by a war to accelerate the downfall of *capitalism."

BAUER, Bruno (1809-1882), German theologian who, with *Marx, was a member of the Young *Hegelian circle at Berlin University around 1840. Later lecturer at Bonn University, he was relieved of his post because of his criticism of Christianity, the so-called "higher criticism" of the Scriptures. He violently opposed both *Feuerbach's, and Marx and *Engels's materialistic reinterpretation of *Hegel. Marx and Engels sharply attacked Bauer, his brother Edgar, and other Young Hegelians in their books: The *Holy Family (*i.e.,* the Bauer family) and The German Ideology, which includes a detailed critique of Max *Stirner (pseud. for J. K. Schmidt), a radical Left Hegelian.

BAUER, Heinrich. See *Communist League.*

BEBEL, August (1840-1913), German socialist leader, founder of Saxon Peoples' Party, which became in 1869 the German Social Democratic Workers' Party, under leadership of Bebel and Wilhelm *Liebknecht; later he helped found the *Second International. During *Engels's lifetime, Bebel was a stout Marxist, though both Engels and *Marx often took him to task for *opportunist or *reformist leanings. From 1867 until his death, except for brief periods, he was a member of the German Reichstag, and after the death of Engels in 1895 he moved toward *Bernstein and moderate *socialism. His chief work is entitled *Woman;* it is both a review of the relations between the sexes and a plea for equal rights for women. *Kautsky says of him: "Bebel was fond of praising mistrust [of government] as a democratic virtue" (Kautsky, 156).

BECKER, Johann Phillip (1809-1896), leader of the Genevan section of the *First International. He participated in the German revolutions at the so-called Hamburg Festival, 1832, and Baden, 1849. From 1866 he was editor of *Vorbote,* the publication of the German section of the First International.

BEEHIVE, THE. From 1862 to 1876 the weekly journal of the London Trades Council, a union workers' group. *Engels called it in 1869 "the only working-class paper in existence." *Marx sought to make it the organ of the *First International, but was unsuccessful in gaining its control; it did, however, become an avenue for Marxist publication until purchased by Samuel *Morley, wealthy Member of Parliament, in 1868. Marx then obliged the Trades Council to withdraw from the paper, which continued in Morley's possession until its dissolution in 1885.

BELINSKY, Vissarion Grigoryovich (1811-1848), with A. *Herzen the founder of Russian pre-Marxist revolutionary *materialism and one of the five writers whose work prepared the way for the spread of *Marxism in Russia (see Section II of this book). The son of a doctor in Chembar, Belinsky was expelled from Moscow University for writing a play, *Dmitri Kalinin,* which attacked the evils of serfdom. Belinsky became a literary critic and contributed to various magazines; from 1846 until leaving for voluntary exile shortly before his death, he was literary critic on *The *Contemporary,* leading *liberal magazine. He sought to expose "autocracy, orthodoxy, and nationality" as enemies of the Russian people. Having contracted tuberculosis, and under threats of imprisonment, he went abroad to die. *Lenin characterized him as seeking all his life for "the correct revolutionary theory." As literary critic he held that the real substance of nationality is the world outlook of a people, and this forms the basis of its art and a standard for judgment of art. Abroad he

27

came into contact with *Marx and Engels through the *German-French Yearbook, but although a philosophical materialist and bitter opponent of Tsarism, Belinsky did not become a Marxist. Writes Berdyaev: "Belinsky was the 'father' of Russian revolutionary intelligentsia."

BELL, THE (*Kolokol*). Important revolutionary periodical published for Russians outside Russia by A. I. *Herzen and N. P. Ogaryov. Its motto at the masthead was *Vivos Voco* — "I call on the living." It appeared in London from July 1, 1857, to April, 1865; then from Geneva, April, 1865, to December, 1868; in editions of around 2,500 copies, most of them smuggled into Russia. It maintained a constant attack upon Russian autocracy, and became the forerunner of the Marxist illegal press. Some work of *Marx and *Engels reached Russia through this medium.

BELTOV, N., pseudonym under which *Plekhanov published his widely read book *The Development of the Monist View of History* (see Section II) illegally in St. Petersburg, 1895. Beltov is sometimes the name used for Plekhanov in Russian literature of the period and after.

BERNSTEIN, Eduard (1847-1932), central figure in the form of *Marxism known as *revisionism, that is, the attempt to fit Marxist views to democratic procedures. By profession a German bank clerk, he became active in the German Social-Democratic Par-

ty, joined the so-called *Eisenachers, and was expelled from Germany in 1881. From Switzerland he edited the paper *Sozial Demokrat,* 1881-1890, and with *Engels's prodding made it a *proletarian revolutionary organ. Exiled to London, he aided Engels, with *Kautsky, in deciphering *Marx's manuscript for the third volume of *Capital* (1895). After the death of Engels in 1896, Bernstein drifted to revisionism, and in a series of articles, "Problems of Socialism," written for the paper *Neue Zeit,* edited by Kautsky, he proposed the "criticism" of Marxism. This "*freedom of criticism" *Lenin called freedom to pervert Marx, and Kautsky, too, differed sharply with Bernstein, though later he also became revisionist. Bernstein replied, "No amount of *historical materialism can get round the fact that history is made by man, that men have minds, and that mental dispositions are by no means so mechanical as to be entirely governed by the economic situation" (*Neue Zeit,* XVI, 749). These theories came to dominate the German Social-Democratic Party. But in 1898 the Stuttgart Congress of the Party rejected any affirmation of revisionism; it refused, however, to follow Rosa *Luxemburg's demand that the Party condemn Bernstein himself. Similar action was taken at Hanover in 1899. In 1901 Bernstein's theories were rejected as official Party line at the Lübeck Congress. Meanwhile, revisionism was taking over the *Second International, and Lenin was launching bitter attacks upon it, collected in the volume *Against Revisionism*. Bernstein developed his views in *Evolutionary Socialism* (first published in 1899) to the effect that, contrary to Marx, *socialism is not inevitable, history is not irrevocably determined by economic factors; the ownership of industry was not being concentrated but dispersed by stock companies. Moreover, he attacked Marx's *Law of Increasing Misery by showing that the *proletariat was enjoying a rising standard of living; and he denied that *capitalism was moving toward any final crisis, such as Marx had foretold. Social gains should be made by legislation, not by *revolution; and the workers, if revolution should come, would in fact be unable to govern, and would fall prey to dictatorship — which prediction was fulfilled in Russia two decades later. Bernstein lived to become the opponent of Marxism in practice, and the target of countless *Bolshevik attacks in press, book, pamphlet, and speech.

BLACK CONGRESS. Name given by Soviets to a conference of landlords, manufacturers, and priests of the Russian Orthodox Church held in Moscow on October 12-14, 1917, in a vain effort to form a united front to defeat the *Bolsheviks. Compare *Private Conference of Public Men*.

BLACK HUNDREDS. Popular designation for the Union of the Russian People, a league of the nobility that employed terrorism against popular and revolutionary movements and figures, including the instigation of *pogroms. It flourished in the mid-nineteenth century.

BLACK REDISTRIBUTION (PARTITION) *(Chorny Peredel)*. A journal published illegally by the revolutionary *Narodnik organization of the same name, from 1880-1881, in total of five issues — 1 and 2 at St. Petersburg and 3-5 at Minsk. *Plekhanov was one of the editors, and the journal sought to stir antagonism against the Tsarist regime by demanding distribution of the landed estates among the peasantry.

BLAGOYEV GROUP. D. Blagoyev, Bulgarian student at St. Petersburg University, became founder of the *Party of Russian Social Democrats in 1883. Later he founded the Bulgarian Communist Party.

BLANQUISM. Name given a trend in the French socialist movement headed by Louis August Blanqui (1805-1881). Its essence is the expectation of a revolutionary overthrow of the existing government from the work of a small group of intellectuals, secretly organized. In this sense the term *Blanquism* occurs repeatedly in Marxist literature. *Lenin: Blanquism "expects mankind's liberation from wage slavery not through the *class struggle of the *proletariat, but through a conspiracy of a small minority of intellectuals" (*Works* X, 34). *Trotsky: "The rules of Blanqui were the demands of a military revolutionary realism. Blanqui's mistake lay not in his direct but in his inverse theorem.

From the fact that tactical weakness condemns an insurrection to defeat, Blanqui inferred that an observance of the rules of insurrectionary tactics would itself guarantee victory .... An active minority of the proletariat, no matter how well organized, cannot seize the power regardless of the general conditions of the country. In this particular history has condemned Blanquism. But only in this. His affirmative theorem retains all its force. In order to conquer the power, the proletariat needs more than a spontaneous insurrection. It needs a suitable organization; it needs a plan; it needs a conspiracy. Such is the Leninist view of this question" (*H.R.R.*, III, 170).

BLOODY SUNDAY (Jan. 9, 1905). On this Sunday more than 140,000 St. Petersburg workers, carrying church banners, icons, and pictures of the Tsar, marched peacefully on the Winter Palace, led by the priest Father *Gapon, to petition the Tsar for various reforms. On orders of the Tsar, or a minister, the crowd was fired upon by soldiers and police. More than 1,000 were killed and over 5,000 wounded, giving the name Bloody Sunday to this day, and giving revolutionary propaganda to the radicals. Gapon is charged by the Communists now with having been working for the police in organizing the march.

BOGDANOV, pen name of Alexander Alexandrovich *Malinovsky (1873-1928). A doctor by profession and revolutionary agitator by avocation, Bogdanov was Marxist in his general views but sympathetic to *Empirio-Criticism in philosophy. For this reason he came under *Lenin's severe criticism in his *Materialism and Empirio-Criticism*. Bogdanov was not active in the *Revolution, but organized a "Proletarian University" in 1918, and later headed a medical institute devoted to studies in blood transfusion. To one experiment he conducted upon himself Bogdanov gave his life.

BOLSHEVIK REVOLUTION. See *Russian Revolution*.

BOLSHEVIKS (Bolshevik Party). This word is simply the Russian term for *majority,* and this is the meaning it had when in 1903 *Lenin drove the *Russian Social Democratic Labor Party to a split on the question of how *revolutionary action should be conducted. The Bolsheviks, under Lenin, held that the aim should be the overthrow of Tsarism through a union of workers and peasants in a tightly organized, Party-led, revolutionary-conscious force. The *Mensheviks, in Russian simply the *minority,* under *Plekhanov and *Trotsky held for revolution by evolution through democratic means. Both parties remained Marxist in basic beliefs. The Bolsheviks became the spearhead of the movement which finally came to power in October 1917, under Lenin and Trotsky, who had joined the Bolsheviks in that year. Up to the *July Days, 1917, the Party had at its disposal no more than forty-one different revolutionary publications appearing in no more than 320,000 copies annually. These were drastically curtailed during the summer of 1917. The treasury of the Party was virtually empty. Yet this Party came to power. "The explanation is very simple: those slogans which correspond to the keen demands of a class and an epoch create thousands of channels for themselves" (*H.R.R.*, III, 304-5). The Party was headed by a Central Committee, which at the time of the successful October revolution had the following members: Lenin, *Zinoviev, *Kamenev, *Trotsky, Nogin, Kallantai, *Stalin, Sverdlov, Rykov, *Bukharin, Artem, Joffe, Uritsky, Miliutin, Lomov. It is the fact that the Bolshevik Party is the only political party in Russia which makes for the peculiar dual form of power there — the *Central Committee of the Party, through its Executive, holds real political power, while the official government has its own President and officers.

BOLSHEVIK-LENINISTS. See *Opposition.*

BOLSHEVIKS, OLD. See *Old Bolsheviks.*

BOLSHEVISM, THREE PILLARS OF. See *Three Pillars of Bolshevism.*

BONAPARTISM (Caesarism). The name given to several types of revolutionary conduct, all having in common the seizure of power by one person who comes as savior of the state, usually against the masses. The name is taken from the performance of Napoleon Bonaparte, who acted thus in France

after the great French Revolution. *Trotsky defines Bonapartism as "The idea of a master of destiny arising between opposing forces," and gaining power by appearing as a balance between them. Marxist theories define the conditions for such an assumption of power as follows: (1) a *revolutionary situation has prevailed; (2) there has been the revolutionary overthrow of one regime by another, but the overthrower lacks power enough to hold on; (3) the army is behind the Bonapartist. From the Marxist point of view, Bonapartism solidifies the domination of the *bourgeoisie over the *proletariat. Says *Kautsky: "When the bourgeoisie, or the peasants, or the workers are alike unable to gain domination in the bourgeois revolution, a disciplined military *coup* takes over" (48). Caesarism is a synonymous term, having reference to Julius Caesar's assumption of power in Rome.

BORBA GROUP. Borba is the Russian word for *struggle*. A group formed in Paris, May 1901, to unify all Russian revolutionary groups abroad. It organized the so-called *Unity Conference, and was at first under guidance of *Lenin. Later it moved away from the Leninist orbit and was officially dissolved by the Second Congress of the *R.S.D.L.P. See *Congresses.*

BOROTBISTS. Ukrainian Party formed in May 1918, and named from their newspaper, *Borotba* (Struggle). The Party held extreme revolutionary views, including terrorism. It joined the Communist

Party of the Ukraine, and later, the Soviet Union, but as an unstable force.

BOURGEOIS DEMOCRACY. This is the Marxist term for capitalist democracy, that is, for the political system of the *bourgeois states. They understand bourgeois democracy to consist in (a) the party system, and (b) representative government. Lenin argued that bourgeois democracy itself is split between those who see the necessity of some economic and social reforms, and those who resist all attempts at change. The former support the "liberal" party, while the latter support the "conservatives." See *Democracy*.

BOURGEOISIE. The term used by *Marx to designate the social class which owns the means of *production and which can live on its resources; that is, it does not (as does the *proletariat) have to sell its labor power in order to exist. *Capitalists* is a term roughly equivalent. The word is French and was originally used to designate city dwellers as distinguished from country dwellers. Then it came to mean the holders of capital and owners of means of production as distinguished from landowners and wage laborers. *Kautsky says: "We understand by the term *bourgeoisie* the whole of the educated and comfortable section of the urban population, the large landowners as well as the peasantry, and the poorer section of the urban population" (36). This view is broader than Marx's, who limited his use of the term to mean the exploiting,

capitalistic owners of the means of production. See *Petty Bourgeoisie*.

BRENTANO, Lujo (1844-1931), German economist and critic of *Marxism (some say one of the best critics) who argued for social equality within the *capitalist framework by social reforms and class co-operation. He frequently used Marxist terminology.

BREST - LITOVSK. City which gave its name to the peace treaty wrought out between the German and Soviet governments between December 1917 and March 1918. The Soviet delegation was headed by *Trotsky, whose views often clashed with those of *Lenin on the negotiations, for which, by the *Stalinists, Trotsky was held solely responsible. The treaty was harsh and cost the Soviets vast land areas which were later recaptured when Germany collapsed.

BRIGHT, John (1811-1889), British manufacturer who, with Richard *Cobden, led the parliamentary struggle for greater democracy in Britain, in opposition to the landowners. He was critical of exploitation of the poor and favored social reforms. *Marx called him *utopian.

BRONSTEIN, Lev Davidovich, given name of *Trotsky, Leon.

BRUSNER GROUP. See *Association of St. Petersburg Workmen*.

BUKHARIN, Nikolay Ivanovich (1888-1938), leading Russian exponent of *mechanistic materialism. After a variety of revolutionary activities in Russia, and during exile abroad, he returned to Russia during the *February 1917 Revolution to become editor of *Pravda and leading figure in the *Third International. He supported *Stalin against *Trotsky, and was rewarded for his services by falling out with Stalin himself over the *sovietization of agriculture — a measure Trotsky had long proposed. He was tried and executed by the last of the great public *purge-trials, in 1938, as a right-wing *deviationist.

BUND, THE (Jewish Bund). The Jewish Workers' Union of Lithuania, Poland, and Russia, founded in 1897. It joined the *R.S.D.L.P. at its First Congress in March 1898, but withdrew at the next Congress when the Bund was denied recognition as sole representative of Jewish workers' interests. It rejoined the Party in 1906 and supported the *Mensheviks in opposition to Lenin's *Bolsheviks. It supported the *Kerensky Government against the *February Revolution in 1917, and in 1921 officially dissolved itself in favor of the Bolshevik Party.

BUREAUCRACY. For the Marxist, a system of government in which power is in the hands of official administrators divorced from the people, uncontrolled by popular will, and serving the interests of exploiting classes. It is characterized, *Marxism says, by formalism, callousness, red tape, and isolation from the masses.

CADETS (Kadets). Nickname given the Russian Constitutional Democratic Party, taken from the (Russian) initials of the Party (K.D.). It was formed in October 1905, after the revolutionary unrest. Its aim was the conversion of Tsarism to a constitutional monarchy, and to this end the Party obtained widespread peasant support. After the *February 1917 Revolution, the Party took a leading role in the government of *Kerensky; after the October 1917 *Bolshevik Revolution, the Party became an oppositionist group under the name *Party of the People's Freedom.* *Lenin called it the "General Staff of the Counter-Revolution."

CADRES. A term which denotes the *Communist Party members in any of their official functions, from positions in the central Party organs down to the lowest Party cells in the *Soviets and among the people. The cadres constitute the self-conscious Communists and the organizational structure upon which the Soviet system rests. In this sense *Stalin frequently spoke of, and to, the cadres, and he could say "the cadres determine everything." See *Communists.*

CAESARISM. See *Bonapartism.*

CALENDAR, RUSSIAN. The Russian calendar was, until the *Bolshevik revision of 1918, the so-called Julian calendar, running thirteen days (in the twentieth century) behind the Western, or so-called Gregorian calendar. This fact must be taken into account when dating events in pre-1918 Russian history. In this *Vocabulary* the dates are given as of the period when the events took place; before 1918, according to the Julian, and after it, according to the Gregorian calendar. The Julian Calendar is so named after Julius Caesar, who was responsible for its use; the Gregorian Calendar is named after Pope Gregory VII, who had it formulated and adopted by Roman Catholic countries around 1580. For further details, see any good encyclopedia.

CAMARILLA. The word means a group, clique, conspiracy of advisors to a king or other ruler. It is used by the Marxists, and others, to point to the small clique led by the priest Rasputin which surrounded the Russian royal family of Tsar Nicholas II and exercised fatal influence over the Tsarina in the period preceding and during World War I.

CAPITAL (*Das Kapital*). The lifework of *Marx, his famous study of *capitalist society, of which the first volume (of three) was the only one published in his lifetime. It appeared in 1867. After Marx's death, in 1883, *Engels took upon himself the task of deciphering Marx's manuscripts and preparing volumes II and III for publication. Vol. II appeared in 1885, and Vol. III in 1894. A collection of Marx's remaining manuscripts, edited by *Kautsky, is sometimes referred to as Vol. IV, but not commonly included in the set. An interesting revelation of Engels's difficulties with Marx's handwriting is provided by Engels's own introduction to Vol. II, and by his correspondence with Laura *Lafargue (Marx's daughter) — see Vol. I of *S.C.* (133-35), Vol. II, letter of

22 May, 1883. The first translation from the German of *Das Kapital* was into Russian, by Nikolai Danielson, published without interference from the Tsar's censors in 1872. A French translation by J. Roy appeared in 1875, and an English translation by Samuel More and Edward *Aveling in 1887. Various abbreviated editions of the huge work have appeared, perhaps the first by Otto Rühle, in German; the most available in English are a Modern Library Giant and Trotsky's *Living Thoughts of Karl Marx.*

CAPITAL. Capital exists, according to *Marx, in two forms; these two forms together provide the means by which the *production of goods is made possible: (1) constant capital — the buildings, machinery, fuel, raw materials, and the like, which Marx calls "congealed labor power"; and (2) variable capital — wages. The profit which capital extracts from the process of production, Marx says, must depend upon one or both of its forms; but constant capital can of itself create no new value; nor can variable capital in itself; but because it commands a creative force — *labor power — variable capital becomes the sole source of profit — by *exploitation. (See *Surplus Value.*) Marx says: "The owner of money can do this [make profit] solely because he finds a *commodity on the *market, whose consumption possesses the special property of being a source of new value. The commodity is labor power" (Dutt, 269). How capital comes into existence (see *Capital Accumulation; Primitive Accumulation*) and how it brings labor power under its dominion, forever estranging the laborer from the fruits of labor (**Alienation*) and thus creates over against the **proletariat both an alien **class (**bourgeoisie*) and much of the permanent work of his own hands, in the form of constant capital — how all this comes about, and what its characteristics are, these are the matters treated in great detail in Marx's lifework, **Capital.* These economic studies are presumed by Marxists to provide the "scientific" foundation for Communism, and the sure proof of its inevitability — Mr. Khrushchev's "We will bury you." (Marx had called the proletariat the "grave-digger of capitalism.") In fact, while much of Marx's analysis rests upon long accepted principles of **classical economics, the whole drive of Communism rests upon the false hope of a **classless society, to be achieved by violent **revolution, and could hardly be more remotely connected with the ponderous tomes of *Capital.* Marxist economic terms may be found throughout this wordbook, in alphabetical order. See particularly *Commodity; Labor Theory of Value; Surplus Value.*

CAPITAL, CONSTANT. See *Constant Capital.*

CAPITAL, VARIABLE. See *Variable Capital.*

C A P I T A L ACCUMULATION. How is capital accumulated? **Marx answers: "The conversion of a sum of money into means of production and labor-power is the first step taken by a quantum of value that is going to function as capital. This conversion takes place in the **market, within the sphere of **circulation. The second step, the process of **production, is complete so soon as the means of production have been converted into **commodities whose value exceeds that of their component parts, and therefore, contains the capital already advanced, plus a **surplus-value. These commodities must then be thrown into circulation. They must be sold, their values realised in money, this money afresh converted into capital, and so over and over again. This circular movement, in which the same phases are continually gone through in succession, forms the circulation of capital" (*Cap.*, I, 564). (See also *Primitive Accumulation.*) "With the accumulation of capital, the specifically capitalistic mode of production develops, and with the capitalistic mode of production the accumulation of capital . . . . The growth of social capital is effected by the growth of many individual capitals . . . . Therefore, the number of capitalists grows to greater or less extent . . . . The increase of each functioning capital is thwarted by the formation of new and the sub-divisions of old capitals. This splitting-up of the total social capital into many individual capitals is counteracted by their attraction, that is, the concentration of capitals already formed, the expropriation of capitalist by capitalist, the transfer of many small into few large capitals" (*Cap.* I, 624-25) .

CAPITALISM/SOCIALISM. "The difference between *socialism and capitalism does not consist in the fact that the one makes a profit and the other not, but in the fact that the one makes a profit for individuals and the other makes a profit for the community" (Kautsky, 212) . See *Socialism/Communism.*

CAPITALISM, STATE. See *State Capitalism.*

CAPITALISM, STATE MONOPOLY. See *State Monopoly Capitalism.*

CAPITALIST. See *Bourgeoisie.*

CAPITALIST ENCIRCLEMENT. Russian theory that every capitalist nation is the enemy of the Soviet State, and that Russia is therefore surrounded by capitalist adversaries awaiting the right time to strike and destroy the Soviet Union. *Stalin pointed repeatedly to the threat posed by such encirclement, and in his Report to the Sixteenth Party *Congress in 1930 he said, "Capitalist Encirclement is not simply a geographical conception. It means that around the USSR there are hostile class forces, ready to support our class enemies morally, materially, and by means of financial blockade; and, when the opportunity offers, by means of military intervention." Stalin used this charge to justify the delay in moving into the Communist, or *classless, society.

CARTELS. See *Imperialism.*

CENTRAL COMMITTEE. Highest Committee of the *Communist Party in the Soviet Union. This Committee is presently composed of 133 full members, with 122 alternates, elected by the All-Union Party Congress, which meets at irregular intervals. Alternate delegates sit in on meetings, participate in discussions, but do not vote. The Central Committee elects its own *Presidium (formerly the Politburo, an abbreviation for Political Bureau) , which acts as executive organ for the Central Committee.

CENTRALISM, DEMOCRATIC. See *Democratic Centralism.*

CENTRISM (Centrist). A position ideologically midway between the right and left wings of a political party. In Marxist literature, it is the position taken by *Kautsky in the *Second International, between the *Left Revolutionaries, who were headed by Rosa *Luxemburg, Karl *Liebknecht, Georg Ledebour, Franz *Mehring; and the *Revisionists (Reformists) headed by Bernstein. *Lenin was a bitter critic of Centrism as being in effect anti-revolutionary and reactionary. The Centrists took the position that the Russian *revolution had first to pass through its *bourgeois stage before *socialism could be envisaged. *Trotsky supported the position in his Vienna *Pravda, and the so-called *Conciliators also joined it.

C H A N G E OF LANDMARKS (*Smena Vekh*) . Name derived from the title of a published symposium which appeared in Prague in 1921, put out by group of Russian *bourgeois exiles who also published a journal in Paris under the same title. Some of these émigrés advocated co-operation with the Soviets in hope of gaining a voice in Russian affairs and of participating in the *New Economic Policy, which permitted small capitalists to function. Others favored non-political co-operation with Russian state economy in NEP. With the introduction of the first *Five Year Plan, in 1927, these aspirations faded away.

CHARTISM. Mass British workers' movement influential in the 1830s. It took its name from the idea of presenting to Parliament a petition or "charter" bearing thousands of signatures and demanding universal male suffrage, secret ballot, annual Parliaments, equal electoral districts, payment of Members of Parliament. It collapsed upon rejection of the Charter on May 13, 1839. Marx looked upon the movement with favor as a limited step forward, but he based no firm hopes upon it.

CHEKA. Soviet Russian secret police (the secret police of the Tsars was known as the *Okhrana). The Cheka was organized by *Lenin as the Extraordinary Committee for Combating C o u n t e r-R e v o l u-tion, Sabbotage, and Speculation. It was headed by Felix *Dzerzhinsky until his death in 1926, and made by him into a dreaded and powerful political police system. Dzerzhinsky was followed by V. R. Menzhinsky, G. G. Yagoda, N. I. Yezhov (who superintended the great

purges, 1936-38), and Lavrenti Beria (whose execution followed by some nine months the death of *Stalin in March, 1953). The Cheka had the power to arrest, try, and execute.

In 1922, the name was changed to State Police Administration, abbreviated to OGPU. In 1934, the name was again changed, this time to Peoples' Commissariat of Internal Affairs, or NKVD. This was changed in 1946 to Ministry of Internal Affairs, or MVD. Since 1953, the name of the secret police has been Commissariat of Internal Security, or KGB, though the MVD has remained as the Ministry in charge of routine police work (as distinguished from political police activities). MVD is also in charge of frontier troops; registration of the populace at birth, marriage, and death; passports, and visas.

Under Stalin the MVD came to have its own army units, airplanes, tanks, and sources of supply. It ran the slave labor camps, which had populations ranging up to ten million inmates. Some relaxation of secret police activities has been attempted since the death of Stalin. See *Socialist Legality*.

CH'EN TU-HSIN. Peking University professor, co-founder with Li Tachao of the *Chinese Communist Party by the formation in 1918 of a Marxist study group at the University.

CHERNYSHEVSKI, Nikolai Gavrilovich (1828-1889), pre-Marxist Russian revolutionary writer and teacher. Exiled to Siberia in 1862 for radical writings in the liberal magazine *The Contemporary,* he returned in 1883. He carried on the work begun by *Belinsky and *Herzen, and introduced the thought of *Feuerbach as a "common sense" *materialism. His revolutionary novel *What Is to Be Done?,* published from prison in 1863, became the "gospel of *nihilism" (Masaryk) and the textbook of radicalism to the younger generation; it taught that society must be reorganized on a communal basis, enterprise must be co-operative, the Tsarist autocracy must be overthrown. From 1859 to his exile, Chernyshevski published a weekly commentary on current events critical of the government. By the Marxists he is classified as a *Utopian Socialist who hoped by moderate reforms to gain equality in the division of the fruits of labor. In philosophy he was a materialist, sometimes guilty of *mechanism: "There is no such thing as absolute truth; truth is concrete. Everything depends upon the conditions of time and space." Lenin: "Chernyshevski was filled with a great love for his country."

CHINESE COMMUNIST PARTY.

The Party began with Marxist study groups, organized in Peking by two university professors, *Li Ta-chao and *Ch'en Tu-hsin. It held its first Congress in July 1921, at Shanghai, with 12 delegates present, one of them *Mao Tse-tung. Its second Congress, held in May 1922, issued a *Manifesto* to the Chinese people, proclaiming *Marxism; Ch'en was chosen as General Secretary and Chairman of the Political Bureau. The Communists infiltrated the Kuomintang Party of *Sun Yat-sen, but were bloodily decimated by Chiang Kai-shek's army in 1927, though *Stalin had ordered co-operation with Chiang. Mao Tse-tung became Chairman of the Party's Central Committee in 1931 and began rebuilding its strength. He led its army on the famous "Long March" of 1935 to get out of range of Chiang's forces and to establish a Communist State in Chensi Province, with capital at Yenan. It gradually expanded its scope of control to final assumption of complete power after World War II.

CHINESE-RUSSIAN SPLIT. Growing friction between Moscow and Peking, apparent since the mid-1950s, burst into open and violent controversy in January, 1963, with blasts and counter-blasts in the Russian *Pravda* and the Chinese *Red Flag,* both official newspapers. At the German Communist Party Congress in the same month, *Khrushchev bitterly castigated the Chinese Communists for breaking Party unity; and Wu Hsiu-Chuan, the Chinese delegate, was hooted off the rostrum when he sought to respond. Khrushchev and *Mao declined mutual invitations to exchange visits in the spring of 1963, and a July meeting in Moscow of lesser dignitaries ended in fraternal frustration. Peking and Moscow agents by the hundreds tour the world Communist Parties seeking support, and the Chinese have come to dominate most of the Asian Communist organizations.

The Chinese resent Russian refusal to honor their treaty of October 1957, which promised fissionable materials to China; they attack Khrushchev as a "Revisionist" for having told the 1956 Party *Congress that East and West can entertain peaceful co-existence, and that violent revolution is not always essential to Communist victory in a capitalist country; they also hold that Khrushchev vacillated on Cuba, and should not have signed the *nuclear test-ban treaty. The Russians, on the other hand, denounce Chinese recklessness in risking war, Chinese *Dogmatism in refusing to recognize co-existence as a Marxist option, and Chinese disloyalty to Moscow's dominance in world Communism. At stake are the leadership of the world Communist movement, the authority to set the *Party Line, a share in world trade, and the growing influence of China in European and South American Communist Parties. (See Crankshaw; a scholarly appraisal, in German, is Klaus Mehnert, *Peking und Moskau,* Stuttgart, 1962). The split is genuine, deep, and growing.

CHORNY PEREDEL. See *Land and Freedom (Liberty) Group; Black Redistribution.*

CHOU EN-LAI (1898-   ), Premier of China since 1949; Foreign Minister. Born in Kiangsu Province, he was educated abroad. He joined the Communist Party in 1914, in France.

CHRISTIAN SOCIALISM. The Christian Socialist movement is specifically the nineteenth-century British development associated with the names of F. D. Maurice, Charles Kingsley, and J. M. Ludlow. They favored trade unionism, co-operatives, the extension of the franchise, the assistance of the poor, the spread of education, and the amelioration of abuses and injustices wherever they found them. A good account of the movement is to be had in Maurice B. Reckitt's *Maurice to Temple.* Gerard Walter holds (in his *Les Origines du Communisme*) that socialism in some sense goes back to the Hebrew prophets and has always been not far from the thinking of the Fathers of the Christian Church.

CHU TEH (1886-   ), War Minister of Communist China; known as the father of the Chinese Communist Army.

CIRCULATION. The name given to the process of *production, sale, and purchase of *commodities. Commodity circulation, according to Marx, moves in this cycle: C (ommodity) — M (oney) — C (ommodity) for all goods sold as use-values; M (oney) — C (ommodity) — M (oney) for all goods purchased for resale. The latter is the basis of *capital accumulation.

CIVIL EXECUTION. The form of punishment employed under the Tsars, intended to frighten and to humiliate political prisoners. The prisoner was obliged to kneel on a public platform while the state executioner broke a sword over his head; or the prisoner faced the firing squad, or had the noose about his neck, when a last-minute reprieve — deliberately planned so — would be announced. Civil execution was often followed by exile, as in the case of the gifted writer N. G. *Chernyshevsky.

CIVIL SOCIETY. "The whole material intercourse of individuals within a definite stage of the development of *productive forces... the true source and theater of all *history" (*G.I.,* 26).

CLASS. *Marxism sees *history as the record of *class struggle. "Classes are large groups of people which differ from each other by the place they occupy in a historically defined system of social *production, by their relations (in most cases fixed and formulated by law) to the means of production, by their role in the social organization of *labor, and, consequently, by the dimensions and the mode of acquiring the share of social wealth of which they can dispose. Classes are groups of people, one of which can appropriate the labor of another owing to the different places they occupy in a definite system of social economy" (Lenin, *Works,* XXIX, 388). In the era of *capitalism, Marxism distinguishes two major classes: (1) capitalists, or *bourgeoisie, (2) workers, or *proletariat. Lesser classes also are to be found: (3) landlords, (4) peasants, or tenant-farmers, (5) *petty bourgeoisie, or small businessmen, (6) intelligentsia, or those engaged in mental work, and (7) the *"Lumpenproletariat" or drifters, ne'er-do-wells.

CLASS CONSCIOUSNESS. One's realization that he belongs to a particular *class and that its interests are his. *Marxism strives to bring the worker to class consciousness as defined by *Lenin: "The worker's understanding that the only way to improve his conditions and to achieve emancipation is to conduct a struggle against the capitalist factory-owners class, his understanding that the interests of all the workers of any particular country are identical, that they all constitute one class separated from all other classes in society. Finally, the class consciousness of the workers means the workers' understanding that to achieve their aims they have to work to influence the affairs of state" (*Works,* II, 112). In *Hegel's terms, class consciousness means to move from thinking of the class-in-itself to thinking of the class-for-itself.

CLASS STRUGGLE. The only explanation, *Marxism holds, of events and changes in society and in *history. "The class struggle is nothing else than the struggle for *surplus-value" (Trotsky). All societies have been shaped by this basic struggle between the possessors and the non-possessors for the fruits of *labor. In the modern world Marxism views the class struggle as having the following forms: (1) Economic: the improvement of working conditions, and in so doing to enlist the support of every worker in further struggle; (2) Ideological: the development of a *class consciousness; (3) Political: the *proletarian revolution, which will destroy the *bourgeois state; it is this last element in the class struggle which distinguishes Marxism from *"utopian socialism" and other *liberal programs.

CLASSICAL ECONOMICS (Economy). The name given the economic theories expressed most systematically by Adam *Smith and David *Ricardo, sometimes called the Manchester or Laissez-faire School. *Marx says: "Once for all I may here state, that by Classical Political Economy I understand that economy which, since the time of William Petty, has investigated the real relations of *production in *bourgeois society, in contradistinction to vulgar economy, which deals with appearance only, ruminates without ceasing on the materials long since provided by scientific economy, and there seeks plausible explanations of the most obtrusive phenomena, for bourgeois daily use, but for the rest confines itself to systematizing in a pedantic way, and proclaiming for everlasting truths, the trite ideas held by the self-complacent *bourgeoisie with regard to their own world, to them the best of all possible worlds" (*Cap.,* I, 81n.).

CLASSLESS SOCIETY. The Communist, and final, stage in *history when there will be no class divisions among men. Only one *class — that is, all people — will both own and work the means of *production, eliminating the possibility of any *class struggle, which is the root of human evil, as the Marxist interprets life. In his *Literature and Revolution,* Leon *Trotsky al-

lows himself to speculate about the achievements of man when he is at last freed from the class struggle: "Through the machine, man in Socialist society will command nature in its entirety, with its grouse and its sturgeons. He will point out places for mountains and for passes. He will change the course of the rivers, and he will lay down rules for oceans. . . . The care for food and education, which lies like a millstone on the present-day family, will be removed, and will become the subject of social initiative and of an endless collective creativeness. Woman will at last free herself from her semi-servile condition. . . . Man at last will begin to harmonize himself in earnest. . . . Emancipated man will want to attain a greater equilibrium in the work of his organs and a more proportional developing and wearing out of his tissues, in order to reduce the fear of death to a rational reaction of the organism towards danger. . . . Man will make it his purpose to master his own feelings, to raise his instincts to the heights of consciousness, to make them transparent, to extend the wires of his will into hidden recesses, and thereby to raise himself to a new plane, to create a higher social biologic type, or, if you please, a superman. . . . Man will become immeasurably stronger, wiser and subtler; his body will become more harmonized. . . . The average human type will rise to the heights of an Aristotle, a Goethe, or a Marx. And above this ridge new peaks will rise" (pp. 252-56, Ann Arbor paperback). This vision of the *new man in the classless society — indeed, produced by the classless society — animates much Communist sacrifice and enthusiasm; it is the Marxist equivalent of heaven. See *Mental versus Manual Labor.*

COBDEN, Richard (1804-1865), Manchester (England) cloth manufacturer who, with John *Bright, led agitation against import duty on corn and favored free trade. He supported the workers in their struggle for the right to vote, and favored the Ten Hour Bill, which limited the working day to ten hours. *Marx wrote in the *New York Daily Tribune* of August 10, 1852, that Cobden and the Free Traders generally were the official representatives of the English *bourgeoisie, "of the England which rules the markets of the world."

COEXISTENCE. See *Peaceful Coexistence.*

COLLECTIVE LEADER-SHIP. The principle that decisions in a Communist state are not to be made by individuals but by the group, theoretically by the whole *Party. After *Stalin's death in 1953, the Party leadership hastened to re-emphasize that collective leadership is the highest guiding principle of party leadership, recalling that even Stalin had once maintained that no individual can possess the wisdom and experience of a collective unity. The principle, however, has received less and less emphasis as the power of *Khrushchev has grown.

COLLECTIVE RESPONSI-BILITY. The principle used in Communist (and other) political oppression and retaliation that a whole family or group is responsible for the acts of any one of its members. Wives and children and even parents and other relatives of a fugitive from political persecution may be deported or otherwise punished if the political suspect himself succeeds in escaping apprehension.

COMINFORM. Abbreviation for the Communist Information Bureau, organized by Stalin in 1947 to include Moscow, the satellite countries, and the Communist Parties of France and Italy in one propaganda and semi-political unity. It was the Soviet response to the Marshall Plan and became a means employed by the Kremlin to exercise tighter control over European Communist Parties. It was dissolved after Stalin's death, and of no importance since 1956. (See W. W. Rostow, pp. 160-62.)

COMINTERN. See *Communist International.*

COMMISSAR. Russian term for *Commissioner,* or *Head of.* Arthur Koestler has given his book which criticizes Communism the title of *The Yogi and the Commissar.* Another synonym might be the bureaucrat.

COMMITTEES OF POOR PEASANTS. Committees set up by the Soviet *Central Committee on June 11, 1918, in almost all Russian villages as representatives of the urban workers among the peasantry. Their principal task was to confiscate grain and other agricultural products which the larger peasant farmers (*kulaks) were refusing to bring to market, and to get these products to the starving cities and army; they also supervised the redistribution of the land, the confiscation of implements and farm animals for distribution among the poor peasants. Before being merged at the end of 1918 with the Village *Soviets — Bolshevik Councils in each village — these Committees had arranged the redistribution of at least one hundred and twenty-five million acres of land and much farm produce. See also *War Communism; Primitive Socialist Accumulation.*

COMMODITY. *Marx begins his study of *capitalism in *Capital with an analysis of this term. He says that a product of *labor becomes a *commodity* only when transferred from one owner to another through *exchange. As product of labor the commodity has value which potentially has the character of: (1) Use Value: it will satisfy a human want, or (2) Exchange Value: it can be exchanged for another commodity. Value itself is given only by the labor a commodity embodies.

COMMUNE. The term from which the word *Communism* derives. It was the name taken by small villages in France early in the feudal period to indicate common use of land and implements, and common sharing in produce. *Engels discusses the history of the term in a footnote to his Preface to the 1888 English edition of the

Communist Manifesto. (See his *S.W., I.*) See *Village Commune.*

COMMUNISM. The term is appropriated from the French word *commune,* which meant the village unit in feudal France, a way of life based on common ownership and sharing of land. The term was used for the *Paris Commune of 1870 when for a few months the City of Paris was governed by a Committee selected from its districts. *Engels indicates in his Introduction to the *Communist Manifesto* (Engl. ed. 1888) that *Marx and he used the term *Communist* to indicate the "scientific" character of their social philosophy as distinguished from the general *"utopianism" of socialist theory of their time. *Lenin developed still more specifically the distinction between Communism and *Socialism. Today Communism and *Marxism may be considered synonymous. "Communism is for us not a stable state which is to be established, but an *ideal* to which reality will have to adjust itself. We call Communism the *real* movement which abolishes the present state of things" (Marx, Engels, *G.I.,* 33). "Communist in the real world means the follower of a definite *revolutionary party" (*G.I.,* 33). "Communism differs from all previous movements in that it overturns the basis of all earlier relations of *production and intercourse, and for the first time consciously treats all natural premises as the creatures of man and strips them of their natural character and subjugates them to the power of individuals united. Its organization is, therefore, essentially economic, the material production of the conditions of this unity; it turns existing conditions into conditions of unity" (*G.I., 70*). See *Socialism/Communism.*

COMMUNIST INTERNATIONAL (Comintern, Third International). The Third International was founded at a congress held in Moscow, March 2-6, 1919, and attended by 52 delegates from Communist Parties in 30 countries. Lenin guided the Congress, and its announced aim was the replacement of *capitalism by Communism all over the world. The Third International held six more World Congresses in various years (1921, 1922, 1924, 1926, 1928, 1935), until it was dissolved by the Presidium of its Executive Committee, under the guidance of *Stalin, on May 15, 1943, as a gesture of unity between Russia and the Western Allies in World War II. The term *Communist International* can, of course, be applied to any one of the international organizations formed by world Communist Parties. The others are discussed here by name: First International, Second International, and Fourth. See also *Communist Manifesto, New; Twenty-one Points, Lenin's.*

COMMUNIST LEAGUE. This is the organization which brought the *Communist Manifesto* into the world by asking *Marx and *Engels to write it. It was organized in 1834 as the Exiles' League by a group of German refugees in Paris. The more extreme broke away in 1836 to form the League of the Just, which had as its motto: *The community of all goods.* Two members, Karl *Schapper and Heinrich Baur, were soon expelled from France and went to London where they set up a London center for the League, now called the Federation of the Just. They were joined by Joseph Moll and with him formed, on February 7, 1840, the German Workers' Educational Association, as a legal group, which tried to establish *communes in both London and Paris. The name was soon changed to Communist Workers' Educational Society, which Moll invited Marx and Engels to join in the spring of 1847. In the summer of 1847, the Society held its First Congress and it was organized "into communes, leading circles, central committee, and congresses" (Engels). At the Second Congress, December 1847, Marx and Engels were asked to draw up a manifesto to set forth the aims of the Society. They did so; and in February 1848 the *Communist Manifesto* saw light. In 1850 there was a split between the Schapper-*Willich group and the Marx-Engels group, and in 1852, on Marx's initiative, the Society was dissolved. Engels has a *History of the Communist League,* published in various collections of his works, including the *Selected Works,* and also in his *Germany.*

COMMUNIST MANIFESTO. The famous declaration of principles and aims which *Marx and *Engels published in February, 1848, at the request of the *Communist League of London. Engels has written the history of how it came to be composed, which is summarized in this *Vocabulary* under the entry for *Communist League*. The *Manifesto* was not widely read at first. It was nobody's "Bible," even in the days of the *First International; it was not often reprinted. Only the spread of Social Democratic parties of various kinds gave it a wide public, and the rise of Soviet Russia gave it grim aspect. Nor did it remain unchanged, in practice: "After the experience of the *Paris Commune, Marx and Engels found it necessary to supplement the, in part, obsolete *Communist Manifesto* with an elucidation of the truth that the working class cannot simply lay hold of the ready-made state machinery, but must *smash* it" (Lenin, *P.R.*, 172). George J. *Harvey gave the *Manifesto* to the world in his paper *The Red Republican,* in 1850. It was translated into German in 1872; it reappeared in English as a pamphlet in 1886; it was translated by *Herzen into Russian in the newspaper *The *Bell,* in the early 1860s, and appeared again in Russian as a pamphlet with preface by Marx in 1882.

COMMUNIST MANIFESTO, NEW. A Manifesto issued on March 10, 1919, by the First Congress of the Third International (see *Communist International*), meeting in Moscow and directed by *Lenin. It called for world *revolution and outlined steps that such a revolution might take. It was signed by *Lenin, *Trotsky, and *Zino-

viev for Russia; by Rakovsky for the Balkan Communist Federation; by Platten for the Swiss Communist Party. (Discussed in Cole, IV, i, 9.) It was first published in the *Communist International,* the newspaper issued by the Third International and edited by Zinoviev, in its first issue, May 1919, in Russian, German, French, and English. It has never taken hold as did the first *Manifesto.*

COMMUNIST PARTY, RUSSIAN. The name adopted by the *Bolsheviks at their 7th Party *Congress, held in St. Petersburg on March 6-8, 1918, which declared the aim of the Soviet Government, now under the Party's control, as "the creation of a Communist society." The Party's official name became Russian Communist Party (Bolsheviks [or B]), abbreviated often as R.C.P. (B). It was changed at the 14th Congress to Communist Party of the Soviet Union (B). At the 19th Congress the (B) was officially dropped. For membership figures, see *Membership, Russian Communist Party.* See also *Party.*

COMMUNIST WORKERS' EDUCATIONAL SOCIETY. See *Communist League.*

COMMUNISTS. "A Communist is one who actively helps to carry out the program of the *Party and necessarily works in one of its organizations under its leadership and control" (Dutt, 413). Communists are "not peculiar in special ways, but are ordinary workers, intellectuals, peasants, distinguished

Compound Labor

only by greater *class-consciousness, ideological steadfastness, and, consequently, by more *revolutionary character" (*Ibid.*, 411).

COMPOUND LABOR. "Sorts of *labor which involve the use of capabilities or knowledge acquired with the expenditure of greater or lesser effort, time and money" (Engels, *A.-D.*, 273). That is, as opposed to "simple labor," which is done without training, *compound labor* is the work performed by trained labor power. "The product of one hour of compound labor is a *commodity of a higher *value — perhaps double or treble — in comparison with the product of one hour of simple labor" (*Ibid.*, 273).

COMPRADOR. A native of a country who represents foreign investors among his own people. Commonly used of China. "Chinese compradorism is the classic form of the colonial *bourgeoisie, and the Kuomintang is the classic party of compradorism" (Trotsky, *H.R. R.*, III, 56).

COMPROMISERS. Derisive name given by *Bolsheviks to leaders of the *Mensheviks and other *socialist parties in Russia who professed socialist principles but who joined the *Cadets in supporting *Kerensky in 1917.

COMRADE COURTS. Present-day Russian elective social units which help educate delinquent young (or old) citizens to fuller understanding of "the Communist spirit," by means of persuasion and public pressure. Members of the Courts are elected to two-year terms by the collectives in industries, in offices, educational institutions, colleges, farms, housing developments, etc. They are guidance and "big brother" units, often used as probation officers, in effect.

CONCERNS, BUSINESS. See *Imperialism.*

CONCILIATORS. The name given a group led by Dubrovinsky, Nogin, *Zinoviev, *Kamenev, and Rykov, which flourished around 1912. With the so-called *Liquidators, this group sought agreement with *Trotsky behind *Lenin's back at a Paris meeting in 1912 in an effort to make Trotsky's Vienna *Pravda* the official organ of the *Bolshevik Party, with Kamenev on its Board. Lenin forced the Congress, meeting in Paris, to condemn the group, as well as *otzovism (terrorism), but had to agree to discontinue his own publication, *Proletary.* The minority kept its own paper, edited by Golos, the *Sotsial-Demokrat,* and the Liquidators kept theirs, *Our Dawn (Nasha Zarya)*, while Lenin started still another, *Dawn (Zarya)*.

CONGRESSES, Russian Social Democratic Labor Party. See next entry.

CONGRESSES, COMMUNIST PARTY SOVIET UNION. At the time of its early Congresses, the present Communist Party Soviet Union was known as the Russian Social Democratic Labor Party, and its first Congresses were known as Congress of Social Democratic Organizations. Following is a list of the Party Congresses, from the first in 1898 to the last in 1961, with

46

some indication of the matters dealt with at the Congress, and the representation present:

First: Minsk, March 1-3, 1898. Organized by N. K. *Krupskaya, later wife of *Lenin. Nine delegates representing Socialist groups in St. Petersburg, Moscow, Kiev, Yakaterinoslav — all called *Leagues of Struggle. This was the founding of the Russian Social Democratic Labor Party (R.S.D.L.P.) A Central Committee of three members was elected and quickly broken by the Tsarist secret police, the *Okhrana.

Second: Brussels and London, July 17—August 10, 1903. There were 51 delegates representing 26 organizations: the *Iskra group had 33; the *Economists, 3; the *Bundists, 5; the Socialist Workers, 10. The Bundists proposed a draft program which excluded the dictatorship of the *proletariat as one of the aims of the R.S.D.L.P. This was rejected. The Congress accepted *Iskra*, Lenin's paper, as officially representative of the Party; and it adopted Lenin's position on the dominant role of the *Central Committee to "guide all practical activities of the Party, allocation of Party funds and forces, and to make rules binding on all Party organizations" (Rothstein, 66). The Congress appointed to the *Iskra* Board: Lenin, *Martov, *Plekhanov: Martov declined appointment. Division in the Congress was so bitter that a split occurred in the R.S.D.L.P., the majority group following Lenin, and taking the name *Bolsheviks (ma-

jority); the minority (*Menshevik) group following Plekhanov. Wrote Lenin later: "As a trend of political thought and as a political party, Bolshevism has existed since 1903" (*Works*, XXXI, 8). The Mensheviks were led by Plekhanov, Martov, *Trotsky, *Axelrod; and through Plekhanov they succeeded in taking over *Iskra* before the end of 1903, and the Central Committee in 1904. (See Deutscher, I, 72ff. for an interesting account).

Third: London, April 12-27, 1905. The history of the Congresses now becomes that of the *Bolshevik group in the R.S.D.-L.P. There were 38 delegates, representing 20 Bolshevik committees. It declared in favor of revolution and dictatorship of the proletariat in Russia; for the confiscation of all lands; for overthrow of the peasants, the Church, and the Tsar. It established another paper, *Proletary,* with Lenin as editor. The Mensheviks held a rival congress in Geneva.

Fourth: Stockholm, April 10-25, 1906. It was called the Unity Congress because both Bolsheviks and Mensheviks attended, a total of 112 delegates, representing 57 organizations, 46 of them Bolshevik and 62 of them Menshevik. Party rules were adopted, including for the first time the concept of *Democratic Centralism advocated by Lenin. Three papers were established: *The Wave (Volna)*; *Forward (Vyeryod)*; *The Echo (Ekko)*. The basic differences between the two factions were not resolved.

Fifth: London, April 30—May

19, 1907. Three hundred and thirty-six delegates represented 147,000 Party members. The Congress determined to use the State *Duma as a forum for the exposure of Tsarism, but not as a means to socialist ends.

Sixth: Prague, January 5-17, 1912. Delegates present from twenty organizations expelled the so-called *Liquidators grouped around the papers *Our Dawn* and *Cause of Life*. They adopted in general the Bolshevik tactics, and Lenin could write: "At last we have succeeded, in spite of the liquidator scum, in restoring the Party to its Central Committee" (*Works,* XXXV, 1).

Seventh: Petrograd, March 6-8, 1918. This was the first Congress after the Bolsheviks had taken power in Russia. Forty-six full delegates and fifty-eight consultative delegates represented 170,000 members; another 130,000 members could not send representatives because they were still behind German lines. The so-called *Left Communists opposed the Peace of *Brest-Litovsk, negotiated by Trotsky with Lenin's concurrence; but they were defeated by Lenin's forces in a vote of 30 to 12 (4 abstentions). The Party name was changed to *Russian Communist Party (Bolshevik), often abbreviated R.C.P. (B) The Congress endorsed Russia's withdrawal from the War.

Eighth: Moscow, March 18-23, 1919. This Congress adopted Lenin's draft of a new Party program, which summed up the re-

sults achieved since 1903 and pointed to the tasks facing the Party in the transition to Socialism in Russia.

Ninth: Moscow, March 29—April 5, 1920. It represented 600,-000 Party members, and adopted Lenin's views of dictatorship of the proletariat against those who favored more democratic procedures.

Tenth: Moscow, March 8-16, 1921. The delegates represented 700,000 Party members, and adopted the *New Economic Policy (NEP). The Congress advocated the rapid sovietization of national groups and a tightened Party discipline.

Eleventh: Moscow, March 27—April 2, 1922. This was the last Congress attended by Lenin. It condemned the so-called *Workers' Opposition, and elected a *Central Committee which in turn appointed *Stalin as its Secretary — the foundation of his forthcoming control of the Party.

Twelfth: Moscow, April 17-25, 1923. The delegates represented 400,000 Party members, a decrease in size brought about by the strict enforcement of the disciplinary measures adopted by the Eleventh Congress. The struggle between the Stalinists and Trotskyites was in evidence, and internal affairs held the stage.

Thirteenth: Moscow, May 23-31, 1924. The delegates represented 643,000 members, of which 445,000 were full Party members (card-carrying), while the rest were candidate members, a distinction begun after the strict regulations adopted in 1923. The Congress condemned Trotsky's conduct versus Stalin, and those who associated with Trotsky. Emphasis was placed upon the continued enrollment of workers in the Party (see *Lenin Enrollment*).

Fourteenth: Moscow, December 18-21, 1925. The delegates represented 643,000 members, 445,000 of them card-carrying. The Congress made a "Party Law" of what it called Lenin's position that Communism can be victorious in one country regardless of its failure to spread to others. It condemned the so-called *New Opposition, composed of the followers of Trotsky. It changed the Party name from Russian Communist Party to Communist Party of the Soviet Union (B). It favored emphasis upon the development of heavy industry and hence came to be known as the "industrialization Congress."

Fifteenth: Moscow, December 2-19, 1927. It approved all-out collectivization of agriculture (see *Kulaks*), adopted directives for the first *Five Year Plan, and approved expulsion of Trotsky and *Zinoviev from the Party, with some 75 others, including *Kamenev, Radek, Pyatakov.

Sixteenth: Moscow, June 26—July 13, 1930. The delegates represented 1,260,874 members, 711,609 of them card carrying. It denounced Trotskyism as anti-Communism, and advocated a "full-scale offensive all along the socialist state front."

Seventeenth: Moscow, January 26—February 10, 1934. The delegates represented 1,874,488 members, 935,298 card-carrying. It approved the second Five Year Plan, and adopted new Party rules without any opposition.

Eighteenth: Moscow, March 10-21, 1939. The delegates represented 1,588,852 members, 888,-814 card-carrying. The decrease in Party membership was due to what the Congress called "verification of Party records, and exchange of membership cards," but it will be noticed that this Congress follows upon the *Purges and *Treason Trials of 1936-38. The Congress considered the third Five Year Plan, and heard Stalin's report on the nature of the State — the necessity of a strong, centralized government not yet ready to "wither away."

Nineteenth: Moscow, October, 1952. The delegates represented 6,013,259 Party members; 868,886 were candidates. It approved the Five Year Plan for economic development from 1951-1955. It officially dropped the designation (B), meaning Bolsheviks, behind the name of the Party, something done long before in practice. (See *Seventh* and *Fourteenth Congresses.*)

Twentieth: Moscow, February, 1956. It represented membership of 6,795,896 of whom 419,609 were candidates. It approved the sixth Five Year Plan, and entertained guest delegates from 55 Communist Parties abroad. *Khrushchev delivered to this Congress his famous *Secret Speech on Stalin. The Congress approved the sixth Five Year Plan.

Twenty-first: Moscow, January 27—February 5, 1959. Membership was at 7,622,356, of whom 616,775 were candidates. This Congress announced the entry of the Soviet Union upon the full-scale development of Communism (see *Socialism/Communism*). It adopted a Seven Year Plan (1959-1965), and set advanced goals in economics, political relations, education, and international relations.

Twenty-Second: Moscow, October 17-27, 1961. The Congress attacked *Revisionism as the chief enemy of Communism. It declared for "peaceful co-existence" with capitalist nations and for disarmament under international control. It set ten- and twenty-year industrial and agricultural goals. The Congress envisioned the development of the *New Soviet Man, and the ultimate transition to full Communism in Russia.

CONSTANT CAPITAL. "That part of capital . . . which is represented by the means of *production, by the *raw materials, auxiliary materials, and the instruments of *labor, does not, in the process of production, undergo any quantitative alteration of *value. I, therefore, call it the constant capital" (Marx, *Cap.*, I, 209). "Constant capital, the means of production, considered from the standpoint of the creation of *surplus-value, only exists to absorb labor" (*ibid.*, 256). "By constant capital advanced for the production of value, we always mean, unless the context is re-

pugnant thereto, the value of the means of production actually consumed in the process, and that value alone" (*ibid.*, 213). See also *Capital*.

CONSTITUENT ASSEMBLY. Russian revolutionary parliamentary body elected between the *February and the *October, 1917, Revolutions. Convened by the Soviet Government on January 5, 1918, it came into quick conflict with the *Bolsheviks, who withdrew. It was dissolved by the All-Russian Central Executive Committee, Bolshevik Party, on January 7, 1918.

CONSTITUTION OF THE RUSSIAN SOVIET OF FEDERATED SOCIALIST REPUBLICS. The so-called "First" Russian Constitution, adopted by the Fifth All-Russian *Congress of Soviets in Moscow, July, 1918. It confirmed the *revolutionary dictatorship of the *proletariat, approved the form of the *Soviet State, guaranteed "democratic" participation in the government, and disfranchised the *bourgeoisie.

CONSTITUTION, CURRENT RUSSIAN. In addition to establishing the form of government of the *Soviet Union, the Constitution provides for the right of every citizen to work, to holidays, to participation in social and cultural life, to pensions and sickness benefits, and to education. The Constitution provides for freedom of conscience, of speech, of the press, and of assembly. It protects the home and provides against all discrimination on the basis of sex or race. It establishes universal direct election by secret ballot, and gives the franchise to all citizens over 18 years of age. It sets minimum age limits for election to public office as follows: Deputy to Supreme Soviet, 23 years of age; to Soviets of member Republics, 21 years of age; to local Soviets, 18 years of age. It must be remembered that many of these provisions exist only on paper.

CONTEMPORARY, The (*Sovremennik*). The most influential *liberal magazine in Russia during the mid-nineteenth century. It was founded in 1836 by the Russian writer Alexander Pushkin, edited after 1847 by the poet N. A. Nekrasov, and published in St. Petersburg. The vehicle for democratic ideas, it was often suspended by the police and suspended permanently in 1866. Its most influential period was from 1854 to 1862, when it took an active role in stimulating the peasant unrest which culminated in the law that freed the peasants from serfdom in 1861. Among others, *Chernyshevsky and *Dobrolyubov were editors and contributors.

CONTRADICTION. According to *Hegel and *Marx, contradiction is the mainspring of *history. Progress rides on the back of conflict, in the form of the *dialectic triad. Every situation has contradiction inherent in it, and history is the process of the *development and resolution of such contradiction. Hegel: "Contradiction leads the way forward." See *Dialectic;* also *Thesis.*

CO-OPERATION (in labor). "When numerous laborers work together side by side, whether in one and the same process, or in different but connected processes, they are said to co-operate, or to work in co-operation" (Marx, *Cap.,* I, 325). "All combined *labor on a large scale requires, more or less, a directing authority . . . . The work of directing, superintending, and adjusting becomes one of the functions of *capital, from the moment the labor under the control of capital becomes co-operative. Once a function of capital, it acquires special characteristics, in form despotic, requiring, like an army, officers (managers) and sergeants (foremen, overlookers) who, while the work is being done, command in the name of capital" (*ibid.,* 330). "As co-operators, as members of a working organism, laborers are but special modes of the existence of capital" (*ibid.,* 333). Co-operation under *capitalism is to be distinguished by two characteristics from *primitive communal ownership: (1) under the primitive form, "ownership was common of the means of *production," and (2) there each member was an integral unit, not function, of the whole (*Ibid.,* 334).

COSMOPOLITANISM. The Soviet term for the failure now to place the Fatherland above all. The Communist praises *"proletarian internationalism," but he is also sensitive to national traditions, and considers that a preference for internationalism and world government so long as *bourgeois nations remain on the earth is Cosmopolitanism, at enmity with true socialist patriotism.

COUNCIL OF MINISTERS OF THE USSR (ALL-UNION COUNCIL, etc.,). The highest executive and administrative organ of the *Soviet Union. Elected by, and responsible to, the *Supreme Soviet of the USSR, the Council is responsible to the Supreme Soviet when it is in session, and at other times to the *Presidium of the USSR. Members of the Council cannot be members of the Presidium. The Council executes the laws, guides the various *Commissariats (Commissions), and may suspend decisions of the constituent Republics.

COUNTER-REVOLUTION. See *Revolution.*

CRAPAUDS. Literally *toads.* Slang used by *Marx and *Engels for the French *bourgeoisie.

CRASS SOCIALISTS. Marx's designation for those socialists who thought themselves above all questions of politics or political action.

CREDO. A declaration of principles set forth by the *Economists, and published at the turn of this century. It was answered by *Lenin's pamphlet *Protest by Russian Social Democrats,* in which *Credo* appears quoted in full. (See Lenin, *A.R.,* pp. 27-30.)

CREMER, W. R. (1838-1908), first Secretary of the General Council of the *First International, 1864. He resigned in 1866. He became a Member of the British Parliament as Liberal in 1885-95 and 1900-1908.

CRETINISM. A term employed by *Marx to denote the psychological effect upon the worker of the monotony of mechanical labor. "Labor produces intelligence, but for the laborer idiocy, cretinism." It is sometimes employed as an epithet to indicate general stupidity or obtuseness, as in *Lenin's favorite phrase "parliamentary cretinism."

CRISES. Periods of unemployment and business depression. *Marxism analyzes these as being due to increased *production of the *means* of production as a result of *capital's drive toward unlimited expansion. The increase of production of consumer goods which follows finally expands beyond the bounds of purchasing power, and crises result. *Lenin considered this the basic contradiction of *capitalism, one it could not escape. *Engels analyzed crises as follows: "The mode of production (social) is in rebellion against the mode of *exchange, the *productive forces are in rebellion against the mode of production which they have outgrown . . . the socialized organization of production within the factory has developed so far that it has become in competition with the anarchy of production in society" (Engels, *A.-D.,* 380).

CRITICISM (Neo - Kantianism). Philosophical movement in Russia. Its adherents held that economics is only one, though an important, factor in social development. This put them at odds with the Marxists, who held the economic factor to be determinative of the social super-structures built upon it. Criticism had two Russian streams: (1) Scientific realism, represented by B. Kistyokovsky and P. *Struve; and (2) Religious *utopianism, represented by N. Berdyaev, S. Bulgakov, S. Frank. Of these latter *Plekhanov said, "They seek the road to heaven simply because they have lost their way here upon earth." Criticism was attacked by *Lenin in *Materialism and Empirio-Criticism*.

CRITICISM AND SELF-CRITICISM. Criticism implies the right of every Communist *Party member to criticize any official at any Party gathering, and to address questions to any Party functionary or group, up to the *Central Committee itself. *Lenin held that criticism must be intended constructively, must aim at practical results, and must not extend to Communist ideology. He also insisted that criticism must be offered, as it were, to the Party as a whole and not to, or for the purpose of creating, factions. Moreover, he held, the right of criticism ends when the subject under criticism has been decided by proper authority; thereafter only obedience is appropriate. Self-criticism means the duty of every Party official, and of every Party member, to examine himself and his conduct, to accept the criticism of others in good grace and with determination to self-correction. Self-criticism often extends to public profession of error in belief or in conduct with promises to change or pleas for mercy. See *Treason Trials; Inner-Party Democracy*.

CRITICISM, FREEDOM OF. See *Freedom of Criticism*.

CULT OF PERSONALITY. Another name for the *Cult of the Individual.

CULT OF THE INDIVIDUAL. Defined by Russian Communists as the worship of an outstanding leader, to whose superhuman merits and virtues no exception may be taken. Specifically, it is the term used by the post-Stalinists to describe the role *Stalin took for himself and was accorded by others. It is considered now to be un-Marxist, bad for practical activity, and tending to absolve the masses of a sense of responsibility for the solution of their problems. It was officially denounced by the Twentieth *Congress of the Russian Communist Party in 1956, after *Khrushchev's *"Secret Speech" concerning the crimes of Stalin.

CUNO, Theodor (b. 1847), helped organize the Milan, Italy, section of the *First International. At the Conference in The Hague he was Chairman of the Commission which expelled *Bakunin from the International. He went to America and edited there the *New York Peoples' Paper*.

DANIELSON, Nikolai Franzevich (Nicolai-on) (1844-1918). The translator of Marx's *Capital* into Russian, completing the work begun by G. A. Lopatin. He published Volume I in 1872, II in 1885, and III in 1896. Danielson was chief theoretician of the *Narodniks, and *Lenin calls him a *utopian for failing to grasp that the *class struggle is a necessary consequence of *capitalism.

DARWIN, Charles (1809-1862), famous British naturalist whose theory of natural selection as the basis of animal evolution was grasped by *Marx as demonstrating in nature the same principles which Marx discovered in society. It is said that Marx offered to inscribe Volume I of *Capital* to Darwin and that he declined the honor. Marx, in a letter to *Engels, December 19, 1860, wrote: "This is the book [*Origin of the Species,* by Darwin] which contains the basis in natural history for our view." And in *Capital* Marx writes: "Darwin has introduced us to the history of Nature's technology" (I, 406, n. 2). See *Social Darwinism.*

DAS KAPITAL. See *Capital.*

DASHNAKS. Armenian anti-Communists who formed a party by this name in the 1890s. It opposed union with Russia in 1917, and took Caucasia from the *Soviet Union. This party headed the Armenian Government from 1918 to 1920 and crushed pro-Communist groups. In November 1920 it succumbed to Soviet power.

DAWN (*Zarya*). Marxist magazine published in Stuttgart, Germany, in 1901-02 by the Editorial Board of *Iskra,* headed by *Lenin. It came out in four numbers, in three issues, April 1901 to August 1902.

DAY OF ENJOYMENT. The name given to the day when the confiscated goods of deportees are made available to those loyal to the Communist regime.

DEBORIN, Abram Moiseyevich (Yoffe) (b. 1881), Russian revolutionary and exponent of *dialectical materialism, considered the most important Russian advocate of *Marxism since *Lenin. He held leading positions in the *Bolshevik Party, and wrote *Introduction to Philosophy of Dialectical Materialism,* in 1916, and other works on *Marx, *Hegel, *Lenin. According to Deborin, dialectical materialism has three moments: (1) materialist dialectic, or general methodology, (2) dialectic of nature, and (3) dialectic of *history, or *historical materialism.

DECEMBRISTS (Dekabrists). Those who participated in the unsuccessful uprising against Tsar Alexander I, in December (*Dekabr*), 1825.

DECLARATION OF RIGHTS OF THE PEOPLES OF RUSSIA. Issued on November 2, 1917, by the Soviet Government, it proclaimed the free development and full equality of all nationalities of Russia. A peoples' Commissariat for the Affairs of Nationalities was then established in the Soviet Government, headed by Joseph *Stalin.

DECLARATION OF THE FORTY-SIX. Statement presented to the *Central Committee of the *Bolshevik Party in October 1923, by *Trotsky and his supporters, charging that the Party appartus had supplanted the Party and demanding freedom for opposition groups. The Central Committee condemned this action, to which Trotsky responded with his pamphlet *The New Course.*

DECREE ON PEACE. The first official act of the Soviet Government, October 8, 1917. The Decree called upon all belligerent governments then engaged in World War I, and their peoples, to make a "just and democratic peace," with no annexation or indemnity (Kennan, pp. 33ff.).

DEFENDERS (Oborontsi). The name given those socialists who favored continuation of the war with Germany after the Russian *Revolution of February, 1917. The *Bolsheviks and other radical groups favored a peace offer to Germany.

DE LEON, Daniel (1852-1914), American socialist, head of the Socialist Labor Party, 1890, who earned the praise of *Lenin as socialist thinker and writer. He wrote much for *The People,* organ of the Socialist Labor Party. De Leon held that *Socialism would come in one massive revolutionary overthrow of "the *capitalist system and its system of wage slavery." De Leon has been called the "best American exemplification of orthodox *Social Democracy" (Hook). In 1905 he helped to found the *Industrial Workers of the World.

DEMOCRACY. *Marxism discriminates between various uses of the term: (1) *Parliamentary* or *political* democracy is, it maintains, the right to vote and hold office; (2) *economic* democracy is equality of opportunity in employment and the fruits of industry; (3) *social* democracy is *class equality. *Democracy* in itself means simply mass, or majority. *Lenin argued that parliamentary democracy "is of enormous importance to the working class in its struggle against the capitalists for its emancipation" (*S. & R.,* 158) because of the freedom given in a democracy to agitate and publish, and the opportunity to hold meetings and to send workers' representatives to governmental bodies. He held, with Marxists generally, that real economic democracy is impossible under *capitalism and that monopoly capitalism, or *imperialism, is characterized by a shift toward *fascism and the elimination of political democracy. The kind of *state a country has may be determined by asking, Whose interests does the state serve? Whose rights and powers does it defend? What policies does it pursue? Lenin: "It is obvious that we cannot speak of 'pure democracy' so long as classes exist; we can only speak of *class* democracy" (*P.R.,* 30). "Democracy is a barometer which permits the strength and the political intelligence of the working class to be measured" (Kautsky, 23). Political democracy clearly reveals the relative strength of various forces in the country. The Communist can, therefore, favor it as a means to his own ends, and can speak of democracy in Russia by meaning mass participation in economic benefits. See *Bourgeois Democracy.*

DEMOCRACY, INNER PARTY. See *Inner-Party Democracy.*

DEMOCRACY, PEOPLE'S. See *People's Democracy.*

DEMOCRACY, PROLETARIAN. See *Proletarian Democracy.*

DEMOCRATIC CENTRALISM. A term commonly employed by *Lenin to combine the ideas of *democracy, by which he meant *mass participation,* and dictatorship. Lenin meant by it to designate administration of affairs by one central authority, or the leadership, and execution of the common will by single persons. In practice it meant: (1) the election of the leading *Party bodies, (2) the accountability of the leaders to the organization, (3) strict Party discipline, subordination of the minority to the majority, and (4) higher bodies absolutely binding lower. Constructive *criticism is encouraged, destructive criticism forbidden — and the difference between these is set by the *Party line. Before a decision, discussion; after a decision, united action. Lenin applied the principle of democratic centralism also to economic management, by centralized control of huge-scale industry, executed by Soviet-appointed directors, with total participation of the workers in the local *soviets, or councils. *Trotsky: "Revolutionary centralism is a harsh, imperative and exacting principle. It often takes the guise of absolute ruthlessness in its relation to individual members, to whole groups of former associates" (*M.L.,* 161).

DEMOCRATIC CENTRALISTS. A group within the Russian Communist Party which, in 1920, advocated that the Presidium or *Supreme Council of National Economy be nominated by the trade unions instead of the *Bolshevik Party, and that single directors of factories be abolished in favor of trade union operation. Not granted.

DEMUTH, Helene (1823-1890), the family companion in the *Marx household who came with Mrs. Marx, *née* Jenny von *Westphalen, into the family and remained until after the death of both Jenny and Karl Marx. She then went to keep house for the *Engels until her death. She was buried in the Marx family plot in Highgate Cemetery. The family nickname for her was *Lenchen.*

DEPRESSIONS, Marxist Analysis of. See *Crises.*

DETERMINISM, ECONOMIC. See *Economic Determinism.*

DEUTSCH — FRANZOESISCHE JAHRBUECHER (*Franco-German Annals*). Publication edited by Marx and Arnold *Ruge in Paris in 1844, after *Marx's expulsion from Germany. The only issue to appear was a double number for February 1844; it contained articles by Marx ("A Critique of the Hegelian Philosophy of Law," and "On the Jewish Question") and by *Engels ("Outlines of a Critique of Political Economy," and "The Position of England"). Marx and Ruge could not agree sufficiently on the nature and aims of the *Annals* to arrive at the publication of another issue.

DEVELOPMENT. In the *Hegelian philosophy, development means the passage of an old *quality* into a new one at a definite stage of *quantitative* modification. The motive power for *development is the struggle of opposites in *contradiction. This, *Marx taught, is literally true of society and figuratively true of organic and inorganic life. *History proceeds "in a spiral, not a straight line. The development of society proceeds through the consecutive replacement, according to definite laws, of one socio-economic formation by another." (Dutt, 153).

DEVIATIONISM. "A deviation is not a fully formed movement. It is something that can be corrected. People have strayed a little from the path or are beginning to stray, but it is still possible to correct." This was *Lenin's view of deviationism (*B. R.,* I, 200). The term can be used to cover any number of "mistakes" and is often the basis of *criticism.

DIALECTICAL MATERIALISM. See *Materialism, Dialectical.*

DIALECTICS (Dialectic, Dialectical). A key term in *Marxism, especially in its philosophy of *history (see *Materialism, Historical*). It has been called the "true soul of Marxism," if Marxism has, or wants, a soul; "the theory of universal connections" (Dutt, p. 69). It is a method of studying, and of changing, reality. The term is Greek in origin, meaning argument, the give and take of logical development. It was developed by *Hegel into the form of a triad (see *Thesis,* etc.). *Engels: "In the Hegelian system — and herein is its great merit — for the first time the whole world, natural, historical, intellectual, is represented as a process, that is as in constant motion, change, transformation, *development" (*A.-D.,* 37). Dialectics is the study of the laws of this development. And dialectics reveals that development proceeds by a process, in which the given situation — or thing, or idea — always gives birth to its exact antithesis, opposite; and in so doing creates a tension, a struggle, which becomes the motive power for change, progress, as the *antithesis* struggles with its mother, the *thesis*, until out of the struggle a new stage in history — be it of the situation, of the thing, or of the idea — is reached, namely, the *synthesis* — and this, in turn, becomes the starting point of another round, by giving birth once more to *its* opposite. The essence of the dialectic method is thus the discernment in *apparent* unity of the reality of *contradictory elements, potentially at strife with one another. *Lenin: "The unity of opposites is conditional, temporary, transitory, relative. The struggle of mutually exclusive opposites is absolute, just as development and motion are absolute" (*Works, XXXVIII,* 358). Thus the dialectic method "sharpens vision; gives insight, flexibility; makes for receptivity to the new; purges the mind of dogma, prejudice, preconceived notions, false 'eternal truths'; and keeps one in touch with life" (Dutt, 106). *Marx and Engels found in material forces, in the economic relations of *production, the basic contradictions which mold history: "Marx and I were pretty well the only people

57

to rescue conscious dialetics from German *idealist philosophy and apply it in the *materialist conception of nature and history" (Engels, *A.-D.*, 16). Dialectics, Engels adds, "comprehends things in their repetitions, in their essential connection, concatenation, motion, origin, and ending. Nature works dialectically, not metaphysically" (*A.-D.*, 36). It is the great fault of *metaphysics, which the Marxists see as the view wholly opposite to dialectics, that it comprehends history and things as static, undeveloping, disconnected. To show that nature is not static, but follows the laws of dialectics, Engels worked for many years collecting materials for his *Dialectics of Nature,* which had to be left unfinished at his death in 1895 because he had given so much of his later years to completing the editing of Marx's last two volumes of *Capital,* unfinished at Marx's death in 1883. Lenin lists sixteen elements in dialectics in his *Philosophical Notebooks* (*Works,* V, 38). *Plekhanov discusses dialectics in his *Monist View,* Engels in *Anti-Dühring,* and Lenin in *Materialism and Empirio-Criticism.*

DIAMAT. The abbreviation, common in philosophical discussion, for *dialectical materialism.

DICTATORSHIP OF THE PRO-LETARIAT. See *Revolutionary Dictatorship of the Proletariat.*

DIFFERENT ROADS TO SOCI-ALISM. A phrase denoting the position that various countries can achieve the socialist state by various means, not necessarily *revolu-

tionary. Local circumstances will according to this position, deter mine the appropriate means. A the 20th *Congress of the Russian Communist Party, in 1956 *Khrushchev took this position, a did other speakers. Before thi time, it had generally been held that only by the road of violent rev olution could *capitalism be over thrown; this had been the stand taken by *Lenin against *Bernstein and *Kautsky. See *Revisionism.*

DIMINISHING RETURNS. See *Law of Diminishing Returns.*

DISTANCE THEORY. A theory enunciated by some Soviet writers in 1958 to the effect that an author who wishes to write creatively abou contemporary problems must "dis tance" himself from political strug gle and Party activity in order to write with *objectivity. In its is sue of August 17, 1958, *Pravda de nounced the distance theory as the invention of "literary idlers" who ignore the principle of *Party mindedness. See *Objectivity.*

DIVISION OF LABOR. For Adam *Smith the division of *labor wa the performance by separate work ers of the parts of a process which together produce the complete product. For *Marx "the division of labor and private *property are identical expressions" (*G.I.*, 22) and the various stages in the division of labor, historically, are just so many different forms of the ownership of property. The first form is tribal ownership, which corresponds to the undeveloped stage of *production. The second form is the ancient communal, or state, ownership, where the *class relationship between citizen and slave is fully developed. The third form of ownership is feudal or estate property, where the producing class is the enserfed small peasantry; and, as its counterpart in the towns, corporate property in the form of the guilds, the feudal organization of the trades. The fourth form of property ownership is modern *capitalistic ownership, which has cast off all semblance of a communal institution and become pure private property. (Adapted from *G.I.*, pp. 9-14, 59). The division of labor between and within the classes reflects property relations.

DOBROLYUBOV, Nikolai Alexandrovich (1836-1861), Russian revolutionary writer, forerunner of Marxist *materialists. Born into the family of a priest and educated for the priesthood, he became a private tutor. He met *Chernyshevsky in 1855 and later joined him as literary critic on the staff of the magazine *Contemporary (*Sovremennik*) and as editor of its satirical supplement *Whistle (*Svistok*). Critical of the Russian autocracy, Dobrolyubov favored the common masses over the elite and worked for the abolition of serfdom and other social reforms. He was materialist in philosophy. At age 25 he died from want and overwork.

DOCTORS' CONSPIRACY (or, Doctors' Plot; Jewish Doctors' Plot). On January 13, 1953, while *Stalin was still alive and dominant, *Pravda announced in its last, inconspicuous paragraph the discovery of a conspiracy on the part of nine doctors on the Kremlin staff to murder high-ranking Party officials. Already, the announcement said, the doctors had killed former Politburo (*Presidium) members Z h d a n o v and Shchenbakov. The doctors were alleged to be in the employ of American and British secret services, as well as serving international Jewry. This announcement signalled the beginning of a wide witch-hunt — in press, on radio and television — in the Soviet Union, with fingers pointed at "enemies of the people" who were serving foreign powers. The witch-hunts ended as mysteriously as they began, with the death of Stalin, announced as having occurred on March 5, 1953. On April 4, *Pravda* announced that the Kremlin doctors had been exonerated and returned to duty. Oddly, however, the number freed was thirteen, four more than had been apprehended; and of the thirteen, two names among the original nine were missing. It has been speculated that the doctors' conspiracy charge heralded another purge, like those of the late 1930's, and that this threat moved some of the most powerful members in the Party hierarchy to undertake the elimination of Stalin before they themselves fell to his suspicions. This is, to date, purely speculative (cf. Gunther).

DOGMATISM, Marxist Definition of. Taking theoretical propositions as absolute, universal truths that can be applied equally and in all cases, regardless of the differences in concrete situations or the emergence of new phenomena. Thus a proposition true in itself becomes a *dogma* if advocated without regard to changing circumstances and concrete surrounding conditions. (See Dutt, 132.) "The Marxist-Leninist theory is not a dogma, but a guide to action" (Dutt, 19). Sometimes it is called *Talmudism* by Stalin. "To master Marxism-Leninism it is not at all enough to memorize formulas and conclusions. . . . You must, in addition, learn to employ this theory in solving practical problems" (Kalinin, 67). Compare *Sectarianism*.

DÜHRING, Karl Eugen (1833-1921), German lawyer and philosophical writer, lecturer at Berlin University. He opposed *dialectical materialism, exhibited anti-Semitism, and became the object of *Engels's attack in his *Anti-Dühring*.

DUMA. The Russian parliament, when called the State Duma; also the term used for Russian municipal elected bodies.

DZERZHINSKY, Felix Edmundovich (1877-1926), founder and first head of the Soviet Secret Police. See *Cheka*.

DZHUGASHVILI, Joseph. See *Stalin*.

ECCARIUS, George (d. 1889), tailor by trade, revolutionary by avocation, a close associate of *Marx and *Engels, a member of the *Communist League, Secretary of the General Council of the *First International. He delivered the opening address at the First Congress of the International, and devoted much of his life to the British trade union movement.

ECONOMIC DETERMINISM. A term used generally to indicate the view that the economic base of a society determines all other social and political characteristics of that society. What *Marxism calls "relations of *production" determine all other relations and all forms of art and institutions of any epoch in *history. Marxism distinguishes between "narrow" economic determinism, the theory which holds that relations proceed in only one direction, namely, from economics to the rest of the social structure; and "broad" economic determinism, which holds that the social relations created by the relations of production can react upon the latter and modify them. Marxism generally holds the "broad" view. (Cf. Plekhanov, *R.I.H.*) See *Materialism, Historical*.

ECONOMIC EPOCHS. *Marxism distinguishes five economic or historical epochs: (1) the tribal, (2) the slave, (3) the feudal, (4) the *bourgeois, and (5) the Communist. "It is not the articles made, but how they are made, and by what instruments, that enables us to distinguish different economic epochs" (Dutt, 35). See *Division of Labor*.

ECONOMIC INTERPRETATION OF HISTORY. See *Materialism, Historical*.

ECONOMISM(-ists). The doctrine that the *social* struggle should be restricted to the use of the strike, so far as the *proletariat is concerned, leaving the *political* struggle to the *bourgeoisie. It was advocated by E. D. Kushova in *Credo* of 1899 and opposed by *Lenin and *Plekhanov in *Iskra*. The Economists believed themselves Marxist, and published their views in papers of their own: *Workers' Thought* (*Rabochaya Mysl*) and *Workers' Cause* (*Rabocheye Dyelo*). Here they proposed that workers limit their demands to purely economic matters (hence the name, Economism), such as shorter working days, higher pay, better conditions, etc. Economism taught the *theory of stages*: first the strike, then unionization of all workers, then political liberation. The Marxists describe Economism as "the Russian variety of international *opportunism" (Rothstein, 54). Lenin wrote against its *Credo* from exile in Siberia, *A Protest by Russian Social-Democrats,* in 1899.

L'ÉGALITÉ. A weekly Marxist newspaper published by Jules *Guesde, in Paris, from 1877 to 1880, in two series of thirty-one and thirty-two issues respectively. It ceased with the August 25, 1880, issue, and was begun again as a daily on October 24, 1882, by Guesde and Paul *Lafargue, son-in-law of *Marx, to replace the Marxist paper *Le Citoyen,* which had been suspended by the police. References to their experiences with the paper appear in Paul and Laura Lafargue's *Correspondence* with Engels.

EISENACHERS. Part of the Social-Democratic Workers' Party of Germany, founded by *Bebel and Wilhelm *Liebknecht at Eisenach in 1869, as an outgrowth of the Saxon Peoples' Party which Bebel had formed in 1866. Their program declared their participation in the *First International. They united with the Social-Democratic Workers' Party in 1875 to form the Socialist Workers' Party of Germany, of which the followers of *Lassalle came to form the right wing.

EMANCIPATION (*Osvobozhdenize*). The paper of a liberal group of Russians headed by Peter *Struve, first published in 1902, which attempted to guide the then revolutionary unrest in Russia into channels of political liberalism rather than to let it flow into channels outlined by *Lenin in *Iskra*, that is, toward violent *revolution.

EMANCIPATION OF LABOR GROUP. Forerunner of the Russian *Bolshevik Party. Founded in Geneva by *Plekhanov in 1883, joined by P. B. *Axelrod, L. G. Deutsch, V. I. *Zasulich, V. N. Ignatov, it was the first Russian Marxist group. These leaders had been *Narodniks who had called themselves General Redistributionists and had been obliged to flee Russia. On September 25, 1883, the Group issued a statement of their program, which followed Marxist revolutionary lines and opposed

Narodnism. The Group translated into Russian, and secretly published, the works of *Marx and *Engels — the *Manifesto; Wage, Labor and Capital; Poverty of Philosophy; Ludwig Feuerbach*, etc. Plekhanov became the foremost Marxist writer of his time, emphasizing over and again the role of the workers in *revolution, the aims of a *socialist society, the ways of taking political power by means of a revolutionary workers' party. In time the Group drifted toward less extreme views, and Plekhanov came to lead the *Mensheviks as opposed to Lenin's Bolsheviks after 1903. The Group tended to underestimate, in *Lenin's view, the role of the peasantry in revolt. Lenin paid the Group and Plekhanov high compliments, but wrote: "The Emancipation of Labor Group only laid the theoretical foundations for the Social-Democratic movement and took the first step toward the working-class movement" (*Works*, XX, 255).

EMERGENCY INTERNATIONAL SOCIALIST CONGRESS. See *Basle Revolution; Second International*.

EMERGENT. See *Leap*.

EMPIRIO-CRITICISM. Philosophical view advocated by *Avenarius and Mach, and (inside Russia) by *Bogdanov, to the effect that reality exists only in the union of the knowing mind and the known world, while being in fact neither the one nor the other. Objective truth is impossible. Modern physics is presumed to validate the philoso-phy which is better known as *Positivism outside Russia. Bogdanov and his Russian colleagues gathered their views into three volumes: *Studies for a Realistic World View; Studies in the Philosophy of Marxism; and Studies for a Philosophy of Collectivism* — all sharply assailed by *Lenin in his *Materialism and Empirio-Criticism*, where he attacks not only their philosophy but their allegiance to *Marx. See *Machism*.

EMULATION, SOCIALIST. See *Socialist Emulation*.

ENGELS, Frederick (1820-1895), co-laborer with *Marx in originating and developing "scientific socialism" or *Communism. Engels was born in Barmen, Germany, November 28, 1820, the son of a German textile manufacturer who also had mills at Manchester, England. At Berlin University he was influenced by the *Left Hegelians and wrote a pamphlet against the philosopher Schelling (*The State and Revolution*) in March 1842 critical of Schelling's effort to harmonize "religion and science." He met Marx in 1844 in Paris after sending to him a "Critique of Political Economy" for the *Deutsch Französische Jahrbücher*. An affinity of mind and personality sprang up at once between the two men, and then and there they outlined a book, The *Holy Family*, as a joint effort. In 1845 they met in Brussels and wrote *The German Ideology* together. Both books were criticisms of the Left Hegelians, in particular of Bruno *Bauer, Edgar Bauer, and

Max *Stirner. Meanwhile, Engels had published in Germany his own book, *Condition of the Working Class in England in 1844* (publ. 1845). In 1848 Marx and Engels composed the *Communist Manifesto*. Together they founded the *First International, and together they wrote articles for Greeley's *New York Daily Tribune*. Engels worked in his father's Manchester mills and contributed heavily to Marx's support, especially after he finally came into his inheritance in the 1870s, when he almost completely supported the Marx family. Engels himself wrote *Anti-Dühring, Origin of the Family* (which *Lenin called "one of the fundamental works of modern socialism") and other books. He died on August 5, 1895, after giving most of the later years of his life to editing Volumes II (1885) and III (1894) of Marx's *Capital*. In a footnote to his booklet on *Feuerbach, Engels says that while he did indeed contribute "to laying the foundations and elaborating the theory" of Communism, "Marx could have gotten along without me"; and that Marx "stood higher, saw farther and took a wider and quicker view." Estimates vary of the role Engels really played in the development of *Marxism, but it was substantial. He dabbled in languages for a pastime and once was chided for "stuttering in twenty languages." Biographies of Engels are not common; the best modern one, no doubt, is that of A. Cornu, now in its third volume (French), entitled *Marx et Engels*.

EPIGONES. Disciples who corrupt the teaching of their masters, "come-lately" and self-important followers. *Trotsky uses the phrase repeatedly of the Soviet officials, including *Stalin.

EQUALITY. *Marxism holds that the *bourgeois conception of equality is limited to equality before the law and at the ballot box, ignoring inequalities in economic status and influence. *Stalin defined the Communist conception of equality as: "(1) the abolition of all *classes, (2) the abolition of *private property, (3) equal duty of all to work according to ability, (4) equal right of all to remuneration according to amount of work performed [that is, in *socialist* society; see *Socialism/Communism*], and (5) the equal duty of all to work according to ability and receive according to needs [that is, in *Communist* society]. Meanwhile, it is recognized that tastes and personal requirements are not and cannot be identical, equal, in quality or quantity" (*S.W.,* 344).

ERFURT PROGRAMME. The program adopted at the Erfurt Congress of the German Social Democratic Party in October 1891 to replace its *Gotha Program of 1875, which had been severely criticized by *Marx (though his criticism had not been freely circulated by the Party leaders). This program was drafted by *Kautsky and had a *revisionist character in that it made no mention of the *class nature of the *state and no reference to its *revolutionary overthrow. The program demanded universal suffrage, secret ballot, proportional representation, biennial elections, payment of the legislators, initiative and referendum, local administrative autonomy. The Left Wing of the Party seceded after the adoption of this program.

ESSAIRES (Socialist Revolutionary Party). A relatively small party, called Essaires from the initials of their (Russian) name. After the *February Revolution the Essaires split into two groups, one called itself the *Left Socialist Revolutionary Party, and moving toward the *Bolsheviks; the other calling itself the Essaires still, but called by the "Lefts" the Right Socialist Revolutionaries, and coming to represent views akin to those of the *Mensheviks during the fall of 1917.

ESTRANGEMENT. See *Alienation.*

ETHICS, MARXIST. *Marxism holds generally that standards of right and wrong are man-made, arise out of *class struggle, and always reflect the form of the class struggle of a given historical epoch. Ethical standards can be understood, Marxism teaches, only in their social context. Communist morality holds that all that contributes to the *revolution is good, all that aids in the abolition of *private property in the means of *production is good, and all that hinders these is bad. (*Trotsky has a pamphlet on this subject, *Their Morals and Ours;* John Lewis has an essay on it in his book, *Marxism and the Open Mind,* and *Lenin

deals with the subject often.) See also *Morality, Class Character of.*

EUROPEAN DEMOCRATIC COMMITTEE. The group founded by Guiseppe Mazzini (1805-1872), Italian revolutionary in London in 1848. It was intended to unite all revolutionary movements in exile. *Marx opposed the group as being essentially *bourgeois in aims.

EVTUSCHENKO, EVGENY. Contemporary Russian poet whose poetry is critical of censorship of the arts in the Soviet Union and proclaims the desirability of greater liberty in all ways of life.

EXCHANGE. In exchange, various kinds of *labor are equated, therefore behind exchange must lie the social *division of labor and exchange itself, *Marx holds is essentially a social relation, making *value, too, social in character.

EXCHANGE VALUE. See *Commodity.*

EXILES LEAGUE. The group founded in Paris in 1834 by German exiles to forward their *revolutionary aims. It split in 1836, and the more extreme wing founded the League of the Just, a forerunner of the *Communist League.

EXISTENTIALISM. The philosophical view variously expounded by thinkers such as K. Jaspers, S. Kierkegaard, J. Sartre, G. Marcel, M. Heidegger, which stresses the individual as opposed to the group. It is critical of *capitalism, but in turn is criticized by *Marxism as ignoring the worth of society which "embodies the true ends of man" (Dutt, 56), and as being demoralizing in its ultimate effect, representative of decadence.

EXPLOITATION. In *Marxism the giving to the worker of less in *wages than is taken from him in the *value of his *labor power. Marx held that exploitation is inevitable under *capitalism, because in this way alone can capital acquire a return on investment. "Every kind of capitalistic production, in so far as it is not only a labor process, but also a process of creating *surplus-value, has this in common, that it is not the workman that employs the instruments of labor, but the instruments of labor that employ the workman. But it is only in the factory system that this inversion for the first time acquires technical and palpable reality" (Marx, *Cap.*, I, 423). The worker becomes a machine, with this difference, that he is a creative machine, capable of producing more value than is returned to him in wages. This "surplus" is taken as profit, and this is exploitation. Wages tend to fall to the minimum necessary for the worker's subsistence and reproduction: "The constant tendency of capital is to force the cost of labor back towards zero" (*Cap.*, I, 600), while the working day tends to be pushed to the longest hours the human body can take, according to Marx.

EXTRACTIVE INDUSTRIES. Those industries "in which the material for labor is provided directly by Nature, such as mining, hunting, fishing, and agriculture (so far as the latter is confined to breaking up virgin soil)" (Marx, *Cap.*, I, 181).

FABIANS (Fabian Society, Fabian Socialists). British socialist organization named after the Roman general Fabius Cunctator (the Delayer), founded in 1884. It advocated gradual transition from *capitalism to parliamentary *socialism, and opposed *Marxism and *revolutionary action. The Society published the *Fabian Tracts, Fabian Essays*, and the like, advocating their views. Its members have often been famous writers, such as H. G. Wells, G. B. Shaw, and the Webbs. *Lenin said that the Fabian Society represented "the most finished expression of *opportunism and liberal labor politics" (see Cole, III, 1, chaps. 3-4).

FACTORY ACTS, British, Early. 1833 — Parliamentary acts which limited the working day from 5:30 a.m. to 8:30 p.m. (15 hours) in cotton, wool, flax, and silk industries. The Acts made it unlawful to employ young persons (13-18 years) more than 12 hours per day and children (9-13) more than 8 hours.

1844 — Acts which protected women over 18 as young persons under Act of 1833, and limited children under 13 to six and one-half hours per day.

1847 — Act which established that after May 1, 1848, the maximum working day should be 10 hours. It was partially nullified by the so-called *Relay System.

"Although the Factory Inspectors unceasingly and with justice commend the results of the Acts of 1844 and 1847, yet they admit that the shortening of the hours of labor has already called forth such an intensification of labor as is injurious to the health of the workman and his capacity for work" (Marx, *Cap.*, I, 417).

The Acts of 1864 extended to potteries, makers of paper-hangings, matches, cartridges, etc. the same regulations that hitherto applied to textile workers.

The Acts of 1867 applied the Factory Acts Extension to large industries and the Workshops Regulation Act to small industries.

FASCISM. Defined by *Marxism as the terroristic dictatorship of the monopolistic *bourgeoisie and landowners, characterized by brutal suppression of workers' and peasants' movements, militarization of the country, and military adventures abroad. *Trotsky wrote several pamphlets on the rise of Fascism in Germany. *Lenin described it in general terms as the last reaction of *capitalism to threats made by the *proletariat against it. (Cf. J. Strachey.)

FEBRUARY REVOLUTION, RUSSIAN. The revolt which overthrew the Tsar and established the *Kerensky Provisional Government in February 1917. It began with a series of strikes in the industrial cities, especially St. Petersburg, followed by a general strike on February 25 (new calendar, March 10) and an armed clash with the police in St. Petersburg. The police and soldiery went into revolt also on February 27, and in St. Petersburg Soviets (Councils) of Workers' and Soldiers' Deputies were formed. A Provisional Government was formed by the State *Duma Provisional Committee, and the *Menshevik leaders surrendered Soviet leadership to the Provisional Government, which was formed under Prince Luov on March 2, 1917. The Tsar abdicated, and Kerensky took the reigns of government in hand.

FEDERATION OF THE JUST. See *Communist League.*

FEUDAL SOCIALISM (Conservative). The state socialism which arose in Germany at the time of Bismarck, when he made concessions to workers' demands for male suffrage and state aid to workers' productive associations. Bismarck's aim was to keep *proletariat and *bourgeoisie apart, lest they both attack the aristocracy. Feudal socialism was attacked by *Marx and *Engels in the *Communist Manifesto.*

FEUERBACH, Ludwig (1804-1872), German theologian who defended *materialism, and found in Christianity the highest expression of materialism. He attacked *Hegelianism in his *Critique of the Hegelian Philosophy* (1839). In 1841 he published *The Essence of Christianity.* The "essence" of Christianity is man's projection into an imagined God all of man's own virtues; therefore man's salvation will consist in his taking the virtues back. Feuerbach held that the world is revealed to man accurately by the senses, and that society can be redeemed by a religion of love, such as was taught by Jesus. He forms the bridge between the idealism of Hegel and the *dialectical materialism of *Marxism, and helped Marx come to the formulation of his own theory of *alienation. *Engels has an essay on Feuerbach (see *S.W.*) and *Lenin pays his respects to him in his *Philosophical Notebooks,* Vol. 38 of his *Works* (pp. 35ff.).

FILOSOFSKIE NAUKI. Russian philosophical journal which began publication in 1958 to provide an additional outlet for philosophical discussion in the Soviet Union to that afforded by the older journal *Voprosy Filosofi.*

FIRST INTERNATIONAL (Working Men's Association). The first international socialist working men's organization, in which *Marx and *Engels played a dominant role. The International began with a public meeting in 1862 called by George *Odger, a shoemaker, President of London Trades Council, and W. R. *Cremer, mason, Secretary of the Mason's Union. At this meeting it was decided to form a Working Man's International Association with a General Council in London to act as permanent intermediary between workers' societies in Germany, Italy, France, and England. A Provisional Committee was appointed, consisting of Odger, Cre-

mer, and others, including Marx. A sub-committee was appointed to draft a declaration of principles, a task Marx managed to obtain for himself by some maneuvering. The First International held congresses as follows: London, 1865; Geneva, 1866; Lausanne, 1867; Brussels, 1868; Basle, 1869; London, 1871; The Hague, 1872. The Russian *anarchist *Bakunin entered the Association with an eye, Marx says, to forming an association within it. His efforts aroused discussion at Basle, and at The Hague he was expelled from the International, but not without such a struggle that the Association was left almost lifeless. Marx, who attended the meeting at The Hague, got the headquarters of the International transferred from London to New York, deliberately making it ineffective, and the First International officially dissolved itself in Philadelphia in 1876. Marx tells the story of the formation and dissolution of the International in two letters, to be found in *S.C.* (pp. 159-165). Marx gave what became a famous address at the First Congress, and drafted the Regulations for the International; both are to be found in *S.W.*, I. The documents arising out of the International, as well as minutes of the Congresses, have been published in two volumes by E. Droz, Geneva. Chapters 6 and 8 in Vol. 2 of Cole are devoted to it. This First International was followed by a Second and Third and Fourth, which are discussed in this *Vocabulary.*

FIVE YEAR PLANS. The Soviet Government, beginning in 1927, established a series of Five Year Plans. These set goals of achievement in industry and agriculture and various social units which were to be achieved within five years, or, if possible, less.

First Five Year Plan: adopted in 1927 with the aims of new construction of productive power — factories, mines, power stations; new towns; collective farms with machine and tractor stations; schools, clubs, hospitals.

Second: adopted in 1932 and declared accomplished April 1, 1937, nine months ahead of schedule, pushing total industrial output to twice that of 1932 and eight times that of 1913. Its aim was the final elimination of all *capitalistic elements in the *Soviet Union, some of which, especially the agricultural capitalists called *kulaks, had been permitted and even encouraged under the *New Economic Policy which preceded 1927.

Third: outlined to the 18th Party *Congress in 1939, involving emphasis on defense industries, fuel and electric production. It was interrupted by World War II.

Fourth: adopted by *Supreme Soviet in 1946 "to restore the ravaged areas of the country, to reach the pre-war level of industry and agriculture and then to exceed it" (Rothstein, 617). Some aspects were not completed, but the body of the Plan was declared accomplished nine months before the end of the five-year period.

Fifth: plan for economic development adopted by the 19th *Congress of the Communist Party, Soviet Union, in October 1952, retroactive to 1951, and declared completed in four years and four months.

Sixth: adopted by the 20th *Congress, February 1956, designed to surpass the output per capita of the capitalist countries; it also denounced the "cult of personality" built up by *Stalin. The Soviet Union now is under a Seven Year Plan, which see.

FORMALISM. A term used frequently in the arts in Communist nations to indicate an undesirable concern with form at the expense of revolutionary content, a version of art for art's sake. In political administration, formalism means the inflexible application of regulations without any concern for circumstances.

FORWARD (*Vperyod*). Revolutionary newspaper founded by the *Bolsheviks on January 4, 1905, to replace *Iskra,* which was lost to the *Mensheviks in 1903 after fifty-two issues. The Editorial Board: *Lenin, Vorovsky, Lunacharsky, Olminsky. The paper ceased publication May 18, 1905, after eighteen issues.

FORWARD. See *Vorwarts*.

FOURTH INTERNATIONAL. After his expulsion from the Soviet Union, Leon *Trotsky sought to organize his own International in competition with the then active *Third International. Trotsky's came to be called the Fourth International, but it never succeeded in wielding great power or influence. It lapsed into decay after Trotsky's murder in 1940.

FRANCO-GERMAN ANNALS. See *Deutsch-Französische Jahrbücher.*

FRATERNAL DEMOCRATS. See *Harvey, George Julian.*

FREE PEOPLE'S STATE. Marxist term for the situation when after the *revolution, as *Marx said, the *state is at last "subordinate to the people" (*Critique of the *Gotha Program*). The role of the state after the revolution and before it "withers away" is a problem in Marxist theory, since the state no longer serves as what Marx defined it to be, namely, the agent of the *bourgeoisie. In an attempt to meet this problem, Marx designated the intervening period as the period of the Free People's State. Marx discussed it (*S.W.,* II, 29-31) and *Lenin (*S. & R.,* 27-37, 103-108) and *Stalin (*P. L.,* 345-348). See also *State.*

FREE WORD (*Volnoye Slovo*). A weekly journal in its first thirty-six issues and bi-weekly thereafter, published in Geneva from 1881 to 1883 under the editorship of A. P. Malshinsky, who was actually a Russian police agent acting in collaboration with the Holy Guard, a secret organization of Russian landed nobility and government officials. To January 8, 1883, the paper appeared in a total of sixty-two issues, advocating freedom and self-government for Russia as a trap for drawing in *revolutionaries, and for drawing off revolutionary fervor within Russia. It was taken over after January 8, 1883, by Dragomanov as the organ for the *Zemstvo League.

FREEDOM, Marxist Philosophical View of. In a world governed by the laws of *dialectical materialism the question naturally arises as to whether or not man has any freedom of will. *Hegel taught that freedom is "recognition of necessity." *Engels says: "Hegel was the first to state correctly the relation between freedom and necessity. To him freedom is the appreciation of necessity. Necessity is blind only in so far as it is not understood" (*A.-D.,* 157). For Engels and *Marx freedom is defined as the knowledge of natural and social laws and acting accordingly. For example, man puts wings on the airplane to defy gravity in compliance with the laws of gravitation. (Engels illustrates his definition in several ways in *A.-D.,* 157ff.) *Lenin: *"Marxism combines complete scientific sobriety in analysis of the objective state of affairs and the objective course of evolution with the most definite recognition of the importance of *revolutionary energy, the revolutionary creative genius, and the revolutionary initiative of the masses" (*Works,* XIII, 21-22). When ideas have the effect of organizing the masses for action they then become "material forces," Marx says. *Plekhanov: "Freedom presupposes necessity, necessity passes entirely into freedom" (*D.M.V.,* 130). Marx and Engels both confess that man does make his own *history, but "within limits." In short, *Marxism wants it both ways: (1) history and all within it, including man, is wholly determined by the laws of *matter;

69

(2) man can act, especially as a revolutionary, in a creative way in history.

FREEDOM OF CRITICISM. The slogan of the *revisionists, especially employed by E. *Bernstein. While the Marxists theoretically recognized the right of *criticism, Bernstein implied by freedom of criticism the necessity of correcting *Marxism, which *Lenin called a disguise for freedom to convert Marxism into its opposite, into *opportunism or reformism. The slogan was used by the *economists, the *Proudhonists in the *First International and, thereafter, the *Blanquists, the *Lassallians, the *"legal Marxists," the *Mensheviks, and the *Trotskyites, all opposed at one time or another by Lenin and the *Bolsheviks. See *Criticism and Self-Criticism.*

FREY. One of Lenin's aliases. See *Unity Conference.*

FRONDEURS. Term for an opposition group within a ruling clique. Name taken from the Fronde, a faction of the French nobility who opposed the government during the minority of Louis XIV, just prior to the great French Revolution.

GAPON, Father Georgi Appollonovich (1870-1906), Russian priest who led the mass procession of workers to the Tsar's winter palace in St. Petersburg on what became *"Bloody Sunday," January 9, 1905. The crowd carried a petition to the Tsar, asking for relief of grievances in labor conditions, for land settlement, and general reforms. Russian troops, probably upon orders of the Tsar (though he may not have been at the winter palace), fired upon the unarmed crowd, killing at least 1,000 and wounding some 5,000 (according to Marxist accounts). The Communists accuse Gapon of being in the pay of the Russian secret police and leading the people to the massacre deliberately. If so, it was a costly blunder, for the news created widespread strikes and unrest and the name "Bloody Sunday" became a *revolutionary symbol. Gapon in 1904 had established a *Union of Russian Factory Workers, with the knowledge of the police, to draw workers away from more radical organizations. The movement spread and began to formulate its own program, which resulted in the plan for presentation of the Bloody Sunday petition. After the massacre Gapon left Russia; later he returned and was murdered as a police spy. This is the Marxist version. Wolfe (pp. 283ff.) maintains Father Gapon's generally high ideals and hopes for social advancement.

GAPONADE. The Marxist term for a form of police-socialism, that is, of socialist movements secretly sponsored by the police to reveal real conspirators and to draw off mob action into controlled channels. It derives from Father *Gapon.

GENERAL, The. The nickname for *Engels given by intimates in respect of his deep interest in military strategy, at which he was adept. He often used the nickname to sign letters to intimate friends.

GENERAL REDISTRIBUTIONISTS. See *Emancipation of Labor Group; Narodniks.*

GEORGE, Henry (1839-1897), American economist whose *Progress and Poverty* has become a classic. In it he advocates a "single tax" on the value of land equal to the economic rent; that is, a tax on the value of unimproved land plus the value added to the same land by its situation and the development of adjacent properties. Such a tax, George believed, would be not only the most just form of taxation but the only one needed.

GERMAN-FRENCH YEARBOOK (*Annals*). See *Deutsch-Französische Jahrbücher.*

GIRONDISTS. A late-eighteenth-century French political group led by men from the Gironde Province, who favored the French Revolution only to the degree that the *bourgeoisie gained the ascendancy over the nobility, but who opposed the transfer of state power to the peasants and city poor, and who finally came to compromise with the royalists to prevent such transfer. *Lenin applied the term "Socialist Gironde" to the *Mensheviks and *opportunists among the Russian Social Democrats.

GOD - SEEKERS (God - Builders). Socialist group formed in Russia in 1905 by Lunacharsky, Bazarov, and others who sought to unite *Marxism with religion and proposed a "new socialist religion."

The group was attacked by *Lenin in *M.E.-C.* and condemned by the Editorial Board of *Proletary,* a *Bolshevik paper edited by Lenin.

GOSPLAN. The State Planning Commission in the *Soviet Union which is entrusted with developing the structure of the *Five Year Plans. It is controlled by the Politburo (*Presidium), which has veto power.

GOTHA PROGRAM. The statement of Social Democratic aims drawn up by the Gotha Congress of the German Social Democratic Party in 1875. It demanded: universal suffrage, direct popular legislation, general arming of the people, equal administration of justice, repeal of certain emergency laws, extension of popular rights and liberties, uniform progressive income tax. It was criticized by *Marx in *C.G.P.* (in *S.W.*) but his criticism was withheld by the Party leadership until published by *Engels in the newspaper *Neue Zeit (New Times)* in 1891, after the adoption of the *Erfurt Program by the Social Democrats.

GREAT PATRIOTIC WAR. The Soviet name for World War II, which began for Russia with Germany's attack of June 22, 1941.

GROUND RENT. The income received by a landowner for the use of land belonging to him. It is one element of agricultural value, which value altogether consists of wages to worker, profit to tenant-farmer, and rent to landowners. *Marx distinguishes among the following: *Differential rent I,* which is the *surplus value obtained on lands of better quality. *Differential rent II*, which is surplus value obtained by additional capital investment on the land. *Absolute rent*, which is the difference between the price of agricultural products and their value. *Rent* represents the excess of surplus value over average profit. "*Ground rent* is that part of surplus-value which remains after the average profit on invested capital is deducted" (Lenin, *Works*, IV, 140).

GUESDE, Jules (1845-1922), publisher of weekly Marxist newspaper *Égalité* from 1877 to 1880, in two series of thirty-one and thirty-two issues each. In 1879 he helped found the French Workers' Party, whose program was formulated with *Marx's advice and with the assistance of Marx's son-in-law, Paul *Lafargue. Guesde became a *Centrist in the *Second International, joining *Kautsky and others who sided neither with *Bernstein nor with the forces of *Lenin.

GUESDISTS. Followers of Guesde, who formed the Marxist wing of the French Socialist Movement. In 1901 they formed the Socialist Movement and the Socialist Party of France (not the French Socialist Party. See *Possibilists*).

GUILD SOCIALISM. The view that industries should be operated by the laborers, organized into guilds, by occupation or by industry. The state comes to own the means of production, but production itself is controlled by the guilds. Power in the factories and in the state is in the hands of elected representatives who are nominated on the basis of industry or occupation. The industrial guilds are headed by a kind of trade union congress. G. D. H. Cole is an exponent of this view in England (see his *Self-Government in Industry*).

HANOVER RESOLUTION. Passed by Hanover Congress of the German Social Democratic Party, October 3-8, 1898, this Resolution rejected the views of *revisionism as advocated by *Bernstein, though it did not condemn him explicitly.

HARVEY, George Julian (1817-1897), radical *chartist leader who edited the paper *The Northern Star* and favored the use of force in *revolutionary action. In 1845 he founded the London branch of international *socialism known as Fraternal Democrats. A member of the London Communist Correspondence Committee, he published the first version in English of the *Communist Manifesto* in his paper *The Red Republican* in 1850. He was a member of the *First International. *Marx mildly chided him for liking "theatrical effect."

HAUSSMANNIST. A label taken from the name of the French Prefect of the Seine under Napoleon III, Haussmann, who built wide and straight streets through the close-knit working districts of Paris to accomplish several ends: (1) to break up the physical unity of the workers, thus undermining their sense of spiritual unity; (2) to make street-barricade fighting more difficult; and (3) to make the building trade workers a virtual government-directed *proletariat. *Engels discusses this in *The Housing Question* (*S.W.* II).

HEGEL, Georg Wilhelm Friedrich (1770-1831), German *idealist philosopher who greatly influenced *Marx and *Engels, even when they reacted against him by seeking, as they said, to "set him on his feet" (they thought of his philosophical idealism as standing on its head). Hegel's highly elaborate and voluminous philosophy can hardly be summarized; the best book, though not an easy one, on the subject is W. T. Stace's *The Philosophy of Hegel* (available in paperback). Hegel gave to Marx the notion of *history as *development, and the concept of the *dialectic as accounting for such development (a progressive process of *thesis, developing its antithesis and thus making for struggle — the motive power of history — and the solution of the struggle at last in synthesis, which immediately becomes another thesis, etc.). Hegel conceived of the visible world as the "other," or *alienation, or, as Marx often said, "estrangement" of the Absolute Spirit with which the world began. But the idea of Spirit as originator of history, this Marx denied; for him *matter came first, and spirit only reflects it. The idea of development, under law, dialectically, however, came to be the foundation of *Marxism, and within this formal scheme Marx developed his own economic interpretation of history. *Lenin outlines and discusses much of

Hegel in *P.N.* (Vol. XXXVIII of *Works*). Marx's first published article was on Hegel's philosophy of right, or law. Hegelians divided, even before the philosopher's death, into two schools: (1) the *Left, or so-called Young, Hegelians, who found in his developmental concepts the impulse to *revolution in thought and state; and (2) the *Right Hegelians, who found, as Hegel himself did, the culmination of history in the Prussian state of the time, and thus became highly conservative. Marx and Engels both belonged to the Left Hegelians at the university, but quickly left them on the ground that matter and not spirit (as the Hegelians believed) was the prime factor in history; and their first jointly published works, The *Holy Family and The German Ideology, were sharp attacks upon their former associates. Some grasp of Hegelianism is very useful in coming to terms with Marxism, both in its structure and in its failures. Engels: "Hegel's merit consists in the fact that he was the first to regard all phenomena from the point of view of development, from the point of view of their origin and destruction" (see Plekhanov, *D.M.V.*, chap. 4).

HEGELIANS, LEFT. See *Left Hegelians*.

HEGELIANS, YOUNG. See *Left Hegelians*.

HELPLAND, A.L. See *Parvus*.

HERO, in History. In contradiction to thinkers like Thomas Carlyle, who held that *history is dominated by single powerful personalities — heroes — the Marxist holds that "it is not heroes who make history but history that makes heroes, and that, consequently, it is not heroes who create a people but the people who create the heroes and move history forward" (Stalin). Heroes play, for the Marxist, a significant role in history only because they clearly understand the conditions and trends of social development more thoroughly than average men. See *Cult of the Individual.*

HERZEN, Alexander Ivanovich (1812-1870), *revolutionary Russian thinker and writer who "played a great role in the preparation of the *Russian revolution" (Lenin) by being the leading spirit among the pre-Marxist *materialists. Herzen was the founder of *Narodnism, the first form of Russian *socialism. He tended to idealize the Russian village *commune, a fact which *Marx criticized on the ground that a modern society could not exist as only agricultural. Herzen founded *The *Bell (*Kolokol*) in London as a revolutionary monthly. It was smuggled into Russia and came to be issued fortnightly. It was the organ of the new thought, critical of Tsarist autocracy, having the aim of developing Russia into the future social leader of Europe. Herzen was acquainted with *Marxism and opposed its dictatorial tendencies, saying, "Communism is Russian autocracy turned upside down." *Lenin said of him, "A thinker who stands head and shoulders above the multitude of modern empiricist natural scientists and the swarms of present-day idealist and semi-idealist philosophers. Herzen stood on the threshold of *dialectical materialism, and halted — before *historical materialism" (*S.W.,* II, 274).

HESS, Moses (1812-1875), German socialist who turned to Communism under the influence of *Marx with whom he served on the staff of the *Rheinische Zeitung (Rhineland Gazette)* in 1844-45. He turned toward *utopian socialism in later life, joined the *"True Socialists," and followed *Lassalle and Jewish Zionism. His admiration for *Marx cooled after the *Communist Manifesto* appeared.

HISTORICAL MATERIALISM. See *Materialism, Historical.*

HISTORY. The Marxist view of history is: "History is nothing but the succession of the separate generations, each of which exploits the materials, the forms of *capital, the *productive forces handed down to it by all preceding ones, and thus, on the one hand, continues the traditional activity in completely changed circumstances and, on the other, modifies the old circumstances with a completely changed activity" (Engels, Marx, *G.I.,* 38). For the Marxist philosophy of history, see *Materialism, Historical.*

HOLY FAMILY, The. The title of the first joint work of *Marx and *Engels, published in 1845, with subtitle: *Or, Critique of Critical Criticism; Against Bruno Bauer & Co.* The book was written between September and November

1844, and published in Frankfort-on-Main, Germany. *Bauer and his group of *Left Hegelians had argued in the *Allgemeine Literatur-Zeitung* that select individuals (like themselves) endowed with the spirit of pure criticism, were in fact the makers of *history, since history followed the lead of *ideas, while the masses were the inert victims of the historical process. Marx and Engels subject this view to devastating attack, advancing as they do their own *materialist point of view (see *Materialism, Historical*). *Lenin remarks in *P. N. (Works,* Vol. XXXVIII) that parts of the book are pedantic and captious, going into minute and fruitless detail, while other parts are of permanent worth in the formation of *Marxism. The book was the fruit of the first lengthy meeting of the two men, and was sketched out in a ten-day session in Paris. Engels wrote his chapters while still in Paris; and after Engels's return to Germany, Marx finished his — the larger part of the book — adding parts of his economic and philosophical manuscripts which were later published in full under the title *Economic and Philosophical Manuscripts of 1844.*

HOLY GUARD. See *Free Word.*

L'HUMANITÉ. French Communist newspaper, founded by the socialist Jean *Jaures in 1904 as the organ of the French Socialist Party. It was taken over by the Communists after a split in the Socialist Party at its Tours Congress of December, 1920. See also *Longuetites.*

HOT LINE. Telegraphic communication, direct between the Kremlin and the White House, to be used in case of apparent atomic attack by either side upon the other, when it is presumed that there may be some error in the preliminary report that such an attack is being launched.

HUTS, British term for *Communes.

IDEALISM. Those philosophical views which contrast most sharply with *materialism; *Lenin tries to reduce all philosophies to one or the other. Lenin: "Everybody knows what a human *idea* is; but an idea independent of man and prior to him, an idea in the abstract, an Absolute Idea, is a theological invention of the idealist *Hegel" (*M.E.-C.,* 232). As Lenin here suggests, idealism holds that mind is prior to matter in time, that ideas are prior to material in activating conduct, that mind is more real, more permanent, of more worth, than matter. For the Marxist, idealism as a philosophy is in fact a defense of religion, of clericalism, of theological views of the world. A good exposition of the Marxist critique of idealism is to be found in Plekhanov, *D.M.V.,* 137ff.

IDEAS, Role in History. *Marxism holds that ideas play a very significant role in *history, but always a secondary one, that is, they must themselves be accounted for. *Reactionary ideas* are those which reflect economic and social orders in decay and resist the approach of new social forms. *Progressive ideas* are those which reflect new economic and social forces emerging and facilitate the approach of new social forms. Ideas are, however, always derived from *material reality, and constitute the "reflection" of matter in the medium of mind or consciousness.

IDEOLOGY. This term has a special significance in *Marxism. "To construct conclusions in one's head, take them as a basis from which to start, and then reconstruct the world from them in one's head is *Ideology"* (Engels, *A.-D.*, 464). Marx says: "Ideology is a process accomplished by a so-called thinker, consciously, indeed, but with a false consciousness. The real motives impelling him remain unknown to him, otherwise it would not be an ideological process at all . . . . represents a stage in thought and never passes outside the sphere of thought" (Ltr. to *Mehring, *S.C.*, 511-512). To the Marxist this is a particular vice of the university professor, and all other armchair, inactive thinkers. "Socialists of the Chair" (*Katheder-Socialisten*) is a German phrase for the same thing. This kind of social philosophy *Engels called "flea-cracking."

ILYN, V., pseudonym used by *Lenin in his early writings, including his first large systematic work, *The Development of Capitalism in Russia,* published 1899. The identity of the writer was known to the police. Probably from this pseudonym he changed to Lenin, by which he came to be permanently known, his real name being Vladimir Ilyich Ulyanov. (See Wolfe, p. 153.)

IMPERIALISM. The doctrine associated with the name of *Lenin in the development of *Marxism. Lenin called it the highest and last stage of *capitalism, the "monopoly stage of capitalism," and meant to include by the term, therefore, not only the foreign extension of investment but also the monopoly aspect of capitalism at home. "Imperialism is a specific stage of capitalism. Its specific character is three-fold: imperialism is (1) monopoly capitalism; (2) parasitic, or decaying capitalism; (3) moribund capitalism" (*Works* XXIII, 94). Lenin also distinguished five fundamental features of imperialism: (1) monopolies, (2) the merger of bank and industrial capital to create finance capital and financial oligarchy, (3) large export of capital, (4) formation of international monopoly combines, (5) territorial division of the world among the largest capitalistic powers (see Lenin's *Imperialism,* p. 193). The essence of Imperialism is the replacement of free competition by monopoly. Various other terms must be distinguished from Lenin's use of Imperialism:

Cartels: agreements among individual producers.

Syndicates: agreements in which participating members give up independent action and have common office.

Trusts: offices which take total control of absorbed units.

Concerns: associations of enterprises in different branches of industry, formerly independent but controlled by one group. Lenin held that monopoly inevitably leads to the decay of capitalism for two reasons: (1) it weakens the impulse to technological improvement in production and in product; and (2) it tends to restrict production and to discourage invention.

INDUSTRIAL PARTY. One of several internal Russian anti-Communist groups exposed and destroyed by the Soviet Government in 1930-31.

INDUSTRIAL WORKERS OF THE WORLD (IWW). American labor organization founded in 1905 by Daniel *De Leon, Eugene V. Debs, and Bill Hayward. It organized anti-war demonstrations, and sent some members into the Communist Party of the U.S. which was formed in September, 1919. It tended toward *syndicalism, and soon dwindled to no influence. It was nicknamed "Wobblies."

INDUSTRIALIZATION CONGRESS. See *Congresses* (14th).

INNER-PARTY DEMOCRACY. This is understood as the basis upon which *criticism and self-criticism are possible, that is, inner-Party *democracy is the right of every Party member to criticize every other Party member, and the duty of the one under criticism to accept the critique, and if it is valid, to act upon it.

INSTRUMENT OF LABOR. "A thing, or complex of things, which the laborer interposes between himself and the subject of his *labor, and which serves as the conductor of his activity . . . . may include all such objects as are necessary to the labor process . . . . workshops, canals, roads, etc." (Marx, *Cap.*, I, 179-180) .

INTERACTION GROUP. See *Spartacus League.*

INTERNATIONAL. See *First International; Second International; Communist International; Fourth International.*

INTERNATIONAL, THIRD. See *Communist International.*

INTERNATIONAL ALLIANCE OF SOCIALIST-DEMOCRATS. *Anarchist group formed by *Bakunin in 1868.

INTERNATIONAL SOCIALISTS BUREAU. Executive body of the *Second International established at its Paris Congress in 1900. *Lenin was a member, being a representative of the *Russian Social Democratic Labor Party from 1905. It ceased to function in 1915.

INTERNATIONAL WOMEN'S SOCIALIST CONFERENCE. Held at Berne, Switzerland, in March 1915, it was called by *Bolshevik women's groups under the leadership of I. F. Armond and N. K. *Krupskaya (Lenin's wife) . It adopted resolutions that condemned the war then in progress.

INTERNATIONALISTS. See *Zimmerwold Conference.*

IRON LAW OF WAGES. The *classical economic doctrine, called "iron" law by *Lassalle, according to which workers' *wages will always tend to a minimum subsistence level, at least in the lowest economic strata, because any increase above this subsistence level permits a population increase which will force wages down once more. *Marx: "The higher wages stimulate the working population to more rapid multiplication, and this goes on until the labor-market becomes too full, and therefore *capital, relatively to the supply of *labor, becomes insufficient. Wages fall, etc." (*Cap.*, I, 637)

ISKRA (*Spark*). First all-Russian, Marxist newspaper, associated with the name of *Lenin, who established it outside Russia in 1900, according to plans formulated while he was in Siberian exile for political crimes. The first Editorial Board was composed of *Plekhanov, *Axelrod, *Zasulich, and Lenin. The first issue, December 11, 1900, was published in Leipzig, Germany, for smuggling into Russia. The epigraph at the masthead read: "The spark will kindle a flame," a phrase taken from the *Decembrists' letter to the novelist Pushkin in a famous exchange of correspondence. The first editorial, by Lenin, was on "The Urgent Tasks of Our Movement," and stated the main task to be the formation of a Marxist Party in Russia, for without it the *proletariat could not come to *class consciousness, upon which rest *class struggle and final emancipation. In the May 1901 issue Lenin wrote, "Where to Be-

gin," and defended the establishment of an all-Russian political newspaper to spread a common understanding of *revolutionary tasks and tactics, to unify separate revolutionary groups; and a network of agents to distribute such a paper. In June 1902, *Iskra* published the program for a Russian Marxist Party, namely, the substitution of *socialism for *capitalism by *revolutionary dictatorship of the proletariat, and the more immediate task of substituting republicanism for the autocracy. The paper formed scattered Marxist groups into cells of one Marxist Party, and kept before all the goals they sought. In 1903, after the split in the *Russian Social Democratic Party, Lenin's *Bolsheviks lost control of *Iskra* to the *Mensheviks. Lenin describes how this transfer took place in "How the Spark was Nearly Extinguished" (*Works*, IV, pp. 333-349). Thereafter the paper declined in power, but it had done its work.

IZVESTIA. Translation: *The News,* or *Gazette.* The official organ of the Soviet Government. It began publication on February 28, 1917, as the newspaper of the Petrograd *Soviet, and became the organ of the Central Executive Committee of all Soviets with its 132nd issue, August 1, 1917. It was controlled by the *Mensheviks in the summer of 1917, and was therefore anti-*Bolshevik. It became the official newspaper of the Soviet Government on October 27, 1917, after the Second All-Russian Congress of Soviets. In March, 1918, its offices were transferred to Moscow, where they remain. See *Press, Soviet*.

JACOBINS. The group in the French Revolution of 1789 which stood for no compromise, demanded land reform and complete change in government. In Marxist terminology the word refers to those who stand for the rule of the revolutionary *proletariat all the way to achievement of Communism. *Lenin writes: "The transfer of power to the revolutionary oppressed class — *that* is the essence of Jacobinism" (*Works*, II, p. 277).

JAURES, Jean (1859-1914), French socialist who belonged to the Marxist *revisionists. His program was the liberation of all humanity from political despotism, economic exploitation, and religious superstition, all of which he held to be interrelated. He did not subscribe to historical *materialism, and had some sympathy for *idealism in philosophy. He was assassinated. His chief work: *History of Socialism from 1789-1900*.

JEWISH BUND. See *Bund, The*.

JEWISH DOCTORS' PLOT. See *Doctors' Conspiracy*.

JEWISH WORKERS' UNION. See *Bund, The*.

JULY DAYS. This phrase refers to mass Russian workers' and soldiers' demonstrations of unrest and dissatisfaction with the economic and political course of the *Kerensky Government. These took place in July 1917, and almost precipitated the *Bolshevik Revolution, which came in October. The demonstrations took place spontaneously, and against the best judgment of both *Lenin and *Trotsky.

JUNIUS. Pseudonym employed by Rosa *Luxemburg, German-Russian Marxist, to write her pamphlet from prison, "The Crisis of Social Democracy," in 1916. She is criticized by *Lenin in his pamphlet "On the Pamphlet by Junius."

KAMENEV, Leo (1883-1936), Russian Marxist, and one of the few *Bolshevik Deputies in the State *Duma in 1914. He was arrested with the other Bolshevik Deputies on November 5, 1914, by police plot, and at the trial which followed he alone of the Deputies turned against *Lenin's theses against Russian participation in the War. (See *Ozerki Conference*.) *Trotsky says: "Kamenev grasped better than most Bolsheviks the general ideas of Lenin, but he grasped them only in order to give them the mildest possible interpretation in practice. Kamenev was always behind the time" (*H.R.R.*, I, 288).

KAPLAN, Fanny, a social revolutionary, known to history because she attempted the assassination of *Lenin on August 30, 1918. She succeeded in wounding him severly by pistol shot but he recovered.

KATHEDER SOCIALISM. German epithet for academic *socialism, advocated by professors from their safe classroom chairs (*Katheder*), which envisioned the state as the unifying force between *classes, and hoped for the gradual introduction of socialism. In Russia these views were espoused by the *"legal Marxists," the party which sought to be both Marxist and legally recognized.

KAUTSKY, Karl (1854-1938), Influential Marxist who gradually came to separate himself from *Lenin and under whose leadership the *Second International turned to *Revisionism. Kautsky was born in Czechoslovakia, and joined the Austrian Social Democratic Party in 1874. He met *Marx and *Engels in London, 1879. Marx writes: "When this charmer first appeared at my place — I mean Kauz ["queer fellow" — a play on Kautsky] — the first question that escaped me was: Are you like your mother? Not in the very least, he assured me, and I silently congratulated his mother. He is a mediocrity with a small-minded outlook, superwise (only 26), very conceited . . . but is otherwise a decent fellow" (*S.C.* 389, the letter is to Marx's daughter Jenny). After Marx's death, Kautsky helped Engels with the editing of Volumes II and III of *Capital, and himself got together manuscripts for a little-used or -known Volume IV. In 1887, Kautsky published *The Economic Doctrines of Marx,* in German, which became a basic text in *Marxism in Germany.

Kautsky became editor of the German Social Democratic paper *Neue Zeit,* in 1883, and used it to oppose the open *Revisionism of *Bernstein, though Kautsky himself was cool to *dialectical materialism and the *revolutionary dictatorship of the *proletariat. In the *Second International Kautsky tried to mediate between the Leninist Left and Bernstein's Right, and earned the dislike of both for what was called his *Centrist position. After the *Russian Revolution Kautsky became a bitter opponent of Marxism-Leninism, and was savagely attacked by Lenin in *P.R.* Lenin says: "Kautsky takes from Marxism what is acceptable to the *liberals, to the *bourgeoisie, and discards, passes in silence, glosses over all that in Marxism which is unacceptable to the bourgeoisie" (p. 31). *Trotsky also entered the fray to defend the stern measures of the Revolution. Kautsky's most important work, *The Material Conception of History,* appeared in 1927. In it he argues that historical forces will take their course by slow steps, and revolutionary violence is unnecessary to help *history along. He favors democratic processes as the best form for solving social problems and moving toward *socialism. In his book *The Labor Revolution* he specifically attacks Lenin and the methods Lenin employed in the Russian Revolution. Lenin's other works against Kautsky are listed by Lenin himself in the Preface to *P.R.* Kautsky thus moved during his life from admiration of and association with

Marx and Engels to a middle position in the Second International, to bitter opposition to the Revolution in practice.

KAZARMA. See *Barracks*.

KERENSKY, Alexander (b. 1881), Russian lawyer, who was first Minister of Justice, then Minister of War, and finally Premier of the Provisional Government which took power in Russia after the *February, 1917, Revolution. Kerensky had achieved a reputation for defending in court some of those accused by the Tsarist government of revolutionary activities; he was a member of the State *Duma (Parliament) at the time of the Revolution. After the *Bolshevik victory in October, 1917, Kerensky fled Russia and came to the United States in 1940, having lived the interim in Paris. He is currently associated with the Hoover Institution, directing Russian studies there.

KETTELER, Wilhelm Emmanuel (1811-1877), German Catholic Bishop whose book *The Labor Question and Christianity* advocated improvement of working-class conditions, and action by the Roman Catholic Church to establish Christian co-operative societies not dependent on the state, but rather financed by capital advanced by loyal Catholics. He advocated state enforcement of fair wages, of safe and decent conditions of labor, and social insurance and security provisions for workers. He was critical of *laissez-faire* *capitalism (see *Classical Economics*) and favored the application of Christian moral principles to economic life. He expounded these views also in later books, especially *Liberalism, Socialism, and Christianity*. He was closely supported by Canon Moufang of Mainz, by various Conferences of German Bishops; and with associates he published *Christian Social Letters*, to spread their views. See *Christian Socialism*.

KGB See *Cheka*.

KHRUSHCHEV, Nikita Sergeievich (b. 1894), Premier of the Soviet Union and First Secretary of the Russian *Communist Party. Born in the village of Kalinovka in the Ukraine, he worked on his father's farm, then became shepherd, coal miner, and locksmith. He joined the Communist Party in 1918, and went to Kharkov University and to the Moscow Industrial Academy, at neither of which he completed degree work. In 1930 he became the General Secretary of the Ukrainian Communist Party, and served on various Commissions during World War II. After the war he again headed the Ukrainian Party and supervised the restitution of Communist rule there. He emerged as ultimate victor in the struggle for *Stalin's post, after the latter's death in 1953. Khrushchev consolidated his hold on the Premiership in 1957 and has since then been sole head of the Soviet Union. (See Werth, *Russia Under Khrushchev;* Kennan, *Russia and the West,* for background material; Seton-Watson, *From Lenin to Khrushchev;* and, for the Communist view of

Khrushchev's visit to the U.S., see the Moscow publication *Khrushchev and America.*)

KIROV, Serge M. (1888-1934), political opponent of Stalin, who was murdered, probably with Stalin's connivance, on December 1, 1934. *Stalin seized the assassination as the opportunity for promulgating the so-called *Lex Kirov, a set of regulations that empowered the police to take swift and merciless measures with all "enemies" of the state, and signaled the beginning of the repressions that culminated in the *Treason Trials and *Purges of 1936-38.

KNIGHTS OF LABOR. The American labor organization founded in 1869 by a Philadelphia tailor named Uriah Smith Stephens (1821-1882). It advocated* class collaboration, and was therefore not Marxist. At first a secret organization, called The Noble Order of the Knights of Labor, in 1878 it came into the open. The organization was active in stimulating strikes for better working conditions, particularly among the miners and railway workers, in 1877. It was in the 1870s the leading trade union force in the U.S., but collapsed from internal dissensions in 1893.

KNOTE. *Marx and *Engels's German term for the man of low mentality, non-proletarian, petty-bourgeois. See *Crapauds.*

KOBA. Pseudonym used by Stalin. See *Stalin.*

KOLCHAK, Alexandr Vasilievich (1874-1920), Russian admiral who led the counter-revolutionary movement in Siberia against the Soviets in 1918, on behalf of the Allied World War Governments. He was captured and executed by the Soviets in Irkutsk Province, February 1920, when his Allied support vanished.

KOLKHOZ. Soviet collective farm, theoretically a voluntary union of farmers who hold their land in common. Such farms were forcibly instituted during the 1930s by *Stalin's sovietization of agriculture. In January 1961, Russia reported 44,000 separate collective farms of this type. See *Sovkhoz.*

KOLOKOL. See *Bell.*

KOMMUNIST. A magazine planned by *Lenin, of which one double issue appeared, in 1915, containing three articles by him (republished in *Works*, Vol. XXI). It is now the name of the official organ of the *Central Committee, C.P.S.U.

KOMSOMOL. Russian Communist youth group. By the spring of 1930 more than a million members had joined, about one half of them rural. The Komsomol joined in the Communist *Emulation movement. The name is an abbreviation for All-Union Leninist Young Communist League. See also *Pioneers.*

KOMSOMOL 'SKAYA PRAVDA. See *Press, Soviet.*

KORNILOV'S REBELLION. The effort led by Russian General L. G. Kornilov, former Commander in Chief of the southwestern front in World War I, to unseat the *Kerensky Government and establish a military dictatorship. Kornilov led a march on St. Petersburg in August 1917, but his troops melted away in silent rebellion before the city was reached. Kerensky in alarm released *Trotsky and other *Bolshevik leaders from prison to gain their support.

KREMLIN DOCTORS. See *Doctors' Conspiracy*.

KRESNAYA SVEZDA. See *Press, Soviet*.

KRESTINTERN. Abbreviation for Peasant's International which was formed in Moscow in October 1923. The organization never became significant and it was dissolved by the *Third International.

KROPOTKIN, Prince Peter Alexeivich (1842-1921), Russian noble who became an anarchist and is considered one of the leading theorists of *anarchism. Born into a family close to the Tsar, Kropotkin was touched by the plight of the Russian peasantry and disillusioned with his class by the refusal of Tsar Alexander to keep his promise to emancipate them. He went abroad, ostensibly to study geology in which he was learned, and met the followers of *Bakunin in the *First International. He returned to Russia for revolutionary activity, and was arrested in 1874. Escaping from prison, he began an active role in the anarchist movement headed by Bakunin. He argued that the worker must remain close to the

soil, his own soil, and do his work by hand. He started an anarchist journal, *Le Revolte,* in Geneva, which he then transferred to London. In 1917 he returned to Russia but was disillusioned with the *Bolshevik manner and *proletarian dictatorship. His book *The Conquest of Bread* (1892) is the first systematic exposition of anarchism. He taught that man is by nature co-operative, if the *state will leave him alone; that is, if the state can be destroyed, all will be well.

KRUPSKAYA, Nadezhda Konstantinovna (1868-1939), wife of *Lenin. They met in the spring of 1894 at a pancake festival in St. Petersburg; she was then 26 and he was 24. They became fast friends, both interested in Marxist revolutionary activity. When Lenin was apprehended by the police (1895) and exiled to Siberia in 1897, Krupskaya carried on in the St. Petersburg *League of Struggle until she, too, was arrested. She requested permission to join her "fiancé" in Siberia, and this was granted; she and Lenin were married in May, 1899. From then until Lenin's death in 1924, they worked closely together, Krupskaya always unobtrusively at her husband's side, copying, translating, caring, warding off visitors when they were unwanted. After Lenin's death, she wrote an intimate *Life* of her famous husband, traveled about the Soviet Union giving encouraging talks, some of them published in a volume *On Education.* See *Testament, Lenin's.*

KUGELMANN, Ludwig (1828-1902), German doctor, pioneer in gynecology, with whom *Marx carried on extensive correspondence on *socialism. Kugelmann joined the *First International and promoted in Germany the sale of the first volume of Marx's *Capital. Marx's correspondence with him has been published separately.

KULAKS. Russian agricultural capitalists. Kulak is translated *fist*. They resisted collectivization of their farms, and in 1918 the *Committees of the Poor Peasants had to be formed by the Soviet Government in many villages in order to extract farm products from the kulaks to keep the workers and the army from starvation. Under the *New Economic Policy, which followed this program (*War Communism) of forced confiscation, the kulaks were permitted to remain, but on January 5, 1930, the Soviet *Central Committee determined to stamp them out, a matter accomplished with much bitter fighting over the next few years.

LABOR. "Labor is in the first place a process in which both man and nature participate, and in which man of his own accord starts, regulates, and controls the material reactions between himself and nature" (Marx, *Cap.*, I, 156). Labor has three elements, *Marx says: (1) the purposeful activity of a human being; (2) an object upon which to act; and (3) a tool which can be used to act on the object. Marx held that by laboring man forms his nature, he "discovers" himself. Man is to be distinguished from the animals in that man *masters* external nature, though both man and animals *use* it (Engels).

LABOR, COMPOUND. See *Compound Labor.*

LABOR, DIVISION OF. See *Division of Labor.*

LABOR, INSTRUMENT OF. See *Instrument of Labor.*

LABOR, MANUAL. See *Mental versus Manual Labor.*

LABOR, NECESSARY. See *Necessary Labor.*

LABOR, PAST. See *Past Labor.*

LABOR, SOCIAL. See *Social Labor.*

LABOR, SOCIALLY NECESSARY. See *Socially Necessary Labor.*

LABOR, SURPLUS. See *Surplus Labor.*

LABOR/WORK. Labor: the process of the creation of *value, *products of exchange. Work: the process of producing *use-values, products for consumption. (Note by Engels in Marx's *Cap.*, I, 186)

LABOR ARISTOCRACY. The Marxist term for the class of workers whose wages, social life, opportunities, and the like, are above the average, and who because of these things lack *class and *revolutionary consciousness. *Marxism views the labor aristocracy as bribed by the *bourgeoisie deliberately to separate them from the labor movement. *Lenin: "They represent a stratum, or groups, or sections of the working class which *objectively* have been bribed by the bourgeoisie (by better wages, positions of honor, etc.) and which help *their* bourgeoisie to plunder and oppress small and weak peoples and to fight for the division of the capitalist spoils" (*A.R.*, p. 356). From this group comes support for *Revisionism, Reformism, *Opportunism, class "peace" movements, and so on. The "bribery" may exist in fact, that is objectively, even though neither the worker nor the capitalist intends it consciously, Lenin believes. What matters is the privilege and its effect.

LABOR PROCESS. Labor as a process involves three factors: (1) personal activity of man; (2) the subject of the work; and (3) the instruments used by the worker (Marx, *Cap.*, I, 178).

LABOR THEORY OF VALUE. The economic doctrine elaborated by Adam *Smith and David *Ricardo which states that all economic value is the creation of *labor. *Engels: "Labor is the creator of all values. Value itself is nothing else than the expression of the socially necessary human labor materialized in an object. Labor *can*, therefore, have *no* value. One might as well speak of the value of value, or try to determine the weight, not of a heavy body, but of heaviness itself, as speak of the value of labor, and try to determine it" (*A.-D.*, 276). *Marx: "The process [of labor] disappears in the *product; the latter is a use-value . . . . Labor has incorporated itself with its subject; the former

is materialized, the latter is transformed. That which in the labor appeared as movement, now appears in the product as a fixed quality without motion" (*Cap.*, I, 180). "In the finished product the labor by means of which it has acquired its useful qualities is not palpable, has apparently vanished" (*Cap.*, I, 183). "The raw material (e.g., cotton) serves merely as an absorbent of a definite quantity of labor. By this absorption it is in fact changed into yarn, because it is spun, because labor-power in the form of spinning is added to it; but the product, the yarn, is now nothing more than a measure of the labor absorbed by the cotton" (*Cap.*, I, 189). The theory was criticized by Bohm-Bawerk, and others, not because labor is not an important factor in the creation of value, but because other factors also contribute.

LAFARGUE, Paul (1842-1911), French Communist, husband of *Marx's second daughter, Laura. He participated in the French Revolution of 1871, fled to Spain, and then to London. He was co-founder with Jules *Guesde of the French Workers' Party in 1879, and a member of the *First International. *Lenin called him "one of the best equipped and most talented disseminators of the ideas of Marx." Lafargue was born in Cuba and went to Paris to study medicine. There he encountered Marxist ideas. He committed suicide with Laura in 1911.

LAISSEZ FAIRE. See *Classical Economics; Ricardo, D.; Smith, A.*

LAND AND FREEDOM (LIBERTY) GROUP. (Zemlya i Volya). A *Narodnik organization, founded in 1876 in St. Petersburg by *Plekhanov and others to forward the establishment of permanent *communes, or settlements, among the peasants. In 1879 the group split into two elements: (1) *Narodnaya Volya, a terrorist organization bent on achieving ends by assassination; called People's Will, or People's Freedom; (2) Chorny Peredel, or *Black Redistribution (Partition), a group which sought to achieve equal distribution of the land. From November 1878 to April 1879 the full organization published a journal, *Land and Freedom,* which appeared in four issues edited by S. Kravchinsky and N. Morozov; and in a fifth issue, for which Plekhanov joined these two as co-editor. The journal favored a program of *revolution, to be accomplished by terroristic acts based on: (1) organization, (2) agitation, (3) establishment of connections with other revolutionary organizations, and (4) propagation of Narodnik views among city workmen and the youth. The group succeeded in organizing a demonstration before Kazan Cathedral in St. Petersburg, December 6, 1876, at which Plekhanov spoke. The demonstration was broken up by the police and some twenty arrests were made, followed by severe punishments. Leaders of the group at its founding were Mark Nathanson and his wife Olga. After the 1879 split, Plekhanov organized his *Emancipation of Labor Group, which was the parent of the Russian Marxist parties.

LAND AND LABOR LEAGUE. The English socialist group founded by J. G. Eccarius and M. J. Boon in 1869, which had leanings toward the *First International. *Marx took an interest in the League and its forty-point program, of which the first was the immediate nationalization of the land. The League lost members to the less radical Land Tenure Reform Association, which was formed in 1870 under the influence of John Stuart Mill, the English philosopher and economist, and was less *revolutionary and not under the influence of Marx.

LASSALLE, Ferdinand (1825-1864) (Lassal by birth), lawyer by profession, revolutionary leader in Germany by avocation. Lassalle took the leading role in the founding of the General Association of German Workers in 1863, which took as its aims universal suffrage, state credits for producers' cooperatives, and general rights. The Association lasted until 1875. Lassalle secretly met with Chancelor Bismarck, and arranged for the success of some of the measures advocated by the General Association in exchange for its staging a pretended revolt in the provinces of Schleswig-Holstein, which Bismarck could then use as excuse for moving into the provinces and annexing them to Prussia. He was killed in a duel which arose in a quarrel over a young lady to whom Lassalle had been engaged. *Lenin credited Lassalle with making the working class in Germany an independent political power. *Marx's attitude toward Lassalle was a combination of appreciation of his organizing talents, his personal courage and magnetism, and suspicion of his loyalties and integrity. Marx accuses him, as does *Engels more violently, of borrowing ideas from him without due credit. (See Marx's letter to Kugelmann, February 23, 1865, *S.C.*, 193-197). In their personal correspondence Marx and Engels refer to Lassalle as *Itzig, Ikey, Ephraim Gescheit,* and other uncomplimentary terms. Lassalle's famous thesis that with respect to the working class all other classes constitute a reactionary mass was adopted in the *Gotha Program of the German Social Democratic Party, and was attacked by Marx as inaccurate. Lenin objected to Lassalle's view of the *state as the authority by which social problems will be solved through its sponsorship of producers' co-operatives. This Marx had termed Royal-Prussian State Socialism. Moreover, Lassalle tended to deny the necessity of the *class struggle, and tended to favor peaceful, parliamentary struggle over *revolution; he underrated the importance of the trade unions and strikes; and he favored German national interests over internationalism: on all of these scores Lenin finds him wanting as a true Marxist. Lassalle's major works are: *Heraclitus the Obscure* (1857), and *System of Acquired Rights* (1861).

LATIFUNDIA. The name given the great landed estates of the nobility of the Roman Empire. *Trotsky uses the term for the Russian nobility, "the lords of the latifundia" (*H.R.R.*, III, 6).

LAVROV, Peter Lavrovich (1823-1900), journalist banished from Russia for his liberal views, and author of *Historical Letters,* which he wrote in exile. In 1870 he participated in the *Paris Commune, and from 1873 he was editor of the journal *Forward (Vpered)*, in which he proposed slow and orderly advance toward *socialism in Russia. Like *Blanqui, Lavrov favored the intellectual elite, and tended to hold that *history was made by great single men, while the masses only followed. *Marx attacked him as *petty-bourgeois in his views.

LAW OF COMBINED DEVELOPMENT. The Marxist view that the same country can exhibit several forms of economic development at the same time; in Russia, for example, the peasantry were developing through medieval stages while the *proletariat in the great industrial centers were moving through modern ones. By this "law" *Trotsky accounts for the fact that the Marxist *revolution occurred in a relatively backward country, Russia (see *H.R.R.*, I, 50).

LAW OF DIMINISHING RETURNS. Each successive application of *labor and *capital to the soil (or other economic enterprise) yields not corresponding, but diminishing returns. On this ground some economists have held that the industrialization of agriculture is impossible; and on this law *Malthus based his contention that a population will always tend to outgrow its food supply. *Marx denied this law, holding that science can so stimulate agricultural production as to evade it see ltr. to Engels, January 7, 1851, *S.C.,* 27-30). *Lenin followed the same line of attack in his pamphlet *The Agrarian Question and the Critics of Marx* (see *Works,* IV, 185ff.). *Marxism holds in general that the law of diminishing returns does not apply to a technologically progressive economy, but is true only in backward epochs. As *Engels put it, "Why discuss over-population when there is wasteland enough in the Valley of the Mississippi for the whole population of Europe to be transplanted upon?" (*MEGA,* IV, p. 400).

LAW OF INCREASING MISERY OF THE PROLETARIAT. See *Theory of Impoverishment.*

LAW OF UNEVEN DEVELOPMENT. Various nations develop their economies at various rates and therefore reach the stage of *revolution at various times. In the dispute between *Trotsky and *Stalin over the question of "revolution in one country," this law was held by Stalin to prove that *socialism in one country could be successfully achieved, even though no other countries in the world were yet ready for it. This Trotsky denied (see Trotsky, *T.I.S.,* pp. 18ff.).

LAW OF VALUE. The economic law that the prices of *commodities tend to gravitate toward their values. This law therefore tends to (1) regulate the distribution of *labor power and the means of *production; (2) motivate technological progress; and (3) drive small producers out of competition.

LAWS OF REVOLUTION. See *Proletarian Revolution; Revolutionary Situation.*

L. D. Initials used by Leon *Trotsky, representing his given name, Leo Davidovitch.

LEAGUE OF RUSSIAN REVOLUTIONARY SOCIAL DEMOCRATS ABROAD. The group of émigré intellectual revolutionists founded in 1894 by the *Emancipation of Labor Group. It had its own printing plant and issued the magazine *Rabotnik.* It affiliated with *Lenin and his paper *Iskra* at first, but the "young socialists" of *"economist" bent gained the upperhand and forced a split with *Plekhanov's Emancipation Group in April 1900, and the League went over to *Menshevik influence after the *Russian Social Democratic Labor Party split of 1903. It dissolved in 1905.

LEAGUE OF STRUGGLE FOR THE EMANCIPATION OF THE WORKING CLASS. The *revolutionary organization formed by *Lenin in 1895 through the participation of some twenty St. Petersburg Marxist workers' reading circles. Branches were soon founded in Moscow, Kiev, and Kharkov. It was headed by a central committee, with Lenin as director, assisted by his wife N. K. *Krupskaya. This, with the *Emancipation of Labor Group, was the origin of Marxist organization in Russia, and became the first internal Russian organization to propagandize the workers on a large scale. Lenin enunciated the principles of the League as being "*centralism, strict discipline, and close contact with the masses" (Rothstein, 46). Lenin and other leaders were arrested on December 9, 1895; and after one year in Russian prisons, Lenin was sent to Siberian exile in early 1897. Meanwhile the League was influential in organizing a strike of some 30,000 textile workers in St. Petersburg in 1896, and it issued thirteen leaflets in one month to support the strike. The Government was obliged to limit the working day to 11.5 hours per day in response to the strike. Lenin called the League "the first real rudiment of a revolutionary party." The affiliates of the League usually called themselves simply League of Struggle.

LEAGUE OF THE JUST. See *Communist League*.

LEAP. In the Marxist philosophy of *history the "leap" is a break in the gradual change; it is the abrupt emergence of the new and unpredictable. The "leap" is the qualitative reflection of quantitative change, as for example the freezing of water, liquification of metals, etc. *Evolution* is the process of *gradual* change in nature and in society; *revolution* is the *leap* in social life. The idea comes from *Hegel, and is useful to Marxism in accounting for the sharp qualitative changes in history, and in justifying revolution. "Hegel demonstrated irrefutably that both in nature and in human society *leaps* constituted just as essential a stage of evolution as gradual quantitative changes" (Plekhanov, *D.M.V.*, p. 96; reference to Hegel is to his *Logic*, Part I, Bk. I, 383ff.). The reader who thinks here of C. Lloyd Morgan's theory of Emergent Evolution, that is, of emergents in the evolutionary process for which the antecedents offer no logical ground, such as the appearance of life and of mind, will find Marxism critical of Morgan's formulation because it is theistic; but the idea is the same.

LEFT COMMUNISTS (Bolsheviks). The term for *Bukarin, Uritsky, Lomov, Bubnov, and associates who favored extreme and radical measures during the *Russian Revolution, including a war against Germany to touch off *revolution there. The group arranged for the assassination of the German Ambassador to the Soviet, Count Mirbach, on July 6, 1918, in an effort to bring such a war about. They were denounced by Lenin.

LEFT HEGELIANS. The disciples of the German philosopher *Hegel were led by Arnold *Ruge, Bruno and Edgar *Bauer, Max *Stirner, and Ludwig *Feuerbach, who drew from the Hegelian philosophy its radical and revolutionary implications, but who differed from *Marx and *Engels in that they worked at philosophy and not at *revolution. In the 1840s the Left Hegelians, to whom Marx and Engels both temporarily belonged, launched a public attack on the Prussian state and society. Because Hegel had taught that the *state represents an idea, they argued that if the idea can be changed, then actual changes in the structure of the state must follow. Meanwhile, they held, practical action is unnecessary. Marx and Engels attacked this "*idealism" in both their early works, The *Holy Family and The German Ideology, as idle speculation, as ignoring the role of the *masses in social change, as blind to the real forces in *history, which are material and not "ideal."

LEFT OPPOSITION. See *Opposition.*

LEFT SOCIALIST REVOLUTIONARY PARTY. This Party arose in Russia in 1917 as the result of a split in the Socialist Revolutionary Party (see *Essaires*), and joined the *Bolsheviks in forming a government in October, 1917. The influence of the Party was strongest in the Department of Agriculture, where the Socialist Revolutionaries held the portfolio (secretaryship) and advocated the distribution of the great estates to the peasants at once, and without compensation to the landlords. This program was that largely followed by the Soviet Government.

LEGAL MARXISTS. The name taken by a group of Russian intellectuals who hoped to make *Marxism legally acceptable by presenting it as a method of gradual social reform. Leader of the movement was P. B. *Struve, who said, "We [Russians] acknowledge our lack of culture and go to *capitalism for schooling." Legal Marxism emptied the *revolutionary content out of Marxism, and on this ground was opposed by both *Plekhanov and *Lenin. Lenin's pamphlet The Economic Content of Narodnism, and his pamphlet Criticism of Interest in Mr. Struve's Book attacked Legal Marxism as "the vermin of police-*bourgeois university science." The Legal Marxists published briefly in 1899 through their periodical Nachalo, The Beginning.

LENCHEN. The nickname for the faithful companion of the Marx family, Helene *Demuth.

LENIN, Vladimir Ilyich (1870-1924), pseudonym for Vladimir Ilyich Ulyanov, the man who more than any single other guided the *Russian Revolution, which he had foreseen and toward which he had worked with singleness of purpose. Without Lenin, said *Trotsky, there would have been no Russian Revolution. Whether in the majority, in the minority, or standing alone, Lenin trusted himself, moving unerringly toward his objectives, never losing his nerve. He was born in Simbirsk, April 10, 1870, into a middle-class home, his father a school inspector and his mother a physician's daughter. His brother Alexander, a quiet and studious lad, was implicated in an attempt to assassinate Tsar Alexander III, and paid for it with his life on May 20, 1887. Lenin went to

Kazan University, where he soon found free-thinking friends, and from which he was expelled for radical views in December 1887. Studying law by himself, he prepared for and passed the bar examinations in 1891. He studied Marx in the works of *Plekhanov, and helped found the *League of Struggle for the Emancipation of the Working Class in 1895. He was arrested for revolutionary activity, imprisoned on December 9, 1895, and exiled to Siberia in February 1897. There he was joined by N. K. *Krupskaya, to whom he was married in exile. In 1900 he escaped to Europe and began the publication of the newspaper *Iskra (Spark). In this paper and particularly in the book *What Is to Be Done?* (1902) he set forth his own conception of a Marxist *revolutionary party for Russia. At the Second Congress of the *Russian Social Democratic Labor Party, held in 1903, Lenin clashed with Plekhanov and the Party was split into *Bolsheviks (Majority) and *Mensheviks (Minority), with Lenin leading the former. In the Russian Revolution of 1905 Lenin played an active role, and he was again sought by the police. He escaped abroad once more, and turned to journalism. He was a delegate to the International Socialist Congress of 1907 at Stuttgart and that of 1910 in Copenhagen. He published *Materialism and Empirio-Criticism,* a defense of Marxist *materialism against the views of *Avenarius, *Mach, and *Bogda-

nov. When World War I broke out Lenin was in Switzerland, and in 1917 he persuaded the German Government to give him safe transit through the German lines to get to St. Petersburg in April. There he found the Marxist leadership wavering and undecided whether or not to support the *Kerensky Government, and he issued his famous *April Theses,* demanding complete overthrow of all existing order, and the formation of a *proletarian dictatorship. From then on Lenin gradually came to take command of the revolutionary forces, and, after the arrival of Trotsky in May, Lenin and Trotsky came to control the Russian Revolution. The *"July Days" of spontaneous workers' uprising called forth repressive measures from the Provisional Government and Lenin was forced into hiding, where he remained until the Bolsheviks took power in October 1917. Trotsky was temporarily in prison, but he was released after *Kornilov's Rebellion. He then took field command of the Bolshevik forces. During his hiding Lenin composed his treatise on revolution, *The State and Revolution.* In October Lenin became Chairman of the Council of People's Commissars, from which post he was leader of the Soviet Government. While Trotsky created the Red Army and fought off the counter-revolution, Lenin ran the civil affairs of the Soviet State. An attempted assassination in 1919 failed, but he suffered a stroke on May 25, 1922, a second in December of that year, and a third fatal attack on January 21, 1924. One of his colleagues, P. B. *Axelrod, wrote: "There is no other man who is absorbed by the revolution 24 hours a day, who has no other thought but the thought of revolution, and who, even when he sleeps, dreams of nothing but the revolution." Another Communist associate, Anatole Lunacharsky, writes in *Revolutionary Silhouettes,* "I believe that Lenin never looks at himself, never glances into the mirror of *history, never even thinks of what posterity will say of him — simply does his work. He does his work imperiously, not because power is sweet to him but because he is sure that he is right and cannot endure to have anybody spoil his work. His love of power grows out of his tremendous sureness and the correctness of his principles, and out of the inability, if you please — an inability very useful in a political leader — to see from the point of view of his opponent . . ." (see Wolfe, 493ff.). Trotsky speaks of Lenin's boldness of conception and his meticulous carefulness in its fulfillment. "Inside that great revolutionary there dwelt a pedantic notary..." (*H.R.R.,* I, 294). Trotsky also writes, "Lenin knew that time, be it ever so relative, was the most absolute of gifts" (*M.L.,* 146). Lenin's body was embalmed and preserved in a mausoleum, which has become a national Russian shrine. (See David Shub's *Lenin* (paperbound) and N. K. Krupskaya's *Lenin.*)

LENIN ENROLLMENT. The opportunity afforded Russian workers to enroll as members of the *Communist Party during the week of national mourning following the death of *Lenin, January 21-28, 1924. About 240,000 new Party members were accepted in this period.

LENINISM. See *Marxism-Leninism.*

LENINIST YOUNG COMMUNIST LEAGUE. See *Komsomol.*

LENIN'S TESTAMENT. See *Testament, Lenin's.*

LENIN'S TWENTY-ONE POINTS. See *Twenty-One Points.*

LEX KIROV. A Soviet law, promulgated on December 1, 1934. This was the day on which S. M. *Kirov, an opponent of Stalin, was murdered. The Lex Kirov instructed the police and judiciary to deal summarily with all defendants accused of terroristic acts, and to carry out the death sentence immediately after it was pronounced. The accused were denied in advance any hope of appeal. The Lex Kirov played a role in the purges which were soon to come.

LI TA-CHAO, Professor at Peking University and co-founder with *Ch'en Tu-hsin of the *Chinese Communist Party, by the formation of Marxist reading groups in 1918.

LIBERATION OF LABOR GROUP. See *Emancipation of Labor Group.*

LIBERDANS. Epithet applied to a group of Russian *Menshevik leaders, followers of Liber and Dan, two relatively minor figures. It was coined in the *Sotsial-Demokrat*, a *Bolshevik newspaper, in its 141st issue, August 25, 1917.

LIEBKNECHT, Karl (1891-1919), German socialist leader, founder with Rosa *Luxemburg of the German Communist Party and German Communist youth movement. He opposed the entry of Germany into World War I, and as a member of the Reichstag stood alone in voting against war credits, that is, funds to pay for carrying on the war. In 1915 he organized the *Spartacus League to act against the war, and wrote the famous *Spartacus Letters* to the same end. On May Day, 1916, Liebknecht distributed his anti-war leaflets in Berlin's Potsdam Square, where he was then arrested and sentenced to prison at hard labor. He was freed by the breakdown of the Imperial Government in November 1918, and at once, with Rosa Luxemburg — also fresh from prison — reorganized the German Communist Party. They headed a rising of the Berlin workers in January 1919, and were arrested. On January 15 some German military officers seized the opportunity to murder both Liebknecht and Luxemburg on pretense of their attempting to escape during a transfer between prisons.

LIEBKNECHT, Wilhelm (1826-1900), by profession a tutor, and by politics a member of the German Social Democratic Party, in which he played a leading role. Friend of *Marx and *Engels, he took part with them in the German Revolution of 1848; he founded the Peoples' Party in Saxony, 1865, and the German Social Democratic Workers' Party in 1869. He was editor of the Social Democratic papers *Volksstaat* and *Vorwarts*. He differed from Marx and Engels in believing that democratic processes could lead to true social reforms, and for this he was roundly criticized by them.

LIQUIDATORS. Those *Revisionists who, after the defeat of the *Russian Revolution of 1905, wanted the *Bolshevik Party to develop a program less revolutionary in tone, which might be sold to the *bourgeoisie and liberal nobility. This, of course, *Lenin hotly refused to do. The group got its name by proposing the "liquidation" of illegal party organizations, and it gained the support of the *Centrists, headed by *Kautsky, in the *Second International.

LIST, Friedrich (1789-1946), German economist who advocated the abolition of customs barriers between the German states and tariff walls around the German nation itself.

LITERATURE, Marxist view of. "Soviet literature must help the *State to educate the youth properly, to meet their requirements, and to bring up a healthy young generation that believes in its cause, is undaunted by difficulties and is prepared to surmount all obstacles" (Central Committee, Communist Party of the Soviet Union).

LITERATURNAYA GAZETA. See *Press, Soviet.*

LITTLE YELLOW BOOKS. The name given to *Lenin's first published work, in 1894, because the pamphlets were hectographed and bound in yellow covers. The title of the first work was *What Are the Friends of the People and How Do They Fight Against the Social Democrats?* The pamphlet was directed against the *Narodniks, whose program of peaceful penetration of the peasantry was, in Lenin's view, not likely to achieve any genuine social reform.

LIU SHAO-CHI (b. 1900), deputy to *Mao Tse-tung, leader of Communist China, and generally presumed to be his probable successor. He holds the post of Chairman of the Peoples' Republic of China.

LONGUET, Charles (1833-1901), husband of Karl Marx's oldest daughter, Jenny (named after her mother). Charles was a French socialist, and delegate to the Lausanne Congress of the *First International in 1867. He was editor of the paper published by the *Paris Commune in 1871, and fled France when the Commune was destroyed. In 1880 he returned to France and was elected a member of the Paris City Council, and gradually drifted away from revolutionary *Marxism. He edited the paper *La Justice,* which took a moderate role in the social struggles of the time.

LONGUETITES, The French followers of Charles Longuet who took a pacifist position on World War I. The group supported the *October Revolution in Russia, but at the Tours Congress of the French Socialist Party they turned against the Russian dictatorship and formed the so-called Two-and-a-Half International, 1920. They later joined the *Second International.

LOSS OF TEMPO. "A dangerous mistake, when the *Party falls behind the course of events or runs ahead, giving rise to a danger of failure" (Trotsky, *H.R.R.,* III, 357). That is, the Party must "lead" the *revolution, by "following" its pulse; it cannot create a revolution as a Party alone. See *Party.*

LUCH. Translated: *Ray,* a paper appearing briefly in 1916, edited by anti-*Bolshevik Marxists just prior to the *Russian Revolution, and opposing *Lenin's conception of the *revolutionary dictatorship of the proletariat.

LUMPEN-PROLETARIAT. *Marx and *Engels recognized a class within the *proletariat which was composed of the dregs of society, the bandits, thieves, beggars, prostitutes, and the like. This they called the Lumpen-Proletariat (the ragamuffin). *Bakunin and the *anarchists generally held this to be the most *revolutionary class in society. Marx and Engels, however, discerned that political instability would lead the Lumpen-Proletariat to sell out to the highest bidder, usually the *bourgeoisie, as, the Marxist holds, was the case with the German Lumpen-Proletarians and Hitler.

LUXEMBURG, Rosa (1870-1919), Russian-born German socialist leader, generally conceded to be the most original Marxist mind of her era, next to *Lenin. She achieved German citizenship by a token marriage to one Gustav Luebeck, in order to agitate in Germany. She took an active role in subversive activities from the age of sixteen, in Russia, and emigrated to Germany in 1899. She attacked *Bernstein's *revisionism and wrote *The Accumulation of *Capital* to vindicate *Marxism against him. She was a close associate of Karl *Kautsky until he drifted toward *Centrist views. She was on the editorial staff of the German Social Democratic Party's paper, *Vorwarts, from 1905. She took part in the Polish Revolt of 1906, and landed in jail. On release she went back to Germany to teach in a Social Democratic training school. She joined Karl *Liebknecht in opposing World War I, and was imprisoned for inciting the youth not to join the army, in the illegal *Spartacus Letters*. While in prison she wrote, under the pseudonym of Junius, her pamphlet *The Crisis of Social Democracy*, a challenge to the Social Democratic Party actively to seek power in Germany. She was freed, with Liebknecht, in 1918, after the breakdown of the Imperial German Government in November, and was murdered with Liebknecht by German army officers on January 15, 1919. "Of all revolutionary Socialists, Rosa Lux-emburg alone can bear comparison with Lenin" (Cole).

LVOV. First pseudonym of Leon *Trotsky, used by him when he formed the *Southern Russian Workers' Union in Odessa in 1897.

MABLY, G. B. (1709-1785), French historian, philosopher, and writer on economics, who condemned private property as the basis of all social inequalities. He was carefully studied and often quoted by *Marx.

MACHINE. "The machine proper is . . . a mechanism that, after being set in motion, performs with its tools the same operations that were formerly done by the workman with similar tools" (Marx, *Cap.*, I, 374). *Marx goes on, "However much the use of machinery may increase the *surplus-labor at the expense of the *necessary labor by heightening the productiveness of labor, it is clear that it attains this result only by diminishing the number of workmen employed by a given amount of *capital" (*Cap.*, I, 407). That is, the machine takes the place of *labor, not only as a fact in *production but also as an implement of capital. "Machinery, by annexing the labor of women and children, augments the number of the human beings who form the material for capitalistic exploitation, confiscates the whole of the workman's disposable time by immoderate extension of the hours of labor, and its enormous increase of production in shorter and shorter periods serves as a means of systematically getting more work done in a shorter time, or of exploiting labor-power more intensely (*Cap.*, I, 418).

MACHISM. The philosophy of the Austrian scientist Ernst Mach (1838-1916). Mach held that the primary elements in the universe are human sense impressions; these we all have, whatever they may mean. Sense impressions are, Mach held, neutral, neither material nor ideal. They simply *are*. Such experience is all we know. *Lenin attacked this view in his *Materialism and Empirio-Criticism,* calling it a form of the philosophy known as subjective *idealism, that is, that reality consists only of experienced impressions. See *Empirio-Criticism.*

MALINOVSKY, Alexander Alexandrovich. See *Bogdanov.*

MALINOVSKY, Roman Vatslavovich (1878-1918), Russian police spy who wormed his way so completely into the confidence of *Lenin after 1912 that he was often used on secret missions for him. Malinovsky reported all he found out to the Russian police. Occasionally Lenin's associates accused him of duplicity, but Lenin never wavered in his faith in him (though *Krupskaya, Lenin's wife, records that once Lenin slapped his thigh, saying, "What *if* it were so . . . ?"). Malinovsky fled Russia in May 1914. When the *Bolsheviks took possession of the *Okhrana (secret police) files in 1917, the record of Malinovsky's duplicity was revealed. When he

foolishly returned to Russia, he was apprehended, tried, and executed. (The story is interestingly told by Wolfe, chap. 31.)

MALTHUS, Thomas (1766-1834), English priest whose *Essay on Population* argued that a population will always increase faster than its food supply; population grows in geometric progression, while food supply increases arithmetically, Malthus argued. There will, therefore, always be some families on the edge of starvation. The *"law of diminishing returns" prevents scientific agriculture from keeping pace with population expansion, Malthus maintained. *Marx called Malthus's views "a libel on the human race," and insisted that the law of diminishing returns was applicable only to backward epochs, and that science could provide food enough for all potential mouths. "The admirers of Malthus do not even know that the first edition of his work on population contains, except in the purely declamatory part, very little but extracts from (Sir James) Stewart and in a less degree from Wallace and Townsend" (*Cap.*, I, 352 n.) The so-called "population explosion" today has once again set people to talking of Malthus', theories, and neo-Malthusianism gains ground. Malthus has, in fact, always been of some influence in social and economic theory. *Lassalle based his enunciation of the *"iron" law of wages (derived from *Ricardo and *Smith) on Malthusian principles.

MAN, Marxist View of. Man makes himself as he molds nature through work, *Marx argues. Man comes to know himself only as he sees his very image in the works of his hand, *Marxism teaches. "As individuals express their life, so they are. What they are, therefore, coincides with their *production, both with *what* they produce and with *how* they produce. The nature of individuals thus depends on the *material conditions determining their production" (*G.I.,* 7). On this view of man's nature, as being determined by material relations outside him and with which he is engaged, Marx based his evolutionary optimism. He accepted Darwin's notion of the survival of the fittest, and of progressive improvement of racial stock; and he proposed that when the *class struggle, which now brings out the worst in men, is over, the "new man" can emerge who will be able to bring in the *classless society and paradise on earth. Marx therefore advocated *revolution as the means for ending class struggle, because in it one class is eliminated, freeing the victorious *proletariat to make of itself, through unexploited work, new men and women of the new age. See *New Man.*

MAN/ANIMAL, Marxist View of. "Man can be distinguished from animals by consciousness, religion, or anything else you like. They themselves begin to distinguish themselves from animals as soon as they begin to produce their means of subsistence, a step which is conditioned by their physical organization" (*G.I.,* 7). Man, therefore, is not primarily distinguished from the animal by having a reason, as the philosophers held, but by consciously turning some of his energy into the means of producing other objects — this the animals do not achieve. *Marx consistently, then, finds true human nature in the work man does.

MANUAL LABOR. See *Mental versus Manual Labor.*

MANUFACTURE / INDUSTRY, Marxist View of. "In Manufacture, the organization of *social labor-process is purely subjective; it is a combination of detail laborers; in its machinery system, Modern Industry has a productive organism that is purely objective, in which the laborer becomes a mere appendage to an already existing material condition of *production." Again: "In handicrafts and manufacture, the workman makes use of a tool, in the factory tools make use of him" (Marx, *Cap.,* I, 386, 422).

MAO TSE-TUNG (b. 1893), Chairman of the *Chinese Communist Party, from which position he controls the government. He was born of a peasant family in Hunan Province. A delegate from Hunan to the first Congress of the Chinese Communist Party at Shanghai, July 1921, he came to head the Party in its dark days in 1935, and led the famous Long March of the Red Army to escape the range of Chiang Kai-shek's forces and to establish the first Communist base in Chensi Province, with capital at Yenan. Mao led the gradual expansion of Communist control to complete domination of China in the late 1940's. A selection of his works, edited by Anne Freemantle, is available in paperback. (See Section II of this book.)

MAOISM. Name given to the version of *Marxism developed in and for China by *Mao Tse-tung, leader of the *Chinese Communist Party and Government. Mao professes allegiance to Marxism-Leninism but has fitted it to China's particular problems (see *Peoples' Democracy*). The term Maoism represents three particular emphases, developed by Mao in guiding the Chinese Revolution: (1) emphasis upon the revolutionary peasantry, rather than, as was the case in Russia, emphasis upon the workers' *proletariat — largely because China had so few industrial enterprises, and because these were under the control of non-Communist forces headed by Chiang Kai-shek; (2) New Democracy, or *People's Democracy, as a policy for uniting the peasantry, the workers, the *petty bourgeoisie or small businessmen, and the intellectuals into one revolutionary party; and (3) development of tactics for guerilla warfare, by which the Revolution was sustained during the pre- and post-World War II years.

MARKET. "The transaction in the market effectuates only the inter-change of the individual components of the annual *product, transfers them from one hand to another, but can neither augment the total annual production nor alter the nature of the objects produced" (Marx, *Cap.*, I, 580). The market, then, is the term used to cover this exchange, wherever and under whatever circumstances it takes place.

MARTOV (Y. O. Zederbaum), one of the founders of the *Bund, Jewish socialist party in Russia. Martov aided *Lenin in founding the *League for the Struggle of the Emancipation of Workers, and then became a leader in the *Menshevik wing of the *Russian Social Democratic Party after the split with Lenin's *Bolsheviks in 1903. Lenin turned on him bitterly for this "desertion." *Trotsky said of him, "A gifted writer, an ingenious politician, a penetrating thinker. . . . But his thought lacked courage; his insight was devoid of will" (*M.L.*, 165). Trotsky adds at another point, "Fate made him a politician in a time of revolution, without endowing him with the necessary resources of will power" (*M.L.*, 246).

MARX FAMILY (Jenny, Laura, Edgar, Heinrich, Franzisca, Eleanor — children of Karl Marx and Jenny Marx, née Jenny von Westphalen). See *Westphalen, Jenny von*.

MARX, Heinrich (1782-1838), father of Karl Marx. A German lawyer, he wished Karl to follow in his footsteps, and so sent him to the university to get a law degree. Karl named one of his sons, who died in infancy, Heinrich Guido, in memory of his father. (For details of the Karl Marx family see entry under *Westphalen, Jenny von,* Karl's wife.)

MARX, Henrietta (1787-1863), mother of Karl Marx. The Marx family was orthodox Jewish in faith until Karl was five, when they were all baptized into Protestantism.

MARX, Karl (1818-1883), founder of international Communism, Marx was born May 5, 1818, in Trier (or Treves), Prussia, the son of a Jewish lawyer, Heinrich. Early a precocious student, Marx studied at Bonn University in law, at Berlin in history, and took his doctor's degree at Jena in philosophy, in 1841. His thesis topic was *The Difference Between the Natural Philosophy of Democritus and Epicurus.* Already a radical thinker, and member of the *Left Hegelians, Marx could find only a newspaper correspondent's job open to him. He took it on the *Rheinische Zeitung (Rhineland Gazette)* which was published in Cologne. He was editor in early 1842, and banished from Germany for his radical views in February 1842. He then went to Paris with Jenny von *Westphalen, his friend and neighbor in childhood, as his bride; met *Engels there, and together they planned and began to write *The *Holy Family* (1845) while Marx edited the *French-German Annuals,* with Arnold *Ruge, of which only one issue appeared. Expelled from France in 1845, he went to Brussels, where he collaborated with Engels in writing *The German Ideology,* which, like the *Holy Family,* was an attack on Left

Hegelianism. Here, too, he published his *Philosophy of Poverty,* a critique of *Proudhon, the French socialist. In 1848 he was obliged to flee to London, where he settled permanently. Here he composed with Engels the famous *Communist Manifesto,* published in February 1848. In 1851 he turned his attention to the French Revolution, and wrote the *Eighteenth Brumaire of Louis Bonaparte,* to analyze the assumption of power by Louis Napoleon after the French Revolution. He was also hard at work in the British Museum on *Capital,* of which Volume I (the only one to appear in his lifetime) was to appear in 1867. In 1864 Engels and Marx organized the *First International Working Men's Association, which brought together the representatives of revolutionary *socialism from many countries. The Association lasted until 1876, when it was dissolved, in Philadelphia, though Marx's interest in it had ceased with its transfer of headquarters to New York in 1872, after his battle with *Bakunin over its leadership had almost wrecked the Association. In 1871 he published *The Civil War in France,* an evaluation of the *Paris Commune of 1870. He worked, wrote, spoke occasionally to the end of his life, March 14, 1883, leaving to Engels the onerous task of getting out volumes II and III of *Capital.*

Marx set himself the task of analyzing *capitalism, tracing its antecedents and outlining its demise — all of which he believed to be governed by the inexorable laws of *matter as they come to expression in economic relations, the relations of *production. As a philosopher he took *dialectical materialism as his guide, developing it out of the views of *Hegel and *Feuerbach. Marx also accepted and enhanced the concept of *historical materialism, namely, that all history is shaped and ordained by the relations of production that appear in its various epochs. As these relations change, the whole structure of society changes, and out of the *class struggle always in progress between the owners of the means of production and those who have nothing in their possession but their *labor power comes historical change and progress. Marx believed that the capitalistic era brought the class struggle into plain view and divided society almost entirely into two classes, the *bourgeoisie (owners) and the *proletariat (workers). The very nature of *capital, Marx taught, is such that it demands a profit, or return, on investment, and because only human labor power can create *value, capital, therefore, creates no value; the only way in which capital can get its profit is by exploitation of labor. Thus capital creates its own "gravediggers," the exploited proletariat, and in the course of time they will inevitably arise and violently destroy the capitalist system. In so doing the proletariat will erase the class struggle, because there will

be only one class remaining, both owning and working the means of production — the *classless society of the new era of the proletariat. From this time onward man will progress to heights of leisure, wealth, and culture for all, now only dreamed of. (See Trotsky, *L. & R.* for a graphic description of the new day.) This, briefly, is Marxism, to the exposition of which Marx gave his life, surrendered his prospects of advancement, lived in great poverty and obliged his family to do likewise. It is this hope of a classless future which drives the genuine Marxist today.

Marx has been evaluated by many writers, and some quotations follow. Moses *Hess, who knew him just after Marx had graduated from the University, wrote, "Imagine Rousseau, Voltaire, Holbach, Lessing, Heine and Hegel united in one person — I say united, not lumped together — and you have Dr. Marx." *Lenin, in his short biographical sketch of Marx, says that he fused together the three most important streams of thought of his time, and made of them a revolutionary doctrine which opened the way to the future for the oppressed and hopeless; the three streams of thought Lenin has in mind are: (1) Classical German philosophy as formulated by Hegel, and (2) French socialism as it came to its head in Proudhon, and (3) Classical economics as it came to finished expression in Adam *Smith and David *Ricardo. Engels says that while he helped

Marx a good deal, it is only true to confess that without Marx there would have been no Communist theory worthy of the name. And this is the best summary of Marx's influence: "Look about you," as Pericles said at Athens. For better and for worse, so it is: Marx made history.

There are, of course, many and various critical estimates of Marx, charging him with pride, intolerance, neglect of family, indifference to human affection. He has been called a chaotic thinker, a mere copiest of other views, an absurd dreamer. Some compilation of such views may be found in the Overstreets' *What We Must Know About Communism*. C. Wright Mills sums it up best in his *The Marxists*: "As with most complicated thinkers, there is no *one* Marx. The various presentations of his work which we can construct from his books, pamphlets, articles, letters written at different times in his own development, depend upon our point of interest, and we may not take any one of them to be The Real Marx. . . . There is indeed no one Marx; every student must earn his own Marx" (p. 41). Though heightened a little for effect, Mills's conclusion might generally be applied not only to judgments of Marx's intellectual work but also to estimates of his personality.

MARXISM, Characteristics of. "These two great discoveries, the materialistic conception of *history and the revelation of the secret of *capitalist production through *surplus value, we owe to *Marx. With these discoveries socialism became a science" (Engels, *A.-D.,* 43). "The great scientific service rendered by Marx is this, that he regarded man's nature itself as the eternally changing result of historical progress, the cause of which lies outside man. . . . Before Marx, writers on social science had taken human nature as their point of departure, and thanks to this, the most important question of human development had remained unanswered. Marx's teaching gave affairs quite a different turn: while man, to maintain his existence, acts on the external world, he changes his own nature. Consequently the scientific explanation of historical development should be begun at the opposite end: it is necessary to ascertain in what way does this process of the productive action of man on external nature take place. In its great importance for science, this discovery can be boldly placed on a par with the discovery of Copernicus, and on a par with the greatest and most fruitful discoveries of science in general" (Plekhanov, *D.M.V.,* pp. 153, 193). And, finally, "Marxism considers itself the conscious expression of the unconscious historical process" (Trotsky, *M.L.,* 334). Marx himself says, "No credit is due me for discovering the existence of *classes in modern society or the struggle between them. . . . What I did that was new was to prove: (1) that the existence of classes is only bound up with particular historical phases in the development of production, (2) that the *class struggle necessarily leads to the dictatorship of the *proletariat, and (3) that this dictatorship itself only constitutes the transition to the abolition of all classes and to a *classless society . . ." (Ltr. to Wedemeyer, Mar. 5, 1852, *S.C.*, p. 57).

MARXISM-LENINISM. S o v i e t writers speak of Marxism now always as the conjunction of *Marx *and* *Lenin, intending thereby to emphasize the original contributions of Lenin to the development of Marxist theory. Lenin himself was always careful to emphasize his complete dependence upon Marx and *Engels, and to view his own work only as an enrichment or logical development of theirs. His contribution lies in the realm of practical revolutionary theory largely, for Lenin worked out the steps to the *revolutionary dictatorship of the *proletariat during the so-called transitional period between the revolution and the *classless society, and insisted upon the absolute character of this dictatorship — which endears him to the heart of the Russian *Presidium. In philosophy Lenin worked out more carefully than had Marx and Engels the implications of *materialism, and he made it more determinative than had they. In economic theory Lenin coined the concept of *imperialism, which he called the "highest stage" of *capitalism, meaning by it both internal monopoly capitalism and external investment of capital abroad.

Marx and Engels had no doubt adumbrated these views, but they had not developed the idea of the dictatorship of the proletariat — in fact had hardly mentioned it, and left open the possibility of gradual and democratic achievement of at least some Communist goals (though this is a hotly disputed point). Marx and Engels had, of course, emphasized materialism, and Lenin draws heavily from Engels (*A.-D.*) for his own work. Finally, Marx had not described the stage of monopoly capitalism in precise enough terms for Lenin, whose book *Imperialism* has, in Marxist eyes, come to take a permanent place next to *Capital*, and is no doubt more read (it is shorter, too).

*Stalin said: "Leninism is the further development of Marxism. Leninism is Marxism in the epoch of imperialism and proletarian revolution" (*Leninism*, 8-9). *Trotsky: "The relationship between master and disciple (Marx and Lenin) became, in the course of history, the relationship of the theoretical precursor and the first realizer. . . . Marx and Lenin, so closely linked historically and yet so different, were to me two unsurpassable summits of man's spiritual power" (*M.L.*, 510).

Official Soviet theory holds that the distinctive characteristics of this world-and-life view are five:

(1) Refusing to recognize supernatural forces of any kind in nature, man, or history; the escape, therefore, from superstition.

(2) Seeing the world as it actually is, with no illusions.

(3) Regarding nature as in constant development, under laws which are wholly independent of man's will but are fully knowable.

(4) Trusting science and resting upon it.

(5) Conceiving of society as in constant development, like all of nature, according to objective laws which can be known, and on the basis of which the future can be foretold. (Dutt, p. 16.)

MARXIST, The. "The revolutionary Marxist differs from the ordinary philistine and *petty bourgeois by his ability to *preach* to the uneducated masses that the maturing *revolution is necessary, to *prove* that it is inevitable, to *explain* its benefits to the people, and to *prepare* the *proletariat and all the toiling and exploited masses for it" (Lenin, *P.R.*, 114).

MASSES, The. The masses play, according to *Marxism, the determining role in the history of this epoch, and in general of all epochs:

(1) as producers of goods,

(2) as creative innovators in periods of *revolution,

(3) as warriors in national defense,

(4) as the real source of all art, literature, science and culture.

*Lenin held that the Party of the People's Will (*Narodnaya Volya*) fell precisely because it was untrue to its name and therefore underestimated the creative worth of the masses. The decisive role in *history is that of the masses, who generate the dynamic and the power by which history is made and changed. The leader is a good one only in so far as he brings to consciousness the movement of the masses. *Fascism, from the Marxist view, aims to eliminate the influence of the masses upon national life. Lenin says, "Victory will go to the exploited, for with them is life, the strength of numbers, the strength of the mass, the strength of inexhaustible sources of all that is unselfish, high-principled, honest, forward-straining, and awakening for the task of building the new, all the gigantic store of energy and talent of the so-called 'common folk,' the workers and the peasants. Victory lies with them" (*Works*, 26, 364).

MATERIAL, RAW. See *Raw Material.*

MATERIALISM. Materialism is the philosophical view that *matter is the real, and mind is the reflection of it; matter is the dynamic force in nature, and mind the copy of it. For *Marx, materialism meant that the forces which shape the nature of man, which form the basis for the whole social structure of any epoch, and which provide the dynamic of *history — all these forces must be sought in the "relations of *production," that is, where matter exposes its relations to society. Marx, therefore, studies *capital to discover what it reveals about the relations of production — the expressions of matter — in the modern era. *Plekhanov defines materialism thus: "*Material-

ism is the direct opposite of *ideal-ism*. Idealism strives to explain all the phenomena of Nature, all the qualities of matter, by these or those qualities of the *spirit*. Materialism acts in the exactly opposite way. It tries to explain psychic phenomena by these or those qualities of *matter*, by this or that organization of the human, or in more general terms, of the animal *body*. All those philosophers in the eyes of whom the prime factor is *matter* belong to the camp of the *materialists;* and all those who consider such a factor to be the *spirit* are *idealists.* . . . Materialism and idealism exhaust the most important tendencies of philosophical thought" (*D.M.V.,* 13-14).

What is primary and governs the other, being or thinking? If it is being, is that matter or spirit? These questions divide philosophers. Those who consider matter as primary, as governing thought, and who think of spirit or mind as a property of matter, these are materialists — as the Marxist is. Marx held that in history the great service of materialism had been to destroy the hold of superstition, especially of religion, on mankind by denying the existence of God and spirit, except as derivatives of matter. Not that the Marxist holds that ideals do not exist, or are not important; all he intends to do is to explain their basis scientifically. *Lenin says, "Matter is the objective reality given us in the senses. Its sole property is that of being an objective reality, that is, of existing outside the mind."

Consciousness is one of the properties of matter. *Trotsky says, "Marx's method is materialistic because it proceeds from existence to consciousness, not the other way around."

Some Marxists trace materialism back to China, India, and Greece; they emphasize the role of Bacon, Descartes, Hobbes, Newton, Priestly, Holbach, and Diderot in its development; in Russian thought they honor *Herzen, *Belinsky *Chernyshevsky, *Dobrolyubov; and, of course, Marx, Engels, and Lenin are credited with explaining the influence of materialistic philosophy on social life and history. For a list of those considered to be the most important contemporary materialists around the world, see Dutt, pp. 65-66.

In their *Holy Family,* Marx and Engels give a brief history of materialism, saying in part, "Materialism is the son of Great Britain. Its scholastic Duns Scotus had already raised the question: whether matter can think? He was a nominalist. *Nominalism is in general the first expression of materialism" (p. 202). They criticize Hobbes for making materialism one-sided, *mechanical, and therefore unhuman; this they presume to correct by making their materialism *dialectical, that is, moving, allowing for some expression of human will and action. Lenin: "Matter is primary. Sensation, thought, consciousness are the supreme products of matter organized in a particular way. Such are the views of materialism in general, and of Marx and Engels in particular" (*Mat.*, 48).

MATERIALISM, DIALECTICAL. Marxists decry the kind of materialism which mechanically defines nature and man as the fixed products of natural law, unable to escape the network of cause and effect. To such materialism they oppose their concept of *dialectical* materialism, that is, of dynamic, acting, moving, developing patterns which, on the one hand, do control man and society and, on the other, are affected by man and society in a living relationship. Material relations come to social expression first of all in the relations of *production, that is, the relations between the possessing class and the working class, and in the relations between the workers and their tools at whatever technological stage production has reached. These relations of production create, in turn, all other social relations, those of law, of politics, of education, and the like. Thus the material basis — the economic basis — of society governs the forms which social life will take; if you want to know why Europe behaves as it does, has the institutions and the art that it has, inquire into the basic relations of production. And so on. But, *Marx taught, these relations of production do not long remain the same; between the owners and the workers there is struggle because there is antithesis; and in the use of tools and machines there is constant change and progress. These "contradictions" in the material relations of life are also reflected in all social relations, in *class struggle and in *revolutionary resolution of struggle as one class comes to supplant another in prestige and power.

This is *dialectical* materialism, a materialism in action, not static, and in an action which proceeds dialectically, that is, by contradiction and revolution. For the manner in which *history has been controlled by dialectical materialism, see *Materialism, Historical;* see also *Dialectics.*

MATERIALISM, HISTORICAL. The Marxist view of the general laws governing the development of society, and a methodology for the particular sciences. *Marx puts it thus: "In the social production of their life, men enter into definite relations that are indispensable and independent of their will, relations of *production which correspond to a definite stage of development of their material *productive forces. The sum total of these relations of production constitutes the economic structure of society, the real foundation, on which rises a legal and political superstructure and to which correspond definite forms of social consciousness. The mode of production of material life conditions the social, political and intellectual life process in general. It is not the consciousness of men that determines their being, but, on the contrary, their social being that determines their consciousness. At a certain stage of their development, the material productive forces of society come into conflict with the existing relations of production, or — what is but a legal expression for the same thing — with the property relations within which they have been at work hitherto. From forms of development of the productive forces these relations turn into their fetters. Then begins an epoch of social *revolution. With the change of the economic relations the entire immense superstructure is more or less rapidly transformed" (*S.W.*, I, 362) .

By *social consciousness* Marx means the sum of all political and legal theories; religion, philosophy, and moral views; social science, art, social psychology. By *social being* Marx means the material life of society, basically the labor processes and power which society devotes to production. The social divisions of society depend, for Marx, on what is the dominant form of ownership at the time. Development proceeds by the replacement of one socio-economic formation by another, and Marx distinguished five such formations in world history:

(1) Primitive-communal system: shared labor, shared instruments of labor, and common goods; becoming

(2) Slave system: private property in the means of production, including human labor power, and the beginning of the *class struggle; becoming

(3) The feudal system: peasant and serf have certain possessions of their own, and class structure depends upon their fealty to the lords; becoming

(4) The capitalistic system: from small manufactories of the feudal ages to the creation of a *bourgeoisie, monopoly *capital; becoming

(5) The *classless society: Communism, appearing after the revolutionary overthrow of the bourgeoisie, in which there will be no classes, hence no struggle, and therefore no history as such any longer.

*Engels wrote: "When it is a question of investigating the driving powers which, consciously or unconsciously, and indeed very often unconsciously, lie behind the motives of men who act in history and which constitute the real ultimate driving forces of history, then it is not a question so much of the motives of singular individuals, however eminent, as of those motives which set in motion great masses, whole peoples, and again whole classes of the people in each epoch" (*S.W.*, II, 392) . In a famous letter to J. Bloch, Engels toned down the fatalistic element which the laws of economics and material forces played in history, writing: "According to the materialistic conception of history the determining element in history is *ultimately* the production and reproduction in real life. More than this neither Marx nor I have ever asserted. If, therefore, somebody twists this into the statement that the economic element is the *only* determining one, he translates it into a meaningless, abstract and absurd phrase

. . . . We make our own history, but in the first place under very definite presuppositions and conditions, among these the economic ones are finally decisive" (September 21, 1890, in *S.C.,* 475-477). The reader will find another statement of historical materialism in *G.I.,* chap. 1; in *A.-D.,* 367; in *C.M.* (Intro.); in Plekhanov, *D.M.V.,* 213ff.

MATERIALISM, MECHANISTIC. The dominant form of materialism prior to the time of *Marx and *Engels, the faults of which, as they saw them, Marx and Engels intended to correct by their concept of *dialectical* materialism. This view — mechanistic — attempts to explain all phenomena by the laws of *matter, that is, largely the laws of motion. In so doing it reduces all *history to mechanics, and denies any self-movement or initiative to any participant in the historical process. It denies *"leaps," and *dialectic. It is represented, the Marxists hold, by Democritus, Hobbes, Descartes, Spinoza, and in general the men of the French Enlightenment. See *Materialism, Dialectical.*

MATERIALISM, S P O N T A N E-OUS. The materialism of those who assume in practice that life is governed by natural laws and who are unaware that materialism is the theoretical basis of their assumption.

MATERIALISM, VULGAR. The characterization employed by *Lenin for a German philosophical tendency, represented by Büchner, *Vogt, and Maleschott, which professed materialism but held that thought exists in its own right as a secretion of the brain — though without any reaction upon *matter. They ignored the *dialectic, and defended *mechanistic materialism. Lenin called it "cheap material-ism," which preached mechanistic materialism and lived practically in its denial.

MATTER. Matter, according to *Marxism, is objective reality existing "outside" man, independent of consciousness, but reflected in it. Matter always exists in motion. "Motion is the mode of existence of matter. Never anywhere has there been matter without motion or can there be" (Engels, *A.D.,* 86). Matter is uncreated and indestructible. "Nothing is eternal but eternally changing, eternally moving matter and the laws according to which it moves and changes" (Engels, *D.N.,* 24). This view, *Lenin held, was first consciously developed by the Greeks, Leucippus, Democritus, and Epicurus, though *Marx and *Engels tended to credit genuine materialism only to later thinkers, beginning with Duns Scotus in England. Matter must not be conceived as dead or inert; it exists in a variety of forms and manifestations. Matter can be thought of as "a philosophical category designating the objective reality which is given to man in his sensations" (Lenin). Advances in science modify man's conception of matter, but not matter itself. Rest is a way of perceiving matter, but it is not a property of matter itself. "From the dialectical standpoint, the possibility of expressing motion in its opposite, in rest, presents absolutely no difficulty. . . . the whole antithesis is only relative; there is no such thing as absolute rest" (*A.D.*, 90).

MAXIMALISTS. The name given to those revolutionaries who, after the reverses in Russia in 1905, turned to terrorism as a method of continuing their agitation. They were criticized by *Lenin and the *Bolsheviks generally as being of no real progressive use to the revolutionary movement.

MAY DAY Celebration. See *Association of St. Petersburg Workmen.*

MECHANISM. See *Materialism, Mechanistic.*

MEGA. The abbreviation for the Marx-Engels Gesamtausgabe, that is, the *Marx-Engels Historisch-kritische Gesamtausgabe,* a complete edition of all their works, with critical annotations, begun by the Marx-Engels Institute of Moscow in 1927 and not yet complete. It is taken as the final authority in textual matters.

MEHRING, Franz (1846-1919), German socialist and writer, leader of the Left Marxists in the German Social Democratic Party. His *History of German Social Democracy*, published in 1897-98, is a definitive study of this subject, and his biography of *Marx (now available in English in paperback) is generally considered one of the best. He was, with Karl *Liebknecht and Rosa *Luxemburg, a leader in the *Spartacus Movement in Germany during World War. I.

MEMBERSHIP, RUSSIAN COMMUNIST PARTY. According to Moscow figures, Party membership for a number of years was as follows:

1905 — 8,400
1917 — 240,000
1918 — 300,000
1920 — 611,978
1923 — 386,000 (deliberate weeding-out)
1925 — 1,088,000 (includes candidates for membership, as do all subsequent figures)
1930 — 1,972,483
1934 — 2,809,786
1939 — 2,474,666
1952 — 7,882,145
1956 — 7,215,505
1959 — 8,239,131

MENSHEVIKS. Russian Marxist party formed in the 1903 split forced by *Lenin in the *Russian Social Democratic Labor Party. The word Menshevik means simply *minority*, and this minority took its stand on the position that the workers must combine with the peasantry to overthrow tsarism and thus to establish a democratic republic. Lenin and the *Bolsheviks (simply, *majority*) held that the workers must lead the peasants — since they are the more class conscious of the *proletarians — not toward a republic but toward the *revolutionary dictatorship of the proletariat after violent *revolution. At the time of the split, the Mensheviks numbered among their leaders *Plekhanov and Leon *Trotsky. They captured the newspaper which Lenin had founded, *Iskra,* in 1903, and took control of the Central Committee of the Social Democratic Party in 1904. Plekhanov tried to reconcile the Menshevik and Bolshevik factions, and earned Lenin's undying opposition both for attempting this, and for writing his article "What Should Not Be Done" in reply to Lenin's "What Is To Be Done?" *Iskra* became a Menshevik paper with issue No. 52, and Lenin turned to writing a pamphlet, *One Step Forward and Two Steps Back* (1904). He charged that the basic error of Menshevism was the confusion of "party with class" (See Rothstein, 77). August *Bebel and Karl *Kautsky supported the Mensheviks, and Lenin drew twenty-two Bolsheviks into a congress in Switzerland, August 1904. The congress issued an appeal, "To the Party," and planned a newspaper to take the place of *Iskra,* to be called *Vperyod* (*Forward*).

The distinctive theoretical characteristic of Menshevism was this: that Russia had not reached the point in its economic development which Marx had established as necessary to make the transition to *socialism possible, or, as some Mensheviks put it, "Russia had not matured for socialism." This is the position that Lenin found dominant among the Russian Marxists when he returned to Russia in April 1917; and it is this position that he attacks in his *April Theses,* saying that the time is ripe to bypass constitutional democracy and forge ahead at once

to proletarian dictatorship. Lenin says, in reply to the Menshevik argument that Russia is not ready for socialism, "Very good. But why could we not first create such prerequisites of civilization in our own country as the expulsion of the landlords and the Russian capitalists, and then start moving towards socialism?" (*A.R.,* 576). After the *October Revolution the Mensheviks tried to play the role of constitutional opposition in Russia, but they were brought to trial for treason; by 1921 the Menshevik Party had ceased to exist in Russia, and had no influence elsewhere.

MENSHEVIK INTERNATIONALISTS. The group of *Mensheviks who tended to agree with the *Bolsheviks, and associated themselves with Maxim Gorky's newspaper *Novaia Zhizn.*

MENTAL VERSUS MANUAL LABOR. *Marx argues that the hard and fast distinction between mental and manual *labor is a characteristic of *bourgeois and other exploiting historical epochs (see *Materialism, Historical* for the epochs of history) in which the hard manual labor is the lot of the *proletariat and other exploited, and the relatively easier mental labor, and the leisure to pursue it, is the lot of the bourgeoisie and other exploiters. Communism, the Marxist says, breaks brown this invidious distinction and recognizes the true worth of manual labor, while opening also the opportunity for mental culture to all. Marx, however, regards manual labor as the true characteristic of *man, and the power which forms humanity in us, while mental labor or leisurely intellectual pursuits are always secondary and derivative and removed from real life; though, of course, correct theories are indispensable to correct work or action.

METAPHYSICS. In the study of philosophy this term means the investigation of what is real, or the nature of reality. *Marx and the Marxists use the term in their own way to mean the tendency to absolutize individual aspects of phenomena, of nature, and to ignore their inter-relations and their movement and change. "To the metaphysician things and their mental reflexes, ideas, are isolated, are to be considered one after the other, are objects of investigation, fixed, rigid, given once for all. . . . For him a thing either exists or does not exist. . . . And the metaphysical mode of thought sooner or later reaches a limit, beyond which it becomes one-sided, restricted, absolute, lost in insoluble contradictions. In the contemplation of individual things, it forgets the connection between them; in the contemplation of their existence, it forgets the beginning and end of that existence; of their repose, it forgets their motion" (Engels, *A.-D.*, 35). All of these faults are, the Marxist holds, corrected by *Dialectics. *Plekhanov says, "*Hegel called *metaphysical* the point of view of those thinkers — irrespective of whether they were *idealists or *materialists — who, failing to understand the

process of development of phenomena, willy-nilly represent them to themselves and others as petrified, disconnected, incapable of passing one into another. To this point of view he opposed *dialectics,* which studies phenomena precisely in their development and, consequently, in their interconnection" (*D.M.V.,* 92).

METHOD, MARXIST DIALECTICAL. The Marxist lays great emphasis on *method.* Approach a subject, and a situation, armed with the correct *method,* he holds, and the battle is half won. Marxist method has the following characteristics: it holds

(1) that nature is interdependent and interconnected: look for background and the context;

(2) that everything is in process, birth, growth, decay: know what stage you are dealing with;

(3) that evolutionary change can be broken by *"leaps," that is, by sudden changes for which the antecedents give no complete ground: watch for these; they are qualitative changes wrought by quantitative changes;

(4) that the motive force behind all change is dialectical, that is, everything embodies its own opposite which time will bring out as a living contradiction; in this process of contradiction there is struggle and release of energy, which is the drive in *history; the struggle is resolved by some kind of synthesis which inherits the lasting worth of both contradictories, and which becomes itself the

birthplace of new contradiction, etc.

The Marxist bears these principles in mind as he studies, as he agitates, as he acts; they form the structure of Marxist *method*. See *Dialectics*.

MIKHAILOVSKY, Nikolai Konstantinovich (1842-1904), Russian revolutionary writer who took leadership among the radical writers after the imprisonment of *Chernyshevsky and *Lavrov in 1860. From 1890 to his death he edited the magazine *Russkoe Bogatstvo* (*Russian Fortune*) and contributed secretly to the illegal journal of the terrorist organization, *People's Will* (*Narodnaya Volya* — the same name as the organization). The Marxists criticized him as "subjectivist," that is, as allowing for individual creativity apart from the economic forces governing, the Marxists held, all life.

MILITARY COMMUNISM. See *War Communism*.

MILITARY OPPOSITION. A group which included the so-called *Left Communists who arose in Soviet Russia in 1918 in opposition to the iron discipline which *Trotsky and the *Bolsheviks imposed on the Army, and in opposition to their using old Tsarist army officers to enforce discipline and rebuild the Red Army. The group was condemned by the Eighth Party *Congress held in Moscow in March 1919.

MILLERANDISTS (Millerandism; Participationism). The name given those *socialists who were willing to join a *bourgeois government. The name arose at the turn of this century from the fact that a French Socialist, Alexandre Millerand, joined the French Government in 1899 and participated in its suppression of his former comrades.

MINISTERIALISM. Similar in meaning to *Millerandism, the term refers to socialist leaders who accept ministerial portfolios in *bourgeois cabinets. Up to World War II, this became a test of the true Marxist — his unconditional refusal to enter bourgeois governments. Those who refused, or opposed, such entrance were considered in Moscow the true revolutionaries; those who accepted, or urged acceptance of, such posts were termed careerist, *reformist, collaborationist, etc. (See Wolfe, 592n.)

MIR. Russian name for *village commune.

MODE OF PRODUCTION. See *Production, Mode of*.

MOHR. A German word meaning *Moor*, given *Marx by his family and intimates because of his swarthy complexion and heavy black beard. His daughter reports Marx's death to *Engels by writing, "Mohr is dead."

MOLL, Joseph. See *Communist League*.

MOMENT. A philosophical term given prominence by the German philosopher *Hegel, who used it for a vital element of thought which is isolated only for the purposes of investigation or discussion, but in fact plays a constantly shifting role in reality. It is used to emphasize the process-character of thought, and the artificiality of seizing upon and holding any one aspect or "moment" of it. The word has come into common use in the philosophy of *Existentialism to indicate that point between the past and the future which is the fleeting and yet everlasting "present."

MONEY, Marxist View of. A special *commodity which acts as the general equivalent of all commodities. See *Capital,* I, ch. 3.

MONTAGNE, LA. See *Mountain.*

MOOR, The. See *Mohr.*

MORALITY, Class Character of. "We maintain that all moral theories have been hitherto the product, in the last analysis, of the economic conditions of society obtaining at that time. And as society has hitherto moved in *class antagonisms, morality has always been class morality; it has either justified the domination and the interests of the ruling class, or, ever since the oppressed class became powerful enough, it has represented its indignation against this domination and the future interests of the oppressed" (Engels, *A.-D.,* 131-32). "The theory of eternal morals can in no wise survive without God. . . . But having torn itself from heaven, moral philosophy has to find earthly roots. To discover these roots was one of the tasks of *materialism. . . . Morality is one of the ideological

functions in the *class struggle. The ruling class forces *its* ends upon society and habituates it into considering all those means which contradict its ends as immoral. . . . A society without social contradictions will naturally be a society without lies and violence. However, there is no way of building a bridge to that society save by revolutionary, that is, violent means. . . . To the revolutionary Marxist there can be no contradiction between personal morality and the interests of the *party, since the party embodies in his consciousness the very highest tasks and aims of mankind. . . . All is permissible which *really* leads to the liberation of mankind." (Quotes taken from various pages in Trotsky's pamphlet *Their Morals and Ours,* which should be studied as a sophisticated exposition of the Marxist viewpoint on morality). See *Ethics.*

MORLEY, Samuel (1809-1886), British industrialist who killed off the British socialist newspaper *Beehive* just as *Marx was gaining an influence in it, simply by buying it and running it his own way.

MOSCOW OPPOSITION. See *Opposition.*

MOST, Johann (1846-1909), German socialist who published the paper *Freiheit* (*Freedom*) in London, beginning in January 1879. In 1882 he was expelled from England and went to the U.S., where he continued the publication of his paper. *Marx said of him that he had *revolutionary terminology but lacked revolutionary backbone.

MOUNTAIN, The. A French political group (La Montagne) of the late eighteenth century, better known as the *Jacobins. They consistently advocated driving the French Revolution on to ultimate *socialist conclusions, or at least to the triumph of republicanism over the nobility and the king. *Lenin applied the term "Mountain" or "proletarian Jacobins" to the *Bolshevik group among the *Russian Social Democrats after the Party split of 1903.

MOUZHIK. Russian peasant; often used as nickname.

MUNICIPALIZATION OF LAND. The transfer to local self-governing authorities of large estates, a step *Lenin approved in itself, but only as one in the right direction. (See Lenin, *P.R.,* 151.)

MUSSAVATISTS. Members of an anti-Communist party formed by the landlords and *bourgeoisie in the Russian province of Azerbijan in 1912. They opposed the unification of the Province with the Soviets and succeeded in holding out until 1920, when the unification was brought about.

MVD See *Cheka.*

MYROGA. Translation: lamprey. *Lenin used the word as a pet name for his wife *Krupskaya, because of her large, bulging eyes.

NARODNAYA DYELO. See *People's Cause.*

NARODNAYA VOLYA (People's Will, or People's Freedom). The name of a terrorist organization operating in Russia in the latter half of the nineteenth century, which succeeded in bringing about the assassination of Tsar Alexander II on March 1, 1881. Originating in the secret *Land and Freedom Group by virtue of a split in that group in August 1879, it ceased to exist as a unit after 1881, when it was broken by the police after the assassination. Lenin's elder brother, Alexander, was a member of a small group which attempted the revival of Narodnaya Volya and unsuccessfully attacked Alexander III in 1886, for which the brother was hanged. *Lenin expressed the highest respect for the courage of the members of the Group, but doubted the wisdom of terrorism as a *revolutionary weapon and attacked the *utopian and liberal democratic theories of the membership.

NARODNICHESTVO. Pre-Marxist *socialism appearing in Russia during the 1870s. See *Narodniks.*

NARODNIKS. The name — taken from Russian *Narod,* meaning the people — of a political party which was opposed to the development of *capitalism in Russia, wishing to keep Russia an agricultural country. It originated among the intellectuals and was headed by *Bakunin, *Lavrov, and *Tkachov, all of whom veered toward *anarchism. The Narodniks saw in the Russian village *commune the hope of social progress in Russia, and saw capitalism as the enemy of the village way of life. Some members formed the *Land and Freedom Group (*Zemlya i Volya*) in 1876, and went to live among the peasants. This group split in 1879 and the minority organized the General Redistributionist Group (Chorny Peredel). The Narodniks ranged in political views from terrorists to mild *socialists and published a paper called *The People's Will* or *The People's Freedom* (*Narodnaya Volya*, the name also assumed by a terrorist branch of the Party).

Narodnism was criticized by *Engels in his pamphlet *On Social Relations in Russia* for being *utopian and extremist, and unaware of the true *revolutionary (that is, Marxist) road to social change. *Plekhanov attacked Narodnism in his booklet *Our Differences* (1885). He argued that capitalism could not be avoided in Russia and should not be; rather, capitalism could itself become a tool for overthrowing the nobility and landed gentry. The peasant commune could not, Plekhanov pointed out, resist capitalism in the form of the *kulak; and, finally, the real hope for the future lay in the workers and their revolution, not in trying to maintain the commune. *Lenin also attacked Narodnism in his *Development of Capitalism in Russia* (1899). Narodnism remained a live political force up to the *Russian Revolution of 1917, and lingered on thereafter but with no influence on the course of events.

NARODNIK COMMUNISTS. A party formed in Russia after the assassination of the German Ambassador to the Soviet, Count Mirbach, by the so-called *Left Socialist Revolutionaries in July 1918. The group was organized in September 1918, with the purpose of controlling terroristic action. In November 1918 it merged with the *Bolsheviks. The membership came from the *Narodnik and Bolshevik Parties.

NASHA ZARYA. See *Our Dawn.*
NASHE DYELO. See *Our Cause.*
NATIONALISM/INTERNATIONALISM. The Communist opposes "proletarian internationalism" to what he calls "bourgeois nationalism." National states are, according to Marxism, the products of revolutions carried out by the *bourgeoisie, and these states represent the interests of the bourgeoisie (see *State*), and each bourgeois state seeks its own ends at the expense, if need be, of those of its neighbors. This results in international divisions and the constant threat of war. "Proletarian internationalism" on the other hand is based, the Marxist holds, on the international solidarity of the workers of the world. Between workers there can be no essential conflicts when their common interests are clearly perceived. One of the charges brought against Tito's Jugoslavia in the Soviet press, for example, is that it represents a "bourgeois nationalism" or separatism as against the international Communist movement. The official Communist attitude toward "bour-

geois nationalism" was defined by the "theses on the National and Colonial Question" adopted by the Sixth Party *Congress in 1928. See, for contrast, *Cosmopolitanism.*

NECESSARY LABOR (or Labor-time). That portion of the working day, according to *Marx, in which the laborer produces the value of goods needed to keep him alive, that is, the value which he receives in wages. Marx writes: "That portion of the working day, then, in which the laborer produces the value of his *labor power (i.e. the actual necessaries which he himself consumes) I call *necessary* labor-time, and the labor expended during that time I call *necessary* labor. Necessary as regards the laborer, because independent of the particular social form of his labor; necessary as regards *capital, and the world of the capitalists, because on the continued existence of labor depends their existence also" (*Cap.,* I, 216-217). See *Surplus Labor; Surplus Value; Socially Necessary Labor.*

NECESSITY. See *Freedom.*

NECHAIEV, Sergei (1847-1882), Russian *nihilist-terrorist who became an associate of the anarchist *Bakunin in exile, and probably collaborated with him in the writing of the notorious *Revolutionaries' Catechism,* which expounded the view that to the *revolutionist all is allowed; there is no moral law. Nechaiev played a peculiar role in relation to *Marx, and probably helped widen the split between Marx and Bakunin which

finally broke the *First International, in this manner: Bakunin had agreed with Marx to translate *Capital* into Russian, a task he lost his taste for before he even started. Not wanting Marx to know, Bakunin persuaded Nechaiev to threaten the would-be publisher of the Russian translation with various mishaps if he continued the contract to publish; the publisher withdrew and thus gave Bakunin a way out, which he took. But Marx suspected trickery, found out the facts, and never forgave Bakunin. The antipathy between the two men thus steadily grew wider and never could be healed. Nechaiev was imprisoned for treason and died behind bars. (See Camus' *The Rebel* on Nechaiev, and Chap. 1 of Shub's *Lenin*).

NEGATION. One of the steps in the process called *dialectics, as conceived by *Hegel. Everything contains within itself its own contradiction, which struggles to *negate* this "thesis." This struggle is the motive power of *history, and as the thesis (first stage) is replaced by *antithesis* (second stage), the process is called *negation.* Negation is "the law-governed replacement in the process of development of an old quality by a new one, which comes into being within the old" (Dutt, 101). "No development that does not negate its previous forms of existence can occur in any sphere" (Marx, *MEGA,* I, 1, 6). Negation must not be thought of, however, as purely destructive; this would be what *Lenin calls "black negation."

Rather, negation is "a factor of connection, a factor of development, with a retention of the positive" (Lenin, *Works*, XXVIII, 218). See *Dialectics; Dialectical Materialism; Thesis-Antithesis-Synthesis.*

NEGATION OF THE NEGATION. A philosophical conception developed by *Hegel as part of his notion of the *dialectic. First, as indicated under *Negation*, all things or situations develop into their opposites by a process called *negation,* or, in other words, the thesis develops into its antithesis. But the antithesis does not remain either, for it develops into the next stage, or synthesis, by another process of negation. This second process is, then, the negation of the negation — which is a cumbersome phrase for a simple repetition. *Marx illustrates it this way: "The *capitalist mode of appropriation, the result of the capitalist mode of *production, produces capitalist *private property. This is the first negation of individual private property, as founded on the *labor of the proprietor. But capitalist production begets, with the inexorability of a law of nature, its own negation. It is the negation of the negation" (*Cap.*, I, 763). Negation of the negation, *Engels says (*A.-D.*), is simply another law of motion, applied differently to each particular form (p. 194). See *Dialectic* and *Dialectical Materialism.*

NEP. See *New Economic Policy.*

NEPMAN. The term for a private trader or manufacturer permitted in Soviet Russia under the *New Economic Policy (NEP) in the 1920s.

NEUE RHEINISCHE ZEITUNG (*New Rhineland Gazette*). When the German Revolution of 1848 broke out, *Marx took all the funds he could lay hands on and hurried from London to Cologne to re-establish the newspaper on which he worked as reporter and editor in 1844-45, the *Rheinische Zeitung.* He established it as a daily, the first issue appearing on June 1, 1848. It continued to appear, with brief suspension during September-October, until May 19, 1849. It was the first genuinely Marxist newspaper, with Marx himself as Editor-in-Chief. Of it *Lenin said, "To this day it remains the best and unsurpassed organ of the *revolutionary *proletariat" (*K.M.*, p. 48). *Engels, writing to *Bernstein, February 2, 1881, recalls that it had about 6,000 subscribers. The paper attacked the existing order, and published at its masthead an appeal not to pay taxes. For this Marx and his associates (Engels and Korff, the first time; *Schapper and Schneider, the second time) were twice taken to court and charged with treasonable conduct. Both times Marx served as the trio's lawyer, and both times the jury freed them — once thanking Marx for enlightening them besides. Contributors included, besides Marx and Engels, W. *Wolff, Werth, *Lassalle, Freilingrath, and others. The tone was revolutionary. On May 18, 1849, Marx was ordered to leave the country (for the second time) and he published the last issue of his paper, May 19, 1849, in red ink, concluding his final editorial with the words: "Everywhere and always our last words will be: Liberation of the Working Class." Engels has an essay on "Marx and the *Neue Rheinische Zeitung*" (*S.W.*, II, 328). See *Rheinische Zeitung*.

NEUE ZEIT (*New Times*). Newspaper of the German Social Democratic Party, published in Stuttgart, 1883-1923. In the period 1885-1895, it published a number of articles by *Engels. After his death the paper was turned into a *revisionist organ under the influence of *Kautsky, who edited it from 1883 to 1917.

NEW DEMOCRACY. See *People's Democracy*.

NEW ECONOMIC POLICY. The Russian economic program adopted by the Tenth *Congress of the Communist Party in 1921 as the first step away from *War Communism. Called NEP, it allowed for private trade, both retail and wholesale, and the re-entry of *capitalists into Russian economic life. Some state enterprises were leased back to their former owners. Free trade was once more permitted. The aim of the Policy was to get the economy moving faster than state control had proved able to accomplish, on the assumption that in time the socialized elements would drive out the private enterprise elements — with, if necessary, forceful assistance from the government. This latter step was accomplished under the first *Five Year Plan.

NEW LIFE (*Novaya Zhizn*). The first legal, official *Bolshevik Party paper published within Russia. It was a daily, appearing first on November 9, 1905, in St. Petersburg. When *Lenin returned from abroad to Russia in November 1905, he assumed editorship of the paper and made it the central organ of the Bolshevik section of the Russian Social Democratic Labor Party (*R.S.D.L.P.). Maxim Gorky, famous novelist, contributed to the paper both financially and by writing for it. The circulation reached about 80,000, despite constant police censorship, 15 out of 27 issues being confiscated. The Tsarist government suspended the paper on December 16, 1905, after the twenty-seventh issue; Lenin issued one more, number 28, illegally, and then fled the country.

NEW MAN (SOVIET MAN). From the time of *Marx, the Communist has recognized that some change in human nature is necessary if the *classless society is to be a success. Marx spoke of the kind of man who had never yet been tried, the new man to be produced by the socialization of industry; *Engels argued that as man changes nature, he also changes himself. The *Program* adopted by the twenty-second *Congress of the Communist Party, Soviet Union, in October, 1961, devotes an entire section to the new Soviet man. The official *History of the Communist Party* indicates that one of the goals of Communism is the formation of a new man (see pp. 694f. of the 1960 ed.). In this sense Communism offers itself to mankind as a means of salvation, that is, as a means of producing a new humanity: "This new man must be imbued with the very finest of human qualities. . . . What are the human qualities that must be instilled? They include, firstly, *love,* love for one's own people, love for the working masses. Man should love his fellow men. . . . Second, *honesty.* . . . Thirdly, *courage.* . . . Fourthly, *a comradely team spirit.* . . . Fifthly, *a love for work"* (Kalinin, 73-75). See *Man, Marxist view of.*

NEW OPPOSITION. The name given to a group within the Soviet Government in the 1920s, headed by *Zinoviev and *Kamenev and *Trotsky which opposed the rise to power of *Stalin. The question at issue was whether or not Communism could be developed in "one country," or had to be exported to others if any one were to be successful. Trotsky was for export; Stalin for concentration on Russia. The Opposition centered in St. Petersburg (Leningrad) but the pro-Stalinists maneuvered its defeat in the Petersburg *Soviet. In the summer of 1926 the New Opposition came out in open appeal to the Communist Party, and declared itself in favor of individual, local groups rather than a nationwide single Party. The *Central Committee of the Communist Party, in October 1927, expelled from their seats both Trotsky and Zinoviev, who had been Central Committee members; in November they were both expelled from the Communist Party itself. Zinoviev compromised with Stalin, as had Kamenev; but Trotsky went into exile. The New Opposition therefore ceased to exist. See *Opposition; Socialism in One Country.*

NEW RHINELAND GAZETTE. See *Neue Rheinische Zeitung.*

NEW YORK DAILY TRIBUNE. A daily newspaper edited by Horace Greely to which *Marx contributed two articles weekly on European affairs, on revolutionary movements in China and Spain, and on other topics of the day, from 1851 to 1862. His small remuneration (one pound — about five dollars — per week) for these was often the only regular income Marx had. *Engels, especially at first when Marx's command of English was faulty, often wrote the articles for him, and a collection of these has been published under the title, *Germany: Revolution and Counter-Revolution.* Marx's grandson, Edgar *Longuet, writes that in fact Marx received payment for only one third or less of what he submitted, the other articles being quashed by Greely or other editors and hence unremunerated (Marx, *Rem.,* 263).

NIHILISM. Russian revolutionary movement, rising in the mid-1900s, committed to terrorism and violence as the means to the overthrow of the existing order. The term itself comes from the novelist Turgenev, who employed it in his *Fathers and Sons* to designate a type of student appearing on university campuses who was slovenly in dress, contemptuous of established views and customs, deliberately unconventional in conduct, and opposed to all but scientifically established opinions. The Nihilists were responsible for assassination attempts on the Tsars, one of which, in March, 1881, was successful, when Alexander II was killed enroute to St. Petersburg by a number of small bombs. Nihilism is associated with, and sometimes used as the equivalent of, *anarchism. Under Tsar Alexander III, severe repressive measures all but eliminated the movement, and revolutionary energies went into other, Marxist, channels.

NIMMY (or Nim, or Papa Nim). Pet nicknames the Marx family had for its faithful servant-companion, Helene *Demuth. They also called her Lenchen.

NKVD. See *Cheka*.

NOMINALISM. The medieval philosophical view that only individual objects are real; the class names or general terms for these have no objective reality. There are good deeds, but *goodness* does not exist, etc. *Marx and *Engels saw in nominalism the "first expression of *materialism," in the sense that it attributed reality only to things, not to mental concepts.

NORTH RUSSIAN WORKERS' UNION (or League). Founded by Victor Obnorsky and Stephan Kjalturin in 1878, the Union was *revolutionary in purpose and Marxist in theory. It stood for the "overthrow of the existing political and economic system" and the "international solidarity of the *prole-tariat." It had some 200 members in the industrial centers in Northern Russia, and managed to inspire several strikes. It was broken up by the police in 1879-80.

NOVOYE VREMYA. The official newspaper of the Tsarist Government in Russia. "One of the most dishonest newspapers in the world — and that is saying something" (Trotsky, *H.R.R.,* I, 369).

NUCULEAR TEST-BAN TREATY. Ratified by the U. S. Senate 80-19, in October, 1963, joining the U.S. with the Soviet Union and 101 other nations in banning all nuclear explosions everywhere except underground.

OBJECTIVE/SUBJECTIVE. See *Subjective/Objective*.

OBJECTIVISM. The doctrine that there can be an objective, unprejudiced, neutral understanding of reality. The Marxist denies this. He holds, on the contrary, that all history, philosophy, art, and politics displays *"Party-mindedness." There are no neutrals. Objectivism is, for the Marxist, merely a *bourgeois falsification of its own bias. *Marx and *Stalin did hold that science can be "objective" in that scientific observation can be verified by methods common to all men and not influenced by economic or political ideology, but the uses to which scientific knowledge is put are not "objective," nor are art, philosophy, politics, and the like.

OBSHCHINA. The term for land belonging to the Russian villages which was held in common by all members of the village, and used as common pasturage. It might be temporarily divided into private gardens.

OCTOBER REVOLUTION. See *Russian Revolution.*

OCTOBRISTS. Party founded in Russia, November 1905, in the wake of the revolution of that year, to support the Tsarist Government and to protect the interests of the landlords and commercial *bourgeoisie. It was headed by Guchkov, a Moscow capitalist. It took its name from the Royal decree of October 1905, which established the State *Duma, Russian national legislature. See *Revolution (Russian) 1905.*

ODGER, George (1820-1877), shoemaker President of the London Trades Council, who convened the meeting which initiated the *First International, in London, in 1864. Later Odger became President of the General Council of the International and broke with *Marx over Marx's determination to abolish the office of President. When Marx published his book *The Civil War in France,* Odger resigned from the International in protest against some of Marx's views; this was in 1871.

OGPU. See *Cheka.*

OKHRANA. Tsarist secret police, "second to no other secret police of its day" (Wolfe, 477).

OLD BOLSHEVIKS. The group within the *Bolshevik Party, including *Stalin, *Kamenev, and *Bulganin, which in April 1917 took a stand against the so-called *April Theses* of *Lenin. These *Theses* advocated a drive for *proletarian dictatorship instead of support of the existing *Kerensky Government.

ON THE EVE (*Nakanune*). See *Self-Emancipation of the Working Class.*

OPPORTUNISM. See *Opportunists.* The term is also used as a synonym for *Reformism, *Revisionism, *Economism.

OPPORTUNISTS. Marxist label for those who assume that the victory of Communism is guaranteed by the laws of *history and that therefore it is not necessary to work, plan, and struggle for *revolution. This is Engels's use of the term in his letter to *Bebel, and others, in September 1879 (see *S.C.,* 362-377). The term is also used for any deviation from the drive for the *proletarian revolution, unless that deviation is made for known tactical reasons. In this sense the term is used to indicate any adaptation of the working-class movement to the interests of the *bourgeoisie, any diversion of the workers from the *class struggle by proclamation of the identity of class interests, or the possibility of *Reformism. The Marxists refer to Opportunists as the "bourgeoisie in the working class movement." See also *Revisionism.*

OPPOSITION (Left Opposition, Moscow Opposition, Opposition of 1923, Bolshevik-Leninists, Trotskyists). All these names represent the same movement within the *Bolshevik Party to thwart *Stalin's rise to absolute dictatorship. Forty-six Party members supported *Trotsky in a letter to the *Central Committee, on October 15, 1923, denouncing the centralization being effected by Stalin. In 1926 the Moscow group was joined by the so-called *New Opposition, which centered in St. Petersburg (Leningrad), and together they presented their *Platform* for Party decentralization to the Fifteenth Party *Congress in 1927. This Congress, however, proved to be under the control of Stalin who, as Secretary of the Party, could control the naming of delegates, and the Opposition was outlawed. Many were imprisoned and exiled; others capitulated. Trotsky was expelled from the Central Committee, from the Party, and finally from Russia. (For the story, see Max Eastman's *Since Lenin Died*.)

ORDER NUMBER ONE. The famous first order issued during the *Russian Revolution by St. Petersburg *Soviet. It declared that Russian troops had no further obligation to obey their superior officers.

OTZOVISTS. The group within the *Bolshevik Party which favored terroristic action, withdrawal from state *Duma and from trade unions. It flourished 1905-1912.

OUR CAUSE. The title of a leaflet issued by Leon Trotsky's first revolutionary group, the *Southern Russian Workers' Union, in 1897. The Group was broken by the police, and *Trotsky arrested, in 1898. Trotsky was sent to Siberia

and escaped. Russian name for the leaflets: *Nashe Dyelo*.

OUR DAWN. The newspaper of the *Liquidators, begun in 1910. Russian name: *Nasha Zarya*.

OZERKI CONFERENCE. A conference of legally elected *Bolshevik deputies to the State *Duma, held secretly at Ozerki (village near St. Petersburg) to discuss Lenin's *Theses on the War*, which were adopted, to the effect that Russia should not have participated in World War I and her own defeat should be sought. The Conference was held November 2 to 4, 1914, and the conferees were arrested through a police spy tip on November 5. They were brought to trial and condemned to Siberia.

PAPER TIGER. Derisive Chinese Communist term for the power of the Western world, particularly that of the United States. The tiger, they say, is in fact only made of paper and hardly to be feared at all. In the *Chinese-Russian split, one of the bones of dispute is this Chinese underestimation (at least for propaganda purposes) of U. S. atomic and military might, an underestimation which at least some of the Russians, including *Khrushchev, think dangerously false.

PARIS COMMUNE. Upon the defeat of the French by the Germans at Sedan, 1870, the government of Napoleon III was replaced by a Provisional Government of National Defense. This Government decided to arm the workers of Paris to act as a National Guard should the Germans advance upon the city. The Paris National Guard, thus armed, set up a Central Committee made up of delegates from twenty districts (*arrondissements*) to rule the city. When the Provisional Government, headed by Thiers, signed a subservient peace with Germany, the National Assembly of France chose to meet outside Paris for fear of reprisals from the workers. All government offices were removed from Paris, leaving the city in the hands of the National Guard Committee. This Committee called a city-wide election, based on universal male suffrage, to elect a "Commune of Paris." It was elected on March 28, 1871, by some 290,000 voters out of 485,000 registered citizens (many of whom had probably fled). Not all members of the Commune were political radicals, and only 19 of the total of 92 elected were Marxist members of the *First International. For two months the Paris Commune ruled the city, but from the beginning Thiers started military action against them, inviting the Germans to participate. In bloody street fighting the Commune and National Guard went down, and its leaders were exiled or executed; some 20,000 Paris citizens were tried by courts and received various sentences. *Marx was vitally interested in the Commune, and analyzed the causes for its failure in his *Civil War in France*. (The story is told in Cole, II, chap. 7.) The chief fault Marx found with the Commune was that it was too "kind," and moved without decision or only after too long delay.

PARTICIPATIONISM. See *Millerandists*.

PARTISANSHIP in Philosophy (or in History, etc.). Lenin's principle that positions in philosophy, or history, or other sciences are related to the *class roots of those who hold them. *Lenin: "The political line of *Marxism is inseparably bound up with its philosophical principles," which are in turn conditioned by the class status and interests of the *proletariat. "History is a party science. A teacher of the history or the Constitution of the USSR must be a passionate propagandist of the ideas of Communism, an ideological guide to the young" (Russian Academy of Pedagogy). Thus, both because one's views necessarily flow from his class status, and because one may not take a neutral stand in any science, the Marxist teaches the "partisanship" of philosophy, and the like. See *Objectivism*.

PARTY, The. In order to teach the *masses and to lead them in their own best interests, a trained group — *organized as a party* — is necessary, "even if at first these elements constitute a negligible part of the *class" (Lenin). The Communist Party is distinguished from other would-be leaders of the masses by the guidance it receives from *Marxism-Leninism, which is, the Marxist holds, the scientific exposition of the fundamental interests of the workers, or masses. The Party not only leads, but also integrates itself with the workers: "If the minority is unable to lead the masses, to link up closely with them, then it is not a party and is of no value whatever, no matter whether it calls itself a party" (Lenin, *Works*, XXXI, 213). The Communist holds that the Party invents nothing, but only leads a spontaneous movement; it can teach the masses because it also learns from close contact with them what their needs are. The *Party Line is elaborated by the leadership and is absolutely binding; it involves: (1) tactics: the line for a relatively short period, adapted to the needs and context of the hour; and (2) strategy: the line for a whole historical epoch, which determines the chief enemy and the main aims. The Party leadership may be looked upon as taking the role of an orchestra conductor, and, as *Lenin says, "iron discipline" prevails all down the line. "The Party is the class-conscious section of the *proletariat, which imparts a socialist consciousness to the spontaneous working-class movement" (Trotsky, *H.R.R.*, 57) See also *Spontaneity*.

PARTY LINE. The strategy and tactics by which the international Communist movement is guided. The Line is established in Moscow by the leadership of the Russian Communist Party and is disseminated by means of newspapers and official communiques. In Russia the Line is set by leading articles in *Pravda*, the central organ of the Communist Party; and in *Kommunist* or *Partinaya Zhizn*, the political newspapers of the *Central Committee. On the average there are seven articles per month on foreign policy, seven articles on domestic policy, five on industrial matters, five on agitation and propaganda, five on agriculture, and one on cultural policy. See *Press, Soviet*.

PARTY OF RUSSIAN SOCIAL DEMOCRATS. Known also as the *Blagoyev Group, this was a Marxist organization in St. Petersburg, organized by student D. Blagoyev in the winter of 1883-84. In 1885 the Group issued two numbers of *The Worker*, (*Rabochy*), the first Social Democratic workers' newspaper in Russia. The Group organized fifteen similar workers' circles for the study of *Marxism, and was broken up by the police in 1887.

PARTY OF THE PEOPLE'S FREEDOM. See *Cadets*.

PARTY OF THE PEOPLE'S WILL. See *Narodniks*, which is another term used for the same movement.

PARVUS (1869-1924). Pen name for A. L. Helpland, Russian-German socialist, a writer for Marxist views among the German Social Democrats. He worked closely with Leon *Trotsky in seeking to unify the *Bolsheviks and *Mensheviks after their split in 1903. He wrote for *Neue Zeit* and *Iskra*, and held that world *capitalism had united the various capitalist nations of the world, and would therefore create a world-*proletariat. He is said to have influenced Trotsky to accept the doctrine of *Permanent Revolution, to the effect that revolution in one country must be followed by revolutions in other countries if any one of them is to become a permanent success.

PAST LABOR. "Past labor always disguises itself as *capital" (Marx, *Cap.*, I, 608). "The powerful and ever-increasing assistance given by past labor to the living labor-process under the form of the means of *production, is therefore, attributed to that form of past labor in which it is alienated, as unpaid labor, from the worker himself, that is, in its capitalistic form" (*Cap.*, I, 88). The tools in the plant, or the building itself, and so on, are all "congealed past labor," which, as the means of production, alone make possible the continued and expanded production of the present and future.

PEACEFUL COEXISTENCE. A Leninist principle, much discussed since World War II: Can the *capitalist and the Communist worlds live peacefully side by side? *Khrushchev replies: "In its simplest expression, peaceful coexistence signifies the repudiation of war.... an obligation to desist from violation of territorial sovereignty and integrity, renunciation of internal interference, equality in political and economic relations" (in the magazine *Foreign Affairs*, No. 10, 1959, p. 3). This, he says, Russia and the West can do, if the will is present. Students of *Marxism, especially in its Chinese form, sometimes argue that its dynamic drive makes a collision with capitalistic countries likely, if not inevitable.

PEN, The (Pero). Nickname given Leon *Trotsky by a friend of *Lenin (Kzhizhanovsky-Clair) because of his great literary ability, displayed in his writing during his first Siberian exile, 1899-1902. *Krupskaya, Lenin's wife, informed her husband of Trotsky's first visit to them, in London, after his escape from Siberia, with "Pero is here." (See Krupskaya's book, *Lenin*.)

PEOPLE'S CAUSE (*Narodnaya Dyelo*). A journal published in Geneva, Switzerland, by Russian *Narodniks, edited by N. I. Utin, secretary of the Russian Section of the *First International, though the very first issue was prepared by *Bakunin, the Russian anarchist. The journal supported *Marx and *Engels against Bakunin in the First International.

PEOPLE'S DEMOCRACY. The name given to the form taken by the Soviet system in Poland, Hungary, Rumania, Jugoslavia, Bulgaria, China, and other Asian countries. Basically the same as the Soviet Government, People's Democracy exhibits these characteristics: (1) it makes a united front of the workers, peasantry, middle strata of city population, the patriotic intellectuals, and even small businessmen; (2) it combines all these under *Party leadership to fulfill the functions of the dictatorship of the *proletariat; (3) it has a multi-party system; (4) it establishes Popular Front governments through which the Communist Party effects its leadership; and (5) it retains some forms of the old order.

PEOPLE'S FREEDOM. See *Cadets*.

PEOPLE'S WILL. See *Narodnaya Volya; Narodniks*.

PERMANENT REVOLUTION. The theory, which exists in two forms, originated by *Marx and developed by *Trotsky, that *bourgeois revolutions, that is, those revolutions which try to overthrow the power of the nobility, can be continued into *proletarian revolutions which overthrow the *bourgeoisie by means of the dictatorship of the *proletariat. In Russia, in the early twentieth century, the theory meant co-operation of the Marxist with the bourgeoisie to overthrow Tsarism, and then co-operation of the Marxist laborers with the peasantry to overthrow the bourgeoisie. *Lenin: "We stand for uninterrupted revolution. We shall not stop halfway" (*Works* IX, 213). In a slightly different form, the theory is commonly associated with the name of Trotsky, to the effect that the revolution in one country cannot succeed unless it be spread to other countries as well. On this question Stalin and Trotsky were bitterly opposed. See *Revolution in One Country*.

PETRUSHKA. A character in Golgol's novel *Lost Souls* who read voluminously by spelling out each word without knowing what any word meant. *Lenin used this term to characterize opponents who quoted *Marx without understanding him.

PETTY BOURGEOISIE. The small owners of means of *production, who hold small *capital. The term may mean those who have small factories, farms, shops, or who are independent workers, artisans, etc., who, if they do employ *labor, work alongside them and do not exploit labor by taking *surplus value. Their outlook is conservative.

PHALANX SOCIALISM. The theory of the Frenchman Charles *Fourier that social problems would be solved by the division of society into small groups — phalanxes — each relatively self-sufficient, within which each member would do the kind of work for which he is best fitted by interest and ability.

PHILOSOPHY, Marxist View of. *Marxism holds certain principles regarding philosophy: (1) Philosophy is not above the battle of life, but takes sides; Marxist philosophy favors *socialism over *capitalism; working class over capitalists; *materialism over *idealism. (2) The history of philosophy is the struggle of materialism against idealism. (3) Dialectical materialism has made a revolution in philosophy — a *"leap." (See *Soviet Dictionary of Philosophy*, Engl. Trans., Preface.)

PHYSIOCRATS. French political economists of the mid-eighteenth century, a school of thought founded by F. *Quesnay. They held that all labor is unproductive of true value except that spent in agriculture, because in all non-agricultural production "the value of the product is merely the sum of the values of the commodities that were thrown into the process of production" (Marx, *Cap.*, I, 192) *Engels says: "The Physiocrats divided society into three classes: (1) The productive, that is, the class that is engaged in agriculture — they are called productive because their labor yields a surplus: rent; (2) the class which appropriates this surplus, including the landowners and their retainers, the prince, and in general all officials paid by the state, and finally also the Church; and (3) the industrial or sterile class; sterile because it adds to raw materials delivered to it by the producing class only as much value as it consumes in the means of subsistence supplied to it by that same class. Quesnay's *Tableau* was intended to portray how the total annual product of a country (concretely, France) circulates among these three classes and facilitates annual reproduction" (*A.-D.*, 335-36). The Physiocrats opposed all state or other interference in freedom of trade and industry under the phrases which have become bywords, "laissez faire, laissez passer." See *Quesnay, Francois.*

PIONEERS (Young Pioneers). Russian Communist children's movement, organized in 1924 to enlist children from the ages of ten to fifteen into study groups and work groups, preparatory to membership in the *Komsomol, the senior youth organization which is the training school for *Communist Party membership.

PISAREV, Dmitri Ivanovich (1840-1868), Russian literary critic who preached rugged individualism founded on "rational egoism," that is, on enlightened self-interest. He trusted the "healthy human understanding" to discover and do the right, if left alone and uncontrolled by outside forces. He was *materialist in philosophy and an enemy of the Church. "There can be nothing more disastrous for the student of nature than to have a general outlook on the universe," he said. His work became one of the sources of Russian *Nihilism and influenced Turgenev, the Russian novelist, especially in Turgenev's famous *Fathers and Sons* (1862).

PLATFORM, The (of the Bolshevik-Leninists) (of 1927). See *Opposition.*

PLEBE, The. Official newspaper of the Italian Section of the *First International.

PLEKHANOV, Georgi (1856-1918), next to *Lenin, and before him in time, the leading Russian Marxist. Lenin says, "It is impossible to become a real and conscious Communist without studying everything Plekhanov wrote on philosophy, studying it directly, for it is the best thing in the whole international Marxist literature." Plekhanov was instrumental in the formation of the first Russian Marxist party, known as The *Emancipation of Labor Group, organized in 1883 in Geneva, Switzerland. This Group set itself in opposition to the *Narodniks in Russia, and in opposition to *Revisionism within the *Second International. Plekhanov joined Lenin in editing the newspaper *Iskra, and it was on this project that the two men came to a parting of the ways (see Lenin's account written as a pamphlet, "How the 'Spark' [Iskra] Was Nearly Extinguished," in Vol. 4 of his Works). In the split of the *Russian Social Democratic Labor Party in 1903, Plekhanov took the leadership in the *Menshevik (Minority) faction in opposition to Lenin's *Bolshevik (Majority) faction. Though *Trotsky and others tried to reunite both the factions and the men, no effort proved successful, and in the *Russian Revolution of 1917 Plekhanov played no important role except that of mild opposition. Lenin believed that Plekhanov erred in his theory of knowledge, in misunderstanding the subordinate role of the peasantry in a *proletarian revolution (the workers must lead it, Lenin believed), and in failing to separate consistently the true *materialist's point of view from that of *idealism. Nonetheless, it was after the split that Lenin still advocated the reading of Plekhanov's works, and said that his Monist View of History had "educated a whole generation of Russian Marxists." Plekhanov's major works are: On the Development of the Monist View of History, 1895; Essays on the History of Materialism, 1896; The Material Conception of History, 1897; and The Role of the Individual in History, 1898. His works in English translation are being published by Moscow in five volumes, only one of which has appeared.

POGROM. Name given anti-Jewish massacres, common in Russia under the Tsars.

POLEMICAL GEMS. Name given to two series of essays published in 1861 in the Russian magazine *Contemporary (first series in no. 6, vol. 87, and second series in no. 7, vol. 88) by N. G. *Chernyshevsky in criticism of the Russian autocracy and its treatment of the peasants. A third series was only partially completed before the author was arrested and imprisoned in 1862, with exile to Siberia, 1864-72.

POLICY OF UNITY OF ACTION. The policy of co-operation of Communist Parties with working-class organizations regardless of the political or religious views of their membership; the co-operation with various other parties despite differences in theoretical outlook. It is a tactical policy, pursued for limited and definite ends, and is referred to as a policy of democratic unity.

POLITBURO. See Presidium.

POLITICAL ECONOMY. "Political economy, in the widest sense, is the science of the laws governing the *production and *exchange of the material means of subsistence in human society" (Engels, A.-D., 203).

POPULIST SOCIALISTS (Trudoviki). Small Russian political party, composed of conservative peasants, leaders of co-operatives, and some intellectuals, representing the views and aims of the *petty bourgeoisie during the revolutionary turmoil of

1917. *Kerensky represented this party in the State *Duma when the *February Revolution, 1917, broke out.

POSITIVISM. The more common name for the philosophical views of Mach, *Avenarius, and *Bogdanov, which *Lenin combatted in *M.E.-C.* Lenin called it a disguise for *idealism, which in fact shuts man up to his own consciousness. Positivism tends to hold that man should accept the universe as science shows it to be, limiting himself to the simple "positive" facts of experience.

POSSIBILISTS. A French socialist group, so-called because it advocated restriction of working-class revolutionary activity to what is *possible* of attainment under *capitalism. In 1902 it was formed into the French Socialist Party, which in 1905 joined the Socialist Party of France (see *Guesdists*). This Party supported France's participation in World War I, and *Lenin then dubbed them "social-chauvinists," that is, blind supporters of their own national society against the interests of world-wide society.

POTEMKIN. Battleship of the Russian Black Sea Fleet. Its crew mutinied in June, 1905, during the revolutionary unrest of the time. The *Potemkin* was the first major unit of the Russian armed forces to go over to the side of revolt, and has been so honored by the Communists ever since. The mutiny ended in severe reprisals as the revolt was subdued by Tsarist forces.

PRACTICE. *Marxism holds that practice is the criterion, or test, of truth. *Marx wrote: "The question whether objective truth can be attributed to human thinking is not a question of theory, but is a practical question. In practice man must prove the truth, that is, the reality and power, the 'this-sidedness' of his thinking. The dispute over the reality or non-reality of thinking which is isolated from practice is a purely scholastic question" (*S.T.F.*). Practice itself is the process in which man, a material being, acts upon his material environment. It is the action of man in altering the world, primarily for the Marxist his *productive and *revolutionary activity See also *Truth, Marxist Definition of.*

PRAGMATISM. The philosophical view popularized by William James, F. C. S. Schiller, and John Dewey (who called his views *instrumentalism*) to the effect that laws and theories are merely guides to action, not accurate accounts of the nature of the world; belief is true if it promotes life, false if it hinders it; the world is plastic to man's action it can be made subservient to his will. The Marxist critique of Pragmatism is that it fosters adventurism and aggression, and is hostile to science and to a progressive world outlook. (See Dutt 137-8.)

PRAVDA. Translation: *The Truth* Official newspaper of the *Bolshevik Party, it originated in St. Petersburg in 1912, with *Stalin as editor The first issue appeared on April

22, as a legal publication. The paper printed news about workers' grievances (some 17,000 such items in its first two years) and police tyranny. Its aim was the creation of a *revolutionary consciousness among the *proletariat, and to this end news of strikes was published and strikers were encouraged. By 1914 daily circulation reached 40,000, with deliveries to 924 localities. It was confiscated forty-one times in its first year by governmental censors, and the editorial staff spent a total of forty-seven months in prison during the period. Eight times it was wholly suspended by the police, and had to reappear under another name (for these see Rothstein, 172 and 181). Finally, on July 21, 1914, the paper was permanently stopped, not to reappear until March 18, 1917, during the *Russian Revolution, when it was published as the central organ of the Bolshevik Party once more. *Lenin took over its direction after his arrival in Russia on April 18, and again governmental censorship obliged the paper to take three different names, until on November 9, 1917, with the Bolsheviks in power, it could once more use Pravda, as it does to this day. *Trotsky: "The Petrograd Pravda, which was edited by Stalin and *Kamenev until Lenin's arrival, will always remain a document of limited understanding, blindness, and opportunism" (M.L., 330). Trotsky had his own Pravda (see below). See also Press, Soviet.

PRAVDA (Viennese). A newspaper issued first in Russian Lvov and then in Vienna, from 1905, edited in Vienna by *Trotsky and controlled by the *Mensheviks. Its staff included Skobelev, later Minister of Labor under *Kerensky; Ryazanov, future head of the Marx-Lenin Institute in Moscow; Uritsky, one of Trotsky's chief aides in the *October Revolution; *Yoffe, also active in the October Revolution and Trotsky's assistant in negotiating the German Peace Treaty signed at *Brest-Litovsk in 1918. In 1910, *Kamenev, who was Trotsky's brother-in-law, was appointed to serve on the Editorial Board, in effect to bring the paper under *Bolshevik influence. When the Bolshevik *Pravda came out in St. Petersburg with *Stalin as its editor in May 1912, Trotsky was enraged at the plagiarism of his title, but his own paper soon disappeared. No issues appeared after early 1912.

PRAVDISTS. The name given the *Bolsheviks after the appearance of their paper Pravada in 1912. See Press, Soviet.

PREDPARLAMENT. A provisional council, specifically that Provisional Council selected by the All-Russian Democratic Conference, which was held September 14-22, 1917. The Conference was attended by the *Mensheviks and other moderate groups, and was called in an effort to stave off the impending victory of the *Bolsheviks. The Bolsheviks boycotted the Conference, and the Predparlament was unable to secure sufficient unity among anti-Bolshevik groups to ward off the Bolshevik triumph the next month.

PRELIMINARY CONFERENCE. See *Private Conference of Public Men.*

PRESIDIUM OF THE USSR. Ruling body in the *Soviet Union, now composed of 32 members elected by the *Supreme Soviet to execute its decisions. The Presidium convenes the sessions of the Supreme Soviet, interprets the laws of the Union, may contravene decrees of the *Council of Ministers if they are found incongruous with the law, and administers internal affairs and foreign relations of the Soviet Union. The *Communist Party of the Soviet Union has its own Presidium (formerly called Politburo) or ruling council.

PRESS, SOVIET. The most important of the 7,246 newspapers published in the Soviet Union (in over one hundred different languages) are the following:

Pravda (founded 1912), organ of the *Central Committee of the Committee of the Communist Party, Soviet Union.

Izvestia (1917), organ of the *Presidium of the USSR.

Trud (1921), organ of the All-Union Central Council of Trade Unions.

Komsomol'skaya Pravda (1925), organ of the Central Committee of the *Komsomol (youth organization).

Krasnaya Svezda (1924), organ of the Ministry of Defense.

Literaturnaya Gazeta (1929),

organ of the Board of the Union of Writers.

Kommunist (1956), theoretical organ of the Central Committee.

Tass, telegraph agency for the foreign press.

PRICE. The value, Marx holds, of a *commodity expressed in *money.

PRIMITIVE ACCUMULATION. The name given in *Marxism to the first appearance in history of *capital in private hands. There are two reciprocal stages in the process of primitive accumulation: (1) the appearance of wage earners (*proletariat) and (2) the accumulation of wealth in the hands of capitalists (*bourgeoisie). *Marx calls primitive accumulation "the path by which the capitalist order of economy emerged from the womb of the feudal order of economy. . . . the historic movement which by divorcing the producers from their means of *production converts them into wage earners while it converts into capitalists those who hold the means of production in their possession" (*S.C.,* 353). Marx says, "A certain accumulation of capital in the hands of individual producers of *commodities forms the necessary preliminary of the specifically capitalist mode of production. We have, therefore, to assume that this occurs during the transition from handicraft to capitalistic industry. It may be called *primitive accumulation,* because it is the historical basis instead of the historical result of specifically capitalist production. In actual history it is notorious that conquest, enslavement, robbery, murder, briefly force, play the great part. . . . The laborer could only dispose of himself after he had ceased to be attached to the soil and ceased to be the slave, serf, or bondsman of another . . . and escaped from the regime of the guilds, and after he had been robbed of his own means of production. The expropriation of the agricultural producer, of the peasant, from the soil, is the basis of the whole process" (*Cap.*, I, 624; 714; 716). "The spoilation of the Church property, the fraudulent alienation of the State domains, the robbery of the common lands, the usurpation of feudal and clan property, and its transformation into modern private property under circumstances of ruthless terrorism, were just so many idyllic methods of primitive accumulation" (*Cap.*, I, 732-33). See Engels's summary in *A.-D.*, 182ff.

PRIMITIVE SOCIALIST ACCUMULATION. See *Primitive Accumulation.* Just as *capitalism requires a first or primitive accumulation of resources at its beginning, so the Soviet Government found that it required resources of capital, or its equivalent, in order to bring its economy to its feet after the devastating era of revolution, 1917-1920. E. I. Preobranzhensky (b. 1886), a member of the Soviet Government, proposed in the early 1920s a program to be called Primitive Socialist Accumulation, a solution of the post-Revolution economic problems by a process of primitive accumulation, that is, by extracting from the peasantry (then relatively independent) and the *kulaks (agricultural capitalists) the capital goods necessary to the stimulation of industry by investment. The idea was rejected by *Lenin, but later put into effect by *Stalin as the program of *sovietization of the farms. See *Committees of Poor Peasants.*

PRIMITIVENESS. The term which refers to the level of production when that level is too low to support the society that rests upon it. See *Production, Mode of; Productive Forces.*

PRIVATE CONFERENCE OF PUBLIC MEN. Sometimes known as the Preliminary Conference, the name refers to a meeting in Moscow, August 8-10, 1917, of representatives of the *bourgeoisie, landlords, and the army, in an effort to establish a common front against the *Bolsheviks. Out of the meeting came a counter-Bolshevik group known as the Union of Public Men.

PRIVATE PROPERTY. *Marxism views private property as a legal relation, established by custom and maintained by the *state. The first claim laid by man to private possession of property in productive means was, *Marx taught, the origin of all *class struggle, with all its ensuing evils; that is, it was the "original sin" in Marxist *theology. "The founder of civil society, and consequently the grave-digger of primitive equality, was the man who first fenced off a piece of land and said, 'It belongs to me.' In other words, the foundation of civil society is property, which arouses so many disputes among men, evokes in them so much greed, so spoils their morality" (Plekhanov, *D.M.V.*, 121).

PRIVATE PROPERTY, HISTORICAL FORMS OF. The first form of property, *Marx says, was tribal, and therefore communal rather than strictly private. In general it existed only in land. "Real private property began with the ancients, as with modern nations, with personal movable property. . . . Tribal property evolved through various stages — feudal landed property, corporative movable property, manufacture-*capital — to modern capital, determined by big industry and universal competition, that is, pure private property, which has cast off all semblance of a communal institution and has shut out the *state from any influence on the development of property. To this modern private property corresponds the modern state" (*G.I.,* 58-59).

PROCURATOR-GENERAL USSR. The Soviet equivalent of the United States Attorney General. He is appointed by the *Supreme Soviet for a seven-year term, and is responsible for the judicial administration of the laws of the Union.

PRODUCTION, MODE OF. *Marx's term for the general method of obtaining the means of life (food, clothing, shelter, tools, etc.). This method consists of: (1) the *productive forces and (2) the *productive relations. Together these form the productive system or mode; and as on the one hand the productive system forms the base of social relations, so on the other hand the social relations modify the productive base upon which they rest. See *Social Labor.*

PRODUCTION RELATIONS (Productive Relations). *Marx's terms for the relations established among people in the process of producing material goods — food, clothing, shelter, tools, etc. Always social in character, these relations are dependent upon the character of the *productive forces, but also modify these. As the production relations change, they reflect and produce changes in the productive forces; and this constant tension is relieved only, Marx taught, under *socialism, when both phases are brought into harmony. See *Materialism.*

PRODUCTIVE FORCES. The name given by *Marx to the instruments of production, which include two classes of objects: (1) the tools by means of which goods are produced and (2) the people who set the tools in motion. The productivity of human *labor is dependent upon the level of the productive forces at the time; and this level marks the degree of mankind's mastery, at the moment, over nature. The evolution of the productive forces underlies the evolution of the mode of *production, which in turn underlies the character of the whole social structure of the epoch.

PROFESSION DE FOI (*Profession of Faith*). The title of a leaflet issued in 1899 by the Kiev Committee (socialist group), setting forth the views of the so-called *Young Socialists. It was similar to the *Credo issued by the *Economists. It was attacked by *Lenin in his pamphlet *Apropos the Profession de Foi.*

PROFINTERN. The international organization of *trade unions set up by the *Comintern in 1921, in Moscow, and dissolved in 1937 without having achieved any notable results.

PROFIT. See *Surplus Value.*

PROGRESS. For *Marxism the measure of progress in *history is the state of development of the so-called *productive forces, for this is the indication of the extent of man's dominion over nature, and all other aspects of life depend upon this. Communist "progress" is toward the *classless society, after the *revolution; *bourgeois "progress" is, the Marxist says, toward what he calls the "slave state," dominated by monopoly *capital. Socialist or Communist "progress" benefits all, embraces all aspects of life, includes all socialist countries, is consciously planned, and is achieved by the participation of the *masses — so, at least, say the Marxists. Writes *Marx, "The very moment civilization begins, production begins to be founded on the antagonism of orders, estates, classes, and finally on the antagonism of accumulated *labor and actual labor. No antagonism, no progress" (*P.P.*, 61).

PROGRESSIVE IDEAS. See *Ideas, Role in History.*

PROLETARIAN DEMOCRACY. The dictatorial rule of the majority over the minority. See *Revolutionary Dictatorship of the Proletariat.*

PROLETARIAN REDEMPTION. The Communist doctrine that the *proletariat has a special task in modern history, namely, to redeem mankind from the shackles of *capitalist exploitation. This task is explained most clearly, Soviet thinkers hold, in the "classics" of Marxism-Leninism, that is, in the works of *Marx, *Engels, and *Lenin (see Section II of this book). These classics function, therefore, as the "Scriptures" of Communism; and the work of Soviet thinkers is confined by the perspectives established by these classics. Proletarian redemption becomes in practice the basic assumption which governs Marxist thought; at the same time it serves as an ideal toward which the proletariat is urged by the Communist to strive.

PROLETARIAN REVOLUTION. The destruction by violence of the old state apparatus and the creation of a new one (Lenin). The proletarian revolution is not a "putsch" or palace revolt; it is a mass movement, directed and organized by the *Communist Party. *Lenin offered some advice on such revolution:

(1) Never play at revolution; once in it, you must go on to the end.

(2) Concentrate great superior-

ity of forces at decisive points and moments.

(3) Act with determination and always keep the offensive — "the defensive is the death of every armed rising."

(4) Try to catch the enemy by surprise, especially when his forces are dispersed.

(5) Strive for daily successes, and thus keep the "moral ascendancy."

(Adapted from *Works*, XXVI, 152). See *Revolutionary Situation*.

*Khrushchev told the 20th Party *Congress that "at present" there is the possibility of peaceful transition to *socialism in some countries by the use of the machinery of *democracy (Report to 20th Congress). *Lenin never thought so. See *Revolutionary Dictatorship of the Proletariat*.

PROLETARIAT. The term employed by *Marx and his followers to indicate the *class of the workers, who have nothing to sell but their *labor power, and who must sell this labor power in order to remain alive. The class is contrasted with the *bourgeoisie, who own the means of production, and thus have resources on which to live if necessary, whether or not goods are produced in their plants. The word proletariat is used more loosely to indicate the exploited, the down-trodden. On the proletariat Marx based his hopes for the *revolution which for him is the gateway to the future. "In every great bourgeois movement there were individual outbursts of that class which was the forerunner, more or less developed, of the modern proletariat. For example, at the time of the German Reformation and the Peasants' War, there were the Anabaptists and Thomas Müntzer; in the English Revolution there were the Levellers; in the Great French Revolution, Baboef" (Engels, *A.-D.*, 29). "In the proletariat the Marxist world outlook has found its material weapon, just as the proletariat has found in *Marxism its spiritual weapon" (Dutt, 19). The historic mission of the proletariat, as a class, is to destroy *capitalism and build *socialism, because:

(1) It is the most exploited class, and therefore the most conscious and irreconcilable opponent of capitalism.

(2) It looks forward and not back, and is therefore in step with *history.

(3) Its liberation will only be achieved by revolution, for which it possesses the following fighting qualities:

(a) Size, mass.

(b) Susceptibility to organization, regimentation, discipline, united action and mutual assistance.

(c) Capability of achieving a world outlook, a political consciousness, based on experience and not books.

(d) A militant attitude.

The proletariat is the "suffering savior" of Marxist "theology." See *Theology, Marxist*.

In an article published in the *Deutsch-Französische Jahrbücher,* 1844, Marx defined, in somewhat rhetorical prose, his conception of the proletariat: ". . . a class of *bourgeois society which is not a class of bourgeois society; a class which is the dissolution of all classes; a sphere of society which has a universal character as a result of its universal suffering; a sphere which demands no particular right, because no particular wrong has been done to it, but wrong as such; a sphere which can no longer appeal to the historical title, but to a human title only; a sphere which does not stand in a onesided contradiction to the consequences, but in a general and all-around contradiction to the very hypotheses of a German state; and finally, a sphere which cannot emancipate itself without at the same time emancipating all other spheres of society also; a class which, in a word, represents the complete loss of humanity and can therefore win itself only through the complete re-winning of humanity. This dissolution of society is the proletariat" (See Mehring, 67ff.).

PROLETARIAT, DICTATORSHIP OF. See *Revolutionary Dictatorship of the Proletariat.*

PROLETARIAT, INCREASING MISERY OF. See *Theory of Impoverishment.*

PROLETARY. Name of the revolutionary paper of which *Lenin was Editor, and which was established by the *Bolsheviks to replace *Iskra* and lost to the *Mensheviks. It appeared abroad and was smuggled into Russia. Fifty issues saw light, the first twenty out of Vyborg, Finland; the next issues, from Feb. 26 to Dec. 14, 1908, out of Geneva; and the remaining, from Jan. 21 to Dec. 11, 1909, out of Paris. In 1910 the paper fell into the hands of the *Conciliators and was allowed to expire.

PROPAGANDA. See *Agitation/Propaganda.*

PROPAGANDA BY DEED. *Anarchist phrase, approved in principle by the Anarchist Congress held in Switzerland, at La Chaux-de-fonds, in 1879. It implies that terroristic acts, including assassination as chief, are the best *revolutionary slogans and advertisement. The phrase was chosen as its password by the Russian organization *Narodnaya Volna, one of whose members (Ignatie Grinevitski) assassinated Tsar Alexander II in 1881.

PROPERTY, PRIVATE. See *Private Property.*

PROPERTY, PRIVATE, HISTORICAL FORMS OF. See *Private Property, Historical Forms of.*

PROTEST, RUSSIAN SOCIAL DEMOCRATIC. Written by *Lenin in exile in Siberia, 1899, as a criticism of the *Credo,* a statement of views adopted by the *Economists. Lenin's Protest was adopted by seventeen Marxists also in exile whom Lenin had managed to convene in Yermakovskoye, Siberia. Other political exiles, unable to attend the meeting, received copies of the Protest and added their support to it. Finally a copy was sent to *Plekhanov's *Emancipation of Labor Group, and published by Plekhanov in 1900 in *The Guide (Vademecum)*, a pamphlet he composed against Economism and *Revisionism.

PROUDHON, Pierre Joseph (1803-1865), French social thinker, classified by *Marx as *petty bourgeois. Proudhon favored small enterprise, and hoped for the establishment of "people's banks" to aid workers in gaining capital interest in the factories in which they worked. He also favored "exchange banks" which would help small producers market their goods. Proudhon opposed *class struggle and minimized the role of the *proletariat in social progress, and wished to minimize the role of the state. He and his followers came into conflict with Marx in the *First International, and were defeated. Proudhon hoped to vindicate his views by the establishment in France by private subscription of a great Central Credit Bank, from which the people's and exchange banks could spring as branches; he advertised for donors, and awaited them at home. None came. His idea of loans was that they should be interest-free, allowing the borrower to receive full return on the value of his labor. Marx attacked him in *P.P.* and gave his views on Proudhon in two letters: to J. B. von Schweitzer, Jan. 24, 1865 (*S.C.*, 169-176) and to P. V. Annenkov, Dec. 28, 1846 (*S.C.*, 5-18).

PROVISIONAL GOVERNMENT. See *February Revolution.*

PURGES, RUSSIAN (Stalin's). The purges of the late 1930s in Soviet Russia were associated with the notorious *Treason Trials, but they must be distinguished from them. Both the purges and the trials were carried out on the orders of *Stalin to secure his own position in Russia. The trials gave a guise of legalty to the execution of some of the co-leaders of Russia who might presumably have challenged Stalin's one-man rule; the purges eliminated lesser *Party officials and terrorized the Russian people. According to *Khrushchev's *"Secret Speech," Stalin disposed of 71 members of the *Central Committee of the Communist Party, leaving only 16 alive; at least 7,000 Party members were killed; while tens of thousands of the Russian people — some of them selected arbitrarily from street to street or house to house — perished or went into slave labor camps. The purges were carried out under the direction of N. I. *Yezhov, then head of the *NKVD, or secret police, from lists of names approved by Stalin. Khrushchev said in the same speech that 383 such lists, comprising thousands of names, were drawn up over a two-year period, 1936-38. In 1938, with the major purges done, Lavrenti Beria succeeded Yezhov as head of the police, and gradually the purges tapered off, though the threat was long present and frequently carried out also under Beria. See *Cheka; Lex Kirov, Treason Trials.* (See Gunther.)

QUALITY. "Anything which exists is definite, determinate" (Lenin), and quality is what makes it so. Those characteristics which determine, define, circumscribe a thing or event are its *qualitative* aspects. At certain stages in *history qualitative changes called *"leaps" — abrupt and unpredictable changes — occur, because of major quantitative changes in *matter and its relations; as, for example, when *revolution breaks out, or, in physics, when water changes into steam — or ice.

QUANTITY. The amount, measure, and weight of physical material which underlie and control its qualitative aspects.

QUESNAY, François (1694-1744), French physician and economist, founder of the school known as the *Physiocrats. Quesnay, *Marx said, properly transferred the investigation of *surplus value (or profit) from the sphere of the circulation of goods in the *market to the sphere of their *production. He thus opened the way to a correct analysis of surplus value, an analysis accomplished, Marx thought, in his own book, *Capital. Quesnay thought that agricultural *labor was the only truly productive labor and, therefore, ground rent the only true form of surplus value. He was the author of the famous *Tableau Économique,* which represented in graphic form the process of reproduction of social capital. Marx called it "incontestably the most brilliant idea of which political economy had hitherto been guilty." For an analysis of the *Tableau,* see Engels, *A.-D.,* 335-343.

RABOTNIK. See *League of Russian Revolutionary Social Democrats Abroad.*

RADISHCHEV, A. N. (1749-1802), author of *A Journey From St. Petersburg to Moscow,* which was the first published attack on Russian serfdom. The Empress Catherine II read the book and had Radishchev sentenced to death, but the sentence was commuted to ten years in Siberia. When again threatened by the police, after his return from exile, Radishchev committed suicide. *Lenin pays him high praise for courage and foresight.

RAW MATERIAL. The subject of *labor, that is, the substance on which labor is performed. Such subject of labor is called "raw material" strictly only when it has been "filtered through previous labor; as for example, ore already extracted and ready for washing" (Marx, *Cap.* 1, 178). *Marx goes on to say, "Raw material may either form the principal substance of a product, or it may enter into its formation only as an accessory. . . . This distinction between principal substance and accident vanishes in the true chemical-industries, because there none of the raw material re-appears, in its original composition, in the substance of the product" (*Cap.,* I, 181).

RED GUARDS. First formed during the *Revolution of 1905, the armed factory workers of Russia were known as the Red Guards.

The association of red with revolution is no doubt due to the fact that blood is spilled and in modern Russian history relates to the so-called *Bloody Sunday. Opposition to the Red Guards came from the so-called White Guards (which see).

REDISTRIBUTIONISTS. See *Emancipation of Labor Group.*

REFORMISM. See *Revisionism.*

RELATIONS OF PRODUCTION. See *Production Relations.*

RELATIVE SURPLUS POPULATION. Term used by *Marx to cover all the unemployed. "Every laborer belongs to it during the time he is only partially employed or wholly unemployed. . . . it has always three forms, the floating, the latent, the stagnant."

(1) Floating: in the centers of modern industry, the laborers are sometimes repelled, sometimes attracted; they come and go.

(2) Latent: agricultural labor is always threatened by permanent displacement and on the point of passing over into an urban *proletariat.

(3) Stagnant: a part of the active labor army that has extremely irregular employment (Marx, *Cap.*, I, 640-643).

"The lowest sediment of the relative surplus population finally dwells in the sphere of pauperism" (*Cap.*, I, 643). Marx divides paupers into three classes: (1) those able to work, (2) the orphans and pauper children, and (3) those unable to work.

RELATIVE SURPLUS VALUE. "The surplus value arising from the curtailment of the *necessary labor time and from the corresponding alteration in the respective lengths of the two components of the working day, I call relative surplus value" (Marx, *Cap.*, I, 315). See *Surplus Value.*

RELAY SYSTEM. An ingenious method, permitted under English law by Justice Baron Parke, for avoiding the ten-hours limitation on the employment of women and children established by the British Factory Act of 1847 (see *Factory Acts*). The Act provided that no more than ten hours work per day could be required of women and children, but failed to specify that the ten hours must be continuous labor. Justice Parke ruled, therefore, that an employer who "relayed" his women and child employees, by giving them off-periods during the day when others were put to work, could thus keep his factory running as far into the night as he pleased so long as no workers put in more than a total of ten hours at their tasks. The relay system was not outlawed until 1874.

RELIGION, Marxist View of. "All religion, however, is nothing but the fantastic reflection in men's minds of those external forces which control their daily life, a reflection in which the terrestrial forces assume the form of supernatural forces . . . , one almighty god, who is but a reflection of the abstract man. Such was the origin of monotheism. When man no longer proposes but also (by taking control of the means of production) disposes, only then will the alien force which is still reflected in religion vanish, and with it will vanish the religious reflection itself" (Engels, *A.D.* 435-37). This is Engels's adaptation of what *Feuerbach had written in *The Essence of Christianity,* which was in turn adapted from *Hegel. *Marx wrote, "The abolition of religion as the illusory happiness of the people is required for their real happiness" (*On Religion,* 42). The volume entitled *On Religion,* published in Moscow by the Foreign Languages Publishing House, is a compilation of Marx and Engels's writing on the subject and can profitably be consulted on this matter. Marx calls religion "the opiate of the people," because, he believes, it serves to keep them satisfied with bad conditions on earth by promising them "pie in the sky"; that is, it lulls their sense of rebellion into drugged sleep.

REPRODUCTION. The term used by *Marx for the process of replacing the continually consumed means of *production by new wealth. Possession of this new wealth is wholly in the hands of the capitalist. Reproduction depends upon a division of the whole productive process into two parts: (1) the production of the means of production (Department I); (2) the production of consumer goods (Department II). From another point of view, reproduction may be analyzed into a three-part process: (1) the replacement of *constant capital, (2) the replacement of *variable capital, and (3)

*surplus value (not strictly reproduction except in so far as it, too, is turned into constant or variable capital).

REVISIONISM (Reformism). Strictly considered, the term belongs to the phase of *Marxism associated with Eduard *Bernstein and with the later work of Karl *Kautsky. Kautsky defines it as follows: "*Democracy makes it possible for the *revolution to be peaceful, bloodless, and without coercion. . . . Our present task is not the forcible overthrow of the constitution [in Germany] but the fullest utilization of the democratic state and rights it confers" (*L.R.,* 29, 33). Kautsky finds in *Marx authority for saying that "the worker may attain his objective by peaceful means"; and in *Engels for saying, "It is conceivable that the old society may peacefully evolve into the new in countries where popular representation has gathered to itself all the power, where one may do what one likes constitutionally" (*L.R.,* 24-25). Bernstein emphasized the necessity of letting *history take its course, arguing that the *Party cannot hasten historical development except at the cost of perversion of its true purpose; he says, "The ultimate goal is nothing, the movement is everything." *Trotsky described revisionism thus: "In practice a reformist party considers unshakeable the foundations of that which it intends to reform. It thus inevitably submits to the ideas and morals of the ruling class" (*H.R.R.,* III, 166). In short, revisionism or reformism assumes that the achievement of *socialism must be by legal, constitutional, long-time means; not, as *Lenin advocated, by violent *revolution and the *revolutionary dictatorship of the *proletariat. Lenin writes, "Revisionism or 'revision' of Marxism is today one of the chief, if not the chief, manifestation of *bourgeois influence on the proletariat, and bourgeois corruption of the workers" (*A.R.,* 185). The threat of revisionism is recognized by the *Program* of the latest *Congress of the Communist Party (22nd Congress, Oct., 1961, *Program,* p. 47) as the most dangerous perversion of Marxism. Modern revisionism declares that *Marxism-Leninism is outmoded, denies the necessity of proletarian revolution and dictatorship, and demands the rejection of Leninist principles of organization as expressed in democratic *centralism; this is Moscow's charge against revisionists both within and without the Soviet Union. A group within the Revisionist Movement, isolated by the name Right-wing Social Democrats, held that (1) *state capitalism will eliminate *monopoly capitalism, or (2) subordinate monopoly to the state; (3) *class distinctions are disappearing, and (4) social ownership can be limited to selected industries. See *Bernstein, Eduard.*

REVOLUTION. "A revolution is certainly the most authoritarian thing there is; it is the act whereby one part of the population imposes its will upon the other part by means of rifle, bayonets, and cannon — authoritarian means, if such there be at all; and if the victorious party does not want to have fought in vain, it must maintain this rule by means of the terror which its arms inspire in the reactionaries" (Engels, *On Authority, S.W.,* I, 578). *Marx held that revolutions are the "locomotives of *history," if, that is, they are genuinely social revolutions, involving great *masses of people in violent overthrow of the existing social and political order. In revolution great significance attaches to the role of the *state and the power it commands. The process of revolution, according to *Stalin, involves first a shift in *productive relations, resulting in the spread of a new consciousness (ideas) which organizes and mobilizes the masses, who become a new political army, create a new revolutionary power and abolish by force the old system (*D.H.M.,* 43-44). If the old *class regains its power, this is known as Counter-revolution, a term used also for all attempts to regain or retain power. *Marxism recognizes several types of social revolution: (1) slave revolts, (2) serf revolts, (3) *bourgeois revolts, (4) *proletarian revolts. The types are defined by the ends sought and the contradictions resolved in the revolution. *Lenin held that revolution was "impossible without a national crisis" in which the "lower classes *do not want* the old way, and the upper classes *cannot continue* in the old way" (*L.W.C.,* 65). See also *Pro-*

letarian Revolution; Revolutionary Dictatorship of the Proletariat, Revolutionary Situation.

REVOLUTION, FEBRUARY. See *February Revolution.*

REVOLUTION, GENERAL LAWS OF. *Lenin formulated his own view on this subject (see *A.R.,* 22-23). See *Proletarian Revolution; Revolutionary Situation.*

REVOLUTION, PERMANENT. See *Permanent Revolution.*

REVOLUTION, PROLETARIAN. See *Proletarian Revolution.*

REVOLUTION, RUSSIAN, 1917. See *Russian Revolution.*

REVOLUTION RUSSIAN, 1905. A period of anti-Tsarist ferment following upon the unsuccessful Russo-Japanese War of 1904-05. The Revolution began with *Bloody Sunday, when Russian workers and peasants who had marched to the Tsar's winter palace in St. Petersburg to petition peacefully for redress of certain grievances were fired upon by Tsarist troops. There were strikes, demonstrations, and a mutiny on the battleship *Potemkin. A *soviet of Workers' Deputies was organized in St. Petersburg, and held its first meeting on October 13, 1905. Other soviets were elected in the major industrial plants of other Russian cities, and set the pattern for the *Revolution of 1917 in this respect. *Lenin arrived in St. Petersburg in November, 1905; on December 6 an armed uprising took place in Moscow, but it was subdued by troops and police by December 8. By 1907 the Govern-

ment had re-established order, Lenin had fled and the so-called Stolypin Reaction (named after the Cabinet minister who organized it) rigorously suppressed all revolutionary activity between the years 1907 and 1910.

REVOLUTION IN ONE COUNTRY. See *Socialism in One Country.*

REVOLUTIONARY CENTRALISM. See *Democratic Centralism.*

REVOLUTIONARY COMMUNISTS. A Russian party formed after the assassination of the German ambassador to the Soviet Government, Count Mirbach (July 1918), to defend such tactics against the criticism of *Narodnik Communists, who favored legal procedures. It united with the *Communist Party officially in 1920.

REVOLUTIONARY DICTATORSHIP OF THE PROLETARIAT. The conception which *Lenin, above all, worked out with care; the process by means of which he hoped to make the transition from *capitalism to the *classless society. Such a dictatorship, formed when the *proletariat gives its power to select leaders, is the only force capable of effecting the revolutionary transformation of society which Communism requires. Lenin writes thus: "Only a definite class, namely, that of the urban and industrial workers in general is able to lead the whole mass of the toilers and exploited in the struggle for the overthrow of the yoke of capital, in the process of this over-throw, in the struggle and consolidation of the victory, in the work of creating the new, socialist, social system, in the whole struggle for the complete abolition of classes" (*Works*, XXIX, 387). A dictatorship is necessary to crush the resistance of the *bourgeoisie, to defeat international meddling, and to correct deviations within the *party and its adherents. Violence is not to be directed against the *masses, but against the counter-revolutionary and outside interference. "Only he is a Marxist," says Lenin, "who extends the recognition of the *class struggle to the recognition of the dictatorship of the proletariat" (*S. & R.*, 54). This dictatorship may be called *Proletarian Democracy, because "the *Soviets are the Russian form of the proletarian dictatorship," and the Soviets represent all the masses. Being a dictatorship in respect to certain classes, the state could also, Lenin held, be democratic in relation to others (*P.R.*, 57). "Dictatorship is rule based directly upon force and unrestricted by any laws," Lenin writes (*P.R.*, 20). "The indispensable characteristic, the necessary condition of dictatorship is the *forcible* suppression of the exploiters as a *class*, and, consequently, the *infringement* of 'pure *democracy,' that is, of equality and freedom in regard to that class." (Lenin, *P. R.*, 54). "Revolution means overthrowing, breaking up, smashing, the state machine." (*P.R.*, 176-77).

REVOLUTIONARY   S I T U A-TION. Conditions which indicate that a country is ripe for *revolu-tion. *Lenin defines them as follows:

(1) When the ruling *classes can no longer maintain their rule in an unchanged form — both upper and lower classes are unable to live in the "old way."

(2) When want and suffering in the *proletariat is more acute than usual.

(3) When the *masses are exceptionally active (see *A.R.*, 228). Lenin advised Communist Parties everywhere to devote all possible attention to finding "forms of transition or approach to the *proletarian revolution" (*Works*, XXXI, 73). See *Proletarian Revolution*.

REVOLUTIONARY SYNDICAL-ISM. See *Syndicalism, Revolutionary*.

RHEINISCHE ZEITUNG (*Rhineland Gazette*). Full name: *Rheinische Zeitung für Politik, Handel und Gewerbe;* translated: *Rhineland Gazette on Problems of Politics, Trade, and Industry*. It was the daily newspaper, printed in Cologne, Germany, from January 1, 1842, to March 3, 1843, which added a new university graduate, one Karl *Marx, to its staff in April 1842, making him Editor in October of the same year. By January 19, 1843, Editor Marx had, by attacking the Prussian Government, earned for the paper an order of permanent suspension, effective on April 1, after various bouts with the Prussian censorship. The paper had been financed by Rhineland businessmen who opposed the Prussian nobility and its grip on political affairs. The paper was briefly re-established in 1848, by Marx and some associates, as the *Neue Rheinische Zeitung* — with the same fate (see entry).

RHINELAND GAZETTE. See *Rheinische Zeitung.*

RICARDO, David (1772-1823), British banker and economist, the last of the so-called *classical school. Ricardo was a disciple in the essentials of Adam *Smith, and developed Smith's views of free trade, *division of labor, enlightened self-interest, and the like. He did original work on rent, and emphasized the idea, found in Smith, that all *value stems from *labor. *Marx seized upon this, and in consequence any attack upon Marx's conception of *"labor theory of value" has also to reckon with Ricardo, and to a lesser degree, with Smith. See Heilbroner for a good chapter on Ricardo.

RIGHT HEGELIANS. See *Hegel.*
RIGHT SOCIALIST REVOLUTIONARIES. See *Essaires.*

RIGHT-WING SOCIAL DEMOCRATS. See *Revisionism.*

RODBERTUS, Karl Johann (1805-1875), also known under the name of Rod-Jagetzow, a German economist who is credited by some with arriving at views like *Marx's before Marx did, and by others (especially *Engels) with borrowing from Marx. Rodbertus was the son of a professor of law, and himself studied law. His first work was entitled *Claims of the Working Class* (1837). He was elected to the Prussian Diet, but after brief service retired to write and farm.

His views are most clearly set forth in his *Social Letters* (1850-51), which were re-issued as *Light on the Social Question* (1875, 1885). He held the *labor theory of value, and believed that workers should be paid their wages in labor-currency, which should be based on *socially necessary labor time. He anticipated a future *socialist society, but expected it to be achieved by a slow evolutionary process, lasting perhaps five hundred years, and thought it would come about under a monarchical state.

ROOT MISSION. Group of American statesmen, headed by former Secretary of State Elihu Root, sent to Russia by President Wilson in June and July of 1917 to spur Russian enthusiasm for continuing in World War I, and to discover the real state of the *Revolution there. Root's message: "No fight; no money." He returned with a favorable report on the Russian future and with the prophecy that Russia would remain in the war. See Kennan, 25-26.

R.S.D.L.P. (sometimes: R.S.D.P.). Initials for Russian Social Democratic Labor Party. It was organized illegally at the second meeting of the Council of Social Democratic Organizations, held at Minsk, March 1-3, 1898, and attended by delegates from six revolutionary organizations. A Central Committee was elected, and almost immediately arrested. The organization guided many strikes, especially on May Day, 1903, when more than 200,000 workers went on strike throughout the Russian industrial centers. At its first Congress as a Party, it decided to publish a newspaper, *The Workers' Gazette (Rabochaya Gazeta)*, but further arrests by the police prevented its publication, though two issues appeared in Kiev — one in August, one in December, 1897. The Party was split in 1903 by *Lenin's struggle with *Plekhanov, and out of it emerged the *Bolshevik (Majority) and *Menshevik (Minority) wings of the Social Democrats, a division that lasted on into the *Revolution of 1917.

RUBINISM. A movement named after a *Menshevik — Rubin — who sought to adapt Marxist views to *Revisionism in the Russian Communist movement.

RUGE, Arnold (1802-1880), German writer, publisher-editor of liberal journals and books. He published the *Hallesche* (later *Deutsche) Jahrbücher* as the voice of the younger, radical progressives, after the work was attacked by the Prussian censor. He collaborated with Marx, in Paris, in publishing the *Deutsch-Französische Jahrbücher*, but this association was short-lived. He went to England in 1850, organized democratic groups, and died there.

RUSSIAN CALENDAR. See *Calendar, Russian.*

RUSSIAN CONSTITUTIONAL DEMOCRATIC PARTY. See *Cadets.*

RUSSIAN REVOLUTION (OF 1917). The fact that the Russian calendar, until late 1917, was the so-called Julian Calendar (see entry under *Calendar, Russian*), running thirteen days behind the Western (Gregorian) calendar is of some importance in describing the Revolution of 1917. According to the Russian reckoning the first stage in the Revolution occurred in February, 1917, and has become known, therefore, as the February Revolution (see this entry), although according to the Western calculation the events occurred largely in March and the student may find them so dated (for example, in William Langer, *Encyclopedia of World History,* p. 1028). Similarly, the decisive transfer of power from the Provisional Government established after the abdication of Tsar Nicholas II in February to the *Bolsheviks took place, according to the Russian calendar, in late October — although the West was then in November. October Revolution, however, is the common name for the Bolshevik victory.

The event was massive, and the story long. It is most brilliantly told by Leon *Trotsky in his *History of the Russian Revolution* (see Section II), and was recorded, sympathetically, with a reporter's eye in John Reed's *Ten Days That Shook the World* (Vintage Paperback). Briefly, the Provisional Government proved unstable from the beginning, experiencing shifts of leadership which finally brought Alexander *Kerensky to the Premiership in the summer of 1917. *Lenin had been granted safe-conduct by the German Army to cross from Switzerland to Petrograd, and arrived at the Finland station on the evening of April 3 (Russian calendar). He immediately denounced every effort the *Bolsheviks had been making to co-operate with the Provisional Government, and next day issued his famous *Theses of April 4,* demanding Bolshevik assumption of power, an end to the war, peasant occupation of landed estates and worker control of industry. Until Leon Trotsky arrived from the United States in mid-May, Lenin stood almost alone for his *Theses;* but Trotsky, who as a *Menshevik had opposed Lenin's Bolsheviks since 1903, now grasped the shrewd accuracy of Lenin's insight into the course of events and together they assumed leadership of the seething revolutionary *proletariat and guided it to victory in October.

But the road was precarious. A Russian offensive against the Austrian front, ordered by Kerensky in late June, was a costly failure; and echoes of the military disaster stirred Petrograd workers to open revolt. This the Kerensky government was able to subdue, and many Bolsheviks, including Trotsky, were jailed; Lenin escaped into hiding in Finland. In late August, however, General Lavr *Kornilov ordered troops from the front to march on Petrograd to reverse an order from Kerensky that dismissed the General for insubordination. This threat persuaded Kerensky to seek Bolshevik aid against Kornilov's presumed attack, and Trotsky was released from prison. The troops melted away into the countryside as they neared Petrograd, and Kornilov's Rebellion came to naught; but now the Bolsheviks were free once more (though Lenin remained hidden behind a false beard, constantly shifting his whereabouts) and able to set the stage for the October "Ten Days." When these came, the factory workers, led by the Petrograd *Soviet which was dominated by the Bolsheviks, and the soldiers on leave, and the sailors from Kronstadt Naval Base, all joined in overthrowing the Provisional Government. On October 24 most of the members of the Provisional Government were arrested, though Kerensky escaped and finally came to America.

Trotsky writes, "At times it seems as though it was easier to capture Petrograd in the autumn of 1917 than to recount the process fourteen years later" (*H.R.R.,* III, 224). In his autobiography (*My Life*) he says, "All the most important points in the city are given over into our hands almost without resistance, without fighting, without casualties. The telephone alone informs us, 'We are here!'" (p. 325). And at the Congress of Soviets on October 25, the Bolsheviks settle accounts with the Mensheviks, Trotsky saying: "What has taken place is an uprising, not a conspiracy. An uprising of the masses needs no justification. . . . Our uprising has won. . . . You are wretched, disunited individuals; you are bankrupts; your part is over. Go to the place where you belong from now on — the dustbin of history!" (*My Life,* p. 328).

And he concludes, "This was the last retort in that long dialogue that had begun on April 3, with the day and hour of Lenin's arrival in Petrograd" (*ibid.*, 328). All this is told in great detail in his *History*, Volume III.

The new government, organized October 25, was headed by Lenin, with Trotsky as commissar for foreign affairs and Stalin as commissar for national minorities. Elections for a national assembly, already planned, were held in mid-November, and an assembly convened in January (the 18th, new calendar, 1918). Because they lacked a majority, the Bolsheviks dispersed the assembly at once with armed troops, and the last democratic flame, hardly alight at all, was out. The Revolution was over, and the Bolsheviks were firmly in control.

RUSSIAN REVOLUTIONARY SOCIAL DEMOCRATS ABROAD. See *League of Russian Revolutionary Social Democrats Abroad.*

RUSSIAN SOCIAL DEMOCRATIC LABOR PARTY. See *R.S.D. L.P.*

RUSSIAN SOCIAL DEMOCRATIC PARTY. A name often used for any left, or socialist, Russian group. It can, however, mean *R.S. D.L.P.*, or *Party of Russian Social Democrats.*

RUSSIAN-CHINESE SPLIT. See *Chinese-Russian Split.*

RUSSIAN SOCIAL DEMOCRATIC PROTEST. See *Protest.*

RUSSKOYE BOGATSTVO, translated, *Russian Wealth.* The leading Russian journal at the turn of this century for economics, sociology, philosophy, and literature. It was edited for a time by N. K. Mikhailovsky, who was a *Narodnik and wrote against *Marxism.

SAINT-SIMON, Claude Henri (1760-1825), French nobleman who participated in the American revolution on the side of the Colonies, and was, according to *Engels, "the most encyclopedic mind of his age." He held that each new form of society was an improvement over its predecessor, and that therefore the Golden Age of mankind lies ahead. Progress is achieved through science, motivated by religion. Simon understood the role of property in social relations as being as determinative as *Marx thought it to be, and analyzed the French Revolution in terms of conflicts in property relations — all to Marx's liking. He, like *Fourier, favored the scientific organization of industry as the means of the emancipation of the workers. His last book, *The New Christianity,* sums up his ideas and envisions the transfer of state power from the rule of men to the "rule of things."

SAY, Jean Baptiste (1761-1867), French economist who popularized the views of Adam *Smith in France, especially favoring *laissez faire,* that is, no government interference with trade and business.

SCHAPPER, Karl (1813-1870), German *émigré* socialist, member of the *Communist League when *Marx and *Engels composed for it their *Communist Manifesto*. With another German, Willich, Schapper formed the "left" wing of the League, siding with Marx, and was active in the *First International. He was associated with Marx on the staff of *Neue Rheinische Zeitung*.

SCHMIDT, J. K. Given name of Max *Stirner.

SECOND INTERNATIONAL. After the demise of the *First International, intentionally brought about at its meeting at The Hague in 1872 by the transfer of its Council to New York, various efforts were made to get another International Workingmen's Association under way. At an International Labor Conference held in London in 1888, plans were laid for a Paris Conference of the same group the next year, to coincide with the International Exposition to be held there, at which the Second International should be launched. Differences haunted the very beginning of the International, and two Congresses were held in Paris: one dominated by *Marx's forces, the other by trade union representatives. The Marxist group numbered 391 delegates, the other (called *Possibilists) had 600; but the Marxists were by far the more noted for the kind of *revolutionary thought and conduct the International required, and they in effect created the Second International. It held no Congress in 1890, as planned at Paris, but had one in Brussels in August 1891, where emphasis was laid on fighting for the eight-hour day and

on getting out *May Day celebrations. Here the *Anarchists again raised their heads, bringing memories of the split of the First International over Marx and *Bakunin. At the next Congress, in Zurich, 1893, an effort was made to force out all "non-revolutionary" organizations, a move aimed at elimination of the trade unions. But the matter was unsettled, and still so at the London Congress in 1896, a situation that revealed the growing influence of the *Revisionists under *Bernstein. From 1900 onwards the major question confronting the International was what to do if world war came. The trend was wholly toward Revisionism, with *Kautsky trying to play the role of mediator — *Centrist — but shifting at last toward Revisionism himself. In 1900, at the Paris Congress, an International Socialist Bureau, housed in Brussels, was established, to provide continuity of leadership between Congresses. At Amsterdam in 1904 the Leninist forces succeeded in getting a condemnation, in words, of Bernstein by having the so-called Dresden Resolution adopted. At Stuttgart in 1907, and at Copenhagen in 1910, the International took a stand against war, but 1912 saw the outbreak of the Balkan War; and at an emergency Congress in Basle there was dispute about what practically could be done. The Congress scheduled for Vienna, in August 1914, was transferred to Paris by the outbreak of the war, and although the International Socialist Bureau was transferred to neutral Holland, the Second International passed into oblivion after January 1915.

SECRET SPEECH ON STALIN, Khrushchev's. A six-hour speech delivered by Khrushchev to the 140 members of the 20th Party *Congress on February 24 and 25, 1956, not intended for publication but obtained by foreign agents and published in the United States, by the State Department on June 4, 1956. In the speech *Khrushchev revealed some of the brutalities practiced under *Stalin, and indicated some of the terror and tyranny that obtained under Stalin's rule. Essentially, he made two major charges against Stalin: (1) that he abolished *collective leadership in the *Party, and (2) that he employed terrorism to achieve personal ends. The speech was not published in Russia, but rumors of its contents spread abroad. In the judgment of some observers the speech did Khrushchev more harm than good in that he, too, had been a part of the Stalin regime, and also in the fact that Stalin's era had been one of massive development and victory over Nazism, despite the tyranny. A good summary, with some direct quotations, may be found in John Gunther's *Inside Russia Today,* Chapter 11.

SECTARIANISM. The dogmatic assumption that theory need not be adapted to circumstances, resulting in loss of touch with reality, clinging to yesterday, and a consequent "revolutionary idleness" (Lenin). Sectarianism is also characterized, in some instances, by a refusal to participate in the trade unions, to adopt flexible tactics, to compromise at the moment for the greater gain later. Though it appears to be the theoretical opposite of *Revisionism, Sectarianism in reality is viewed by the Marxist as equally destructive of the *Party and its hopes. See *Dogmatism.*

SELF-CRITICISM. See *Criticism and Self-Criticism.*

SELF-EMANCIPATION OF THE WORKING CLASS. Name taken by the small group of *Economists who organized in St. Petersburg in the fall of 1888. They issued a statement of aims, published in the magazine *Nakanune* (*On the Eve*) in London. They were criticized by *Lenin for their "economism" in Chapter 2 of his *What Is To Be Done?*

SEVEN YEAR PLAN. *Khrushchev's modification of the traditional *Five Year Plan pattern. It was adopted by the 21st *Congress of the Communist Party in 1959 to continue the social and economic goals of the *Five Year Plans of *Stalin. It laid down aims in economics, politics, education, and international relations for the years 1959 to 1965.

SHAKHTY CASE. Taking its name from the region where it occurred, this incident involved sabotage in the mines of the Donets coal field. The plot was uncovered by the Soviet Government in 1928. Some 300 former mine owners were implicated.

SHAMEFACED MATERIALISTS. A term coined by *Lenin for those materialists who, like T. H. Huxley for example, hold views which are unquestionably *materialistic but who hesitate for social or other reasons to assume the name of Materialists.

SHOCK BRIGADES. The name for Russian workers' units, organized in 1927 and thereafter, committed to the full use of all their talents in an effort to do the *Five Year Plan in *four years,* and to give in general extra effort to the achievement of advances in the Russian economy. By the end of 1933 over five million industrial and transport workers were enrolled. See also *Socialist Emulation* and *Stakhanov Movement.*

SINO-RUSSIAN SPLIT. See *Chinese-Russian Split.*

SMITH, Adam (1723-1790), philosopher and economist whose book *The Wealth of Nations* is the definitive statement of the principles of political economy (*classical, or Manchester School economic theory) underlying the industrial revolution. His work dealt with *division of labor, *surplus value, *labor theory of value, and the harmony which develops in the market if no state restraints are placed upon trade. He believed that, if left alone, economic enterprise would continually provide more for all in an ever rising standard of living. *Marx appropriated Smith's ideas as he could use them, especially his labor theory of value, but criticized Smith for failing to solve the con-

tradictions which Marx found inherent in *capitalism between *proletariat and *bourgeoisie. *Engels called Smith an "economic Luther who hypocritically eulogized trade as a bond of union and friendship among nations as among individuals" (see Heilbroner).

SOCIAL DARWINISM. The application of *Darwin's principles of natural selection by survival of the fittest to human history and social relationships, with the implication that the fittest always come out on top and the unfit deservedly appear at the foot of the social and economic ladder. The notion was popularized by Herbert Spencer, English philosopher, who held that the ruling classes of Britain were naturally superior persons. *Engels writes: "Marx considered the mechanical transference of laws of animal societies to human societies as incorrect."

SOCIAL DEMOCRATS. Russian political party based on Marxist theories, more commonly known as Russian Social Democratic Labor Party, or *R.S.D.L.P. It is also the name generally taken by socialist parties.

SOCIAL LABOR. That labor performed by the mutual co-operation of a large number of workers. "The productiveness of social labor presupposes co-operation on a large scale; only on this supposition can *division and combination of labor be organized, and the means of *production economised on a vast scale; instruments of labor which, from their very nature, are fit only for use in common, such as a system of machinery, be called into being; huge natural resources be pressed into the service of production; and the transition can be effected of the powers of production into a technological application of science" (Marx, *Cap.*, I, 623-24). Because *capitalistic production is in fact social in character, Marx assumed that the relations of production would eventually and inevitably take on a *socialistic form.

SOCIAL LIQUIDATION. The abolition of the *state, in the theory of *Bakunin (*anarchism).

SOCIAL REVOLUTIONARIES. The peasant socialist party, in Russia, which split into two wings during the *Revolution of 1917: (1) the Left Socialist Russians, who tended to *anarchism; and (2) the Right Socialist Russians, who supported the Provisional Government of *Kerensky.

SOCIAL-DEMOCRATIC DEVIA-TIONISM. Another name for *Trotskyism, and the charge on which Trotsky himself was expelled from the Communist Party and the *Third International in 1927. See also *Socialism in One Country*.

SOCIALISM, CHRISTIAN. See *Christian Socialism*.

SOCIALISM, FEUDAL. See *Feudal Socialism*.

SOCIALISM, GUILD. See *Guild Socialism*.

SOCIALISM, PHALANX. See *Phalanx Socialism*.

SOCIALISM/COMMUNISM. What is the difference in meaning between the two terms? Often they are used as essentially synonymous, though usually Socialism is taken to be the broader term, of which Communism is one special form. *Engels says in his Preface to the German edition of the *Communist Manifesto* (1890) that they "could not have called it a *Socialist* Manifesto" because the term had too many meanings; and that, therefore, *Marx and he chose *Communist* to indicate what they believed to be the "scientific" character of their social views. *Lenin says that "socialism is the society which grows out of *capitalism directly, is the initial form of the new society (after the *revolution). Communism, however, is a higher form of socialism and it can develop only when socialism is fully entrenched" (*Works*, XXX, 260). Socialism and Communism may be said to coincide in regard to four aims: (1) the important means of *production must be collectively owned; (2) society must have a high level of social services; (3) no one has the right to live on the labor of another; and (4) building the new society is primarily the task of the working *class. (See Dutt, 447.) In *S. & R.*, Lenin distinguished Socialism from Communism by two separate formulae:

(1) From each according to his ability, and to each according to his *work*: the principle of *Socialism*.

(2) From each according to his ability, and to each according to his *need*: the principle of *Communism*.

Both, Lenin said, are equally characterized by social unity, a heightening of ideological consciousness, the disappearance of *religion, Communist morality, and a general culture. When, on this basis, Russia will pass from Socialism to Communism is a question long discussed both within and outside the Soviet Union. Marx set no period for that "withering away of the *state" which would mark the advent of Communism; Lenin was vague; and *Stalin tried to explain it away. Presently, Soviet writers show an expectation that the time is almost at hand for the transition to full Communism: "Its main elements should be completed within the next fifteen years" (T. Stepanion, in *Communist,* Sept. 1959). See Werth, chap. 12. See also *Program* (adopted by 22nd Party *Congress, Oct. 1961, which aims at achieving Communism).

SOCIALISM IN ONE COUNTRY. Can the new *socialist society envisioned by *Marx, *Engels, and *Lenin be brought into being in one country alone, surrounded by foes, or must the *revolution spread into many if it is to succeed in any one? This is the question of "Socialism in One Country." Trotsky says, "It would be hopeless to think that a revolutionary Russia, for instance, could hold out in the face of Europe" (see his *The Peace Program,* written in 1915) ; and in his analysis of the draft program for the *Third International, Trotsky insists that on this point Lenin agreed with him (see his *The*

Third International After Lenin). *Stalin held to the contrary, and insisted that Lenin agreed with him, namely, that Russia could successfully develop its socialist economy and society without spreading revolution abroad. Trotsky's views were condemned by the Third International as *"Social-Democratic Deviationism." Stalin writes: "The *party always took as its starting point the idea that the victory of socialism in one country means the possibility to build socialism in that country, and that this task can be accomplished with the forces of a single country" (*Pravda,* Nov. 12, 1926).

SOCIALIST EMULATION. Soviet challenge to the Russian workers "to display their abilities, develop their capacities, and reveal their talents," in an effort to achieve the First *Five Year Plan in four years (Lenin, *Works,* XXVI, 367). The slogan: *Five Year Plan in Four Years.* "Youth shock brigades" were part of the program (see *Komsomol*), formed first in Leningrad in 1928. By the end of 1929, 63 percent of the workers in large enterprises were engaged in various forms of "emulation" and by 1932 the figure was 75 percent. Emulation was celebrated on a nationwide *May Day, 1942. The First All-Union Congress of the Shock Brigades was held in Moscow, December 1929. *Stalin wrote, "Socialist emulation transforms labor from the disgraceful painful burden it was considered before into a matter of *honor,* a matter of *glory,* a matter of *valor* and *heroism"*

151

(Kalinin, 135). See also *Stakhanov Movement; Subbotniks.*

SOCIALIST LEGALITY. The name given the shift in Russian police methodology since the death of *Stalin. It has placed the administration of the police and the courts on a legal rather than on an arbitrary basis, abolishing illegal arrests and secret trials. But it is, of course, subject to a degree of unpredictable change. (see Werth, chap. 6).

SOCIALIST REVOLUTIONARY PARTY. See *Essaires.*

SOCIALIST - REVOLUTIONARIES (S-R's). A Russian political party formed in 1902 through the union of several *Narodnik groups. It held its first Congress in 1905, at which it adopted the Marxist *Revisionism of *Bernstein but added to it terrorism as the basic method of *revolutionary struggle. In 1905-06 the S-R's formed an alliance with the *Cadets and founded the People's Socialist Labor Party. After the *February, 1917, Revolution, that Party split three ways, part led by *Kerensky and supporting the *Provisional Government, part joining the *Bolsheviks, and part the *Mensheviks.

SOCIALISTS, POPULIST. See *Populist Socialists.*

SOCIALISTS, YOUNG. See *Young Socialists.*

SOCIALLY NECESSARY LABOR. "The labor-time socially necessary is that required to produce an article under normal conditions of *production, and with the average degree of skill and intensity prevailing at the time" (Marx, *Cap.,* I, 39). The labor itself socially necessary is that labor expended upon things which society needs for its existence, reproduction, and gradual advancement — not that spent on luxuries, trinkets, trifles, and the like. See *Necessary Labor.*

SOLDIERS TRUTH (*Soldatskaya Pravda*). A *Bolshevik newspaper published from April 15, 1917, to March 1918 (except for police suppression from July to October, 1917) as the official organ of the army section of the Central Committee of the *Russian Social-Democratic Labor Party (Bolsheviks). Its circulation rose to around 50,000, at least half of which made its way to the front lines.

SOMBART, Werner (1863-1941), German economist and professor who was one of the most acute critics of *Marx, though he used Marxist language and took many of his ideas from him.

SOPHISTRY, Marxist. A term employed by *Lenin to define his differences with *Plekhanov in 1915. Sophistry, says Lenin, is "the method of clinging to the outward similarity of cases without a connection between the events." Opposed to Sophistry is *Dialectics, which is "the study of all the concrete circumstances of an event and of its development" (*Works,* XVIII, 113). See *Dialectics.*

SORGE, Friedrich Albert (1826-1906), German Communist who participated in the German Revolution in Baden in 1849, and then fled to the U.S., where he became active in the U.S. labor movement. When the General Council of the *First International was transferred to New York in 1872, Sorge became its General Secretary, an office he resigned the same year. In a letter to him of September 12, 1874, *Engels wrote that the First International now was dead in fact (though it lasted in name until dissolved officially in Philadelphia in 1876) and that any effort to revive it "would be folly and waste of energy" (*S.C.*, 329).

SOTSIAL-DEMOKRAT. The newspaper of the *Russian Social Democratic Labor Party, published illegally, from 1908 (Feb.) to 1917 (Jan.) in a total of fifty-eight issues, the first in Russia and the rest in Paris or Geneva. *Lenin edited it from 1911, and to it contributed some eighty articles. After the *Revolution it was continued by the Moscow *Soviet as its newspaper. A magazine of the same title was published in 1890-92 by the *Emancipation of Labor Group, in four issues.

SOTSIAL-DEMOKRATIC OR-GANIZATION. A group formed by the *Emancipation of Labor Group in May 1900, after the split in the *League of Russian Social Democrats Abroad (May 1900). It published translations into Russian of *Marx and *Engels's works. In 1901 it joined the *Iskra group, headed by *Lenin, to form the *League of Russian Revolutionary Social Democrats Abroad.

SOUTH RUSSIAN WORKERS' UNION. The first workers' *revolutionary organization formed on

Russian soil, it was founded in 1875 by a student, Y. O. Zaslavsky, and soon had a membership of some 200 in Rostov-on-Don, Kharkov, Oral, Taganrog. It was broken up by the police in 1876, and its leaders were sentenced to hard labor.

SOUTHERN RUSSIAN WORK-ERS' UNION. A *revolutionary group formed by Leon *Trotsky as his first adventure into radicalism, in Odessa in 1897. It circulated leaflets called *Nashe Dyelo* (*Our Cause*). It was broken up, and Trotsky was imprisoned and then exiled to Siberia in 1898.

SOVIET. Russian term for *Council* or *Committee*. The Soviet is the basic unit of Russian Communist government. These Councils were first created in the Russian *Revolution of 1905, when they were elected in the factories by the workers to direct strike action and to represent the workers to the factory managers and owners. The workers' Soviets became, however, instruments of *revolution, and some of them issued decrees establishing the eight-hour day. Though the 1905 Revolution was stamped out, the Soviets remained and *Lenin saw in them the organizational units he needed. The Councils were elected on industrial rather than regional principles, in the factories, and in the villages, and in the Armed Forces. The most important of the Soviets was that of St. Petersburg, which took the form of a General Council representing a large number of industrial Soviets, and was established by the election of an Executive on October 17, 1906. It was never entirely disbanded by the Tsarist police. For a time the St. Petersburg Soviet published its own newspaper, *Izvestia,* edited by Joseph *Stalin. (See Deutscher, I, 130ff.). Says Lenin, "The Soviets are the direct organization of the toiling and exploited *masses themselves, which help them organize and administer their own state in every possible way" (*P.R.,* 38). The Russian state organization rests upon a hierarchy of Soviets, each single Council sending deputies to more general Councils, on up to the *Supreme Soviet, which rules the country.

SOVIET FARMS. "Large farms cultivated by associations of workers on behalf of the *state" (Lenin, *P.R.,* 156).

SOVIET MAN. See *New Man.*

SOVIET PRESS. See *Press, Soviet.*

SOVIET UNION (Soviet State, Government). A federation of fifteen theoretically independent Republics, each having its own Constitution, Government, and Communist Party. The Soviet Union has a dual system of power because of the fact that only one political party is recognized, and therefore office in that Party is tantamount to office in the State. The Party is headed by a First Secretary (*Khrushchev today — 1963), who is chosen by the *Central Committee of the Party. The Secretary presides over the Secretariat, or *Presidium, of the Central Committee. The All-Union *Congress of Deputies — the 22nd was held in October, 1961 — elects the Central Committee from a slate predetermined by the Committee itself. Delegates to the Congresses are elected on regional bases. The regions are divided into districts, and the districts into *Soviets. In practice the First Secretary can control to a large measure the selection of delegates to the Congresses, and it was thus that *Stalin consolidated his power. The State machinery is headed by the Chairman of the *Council of Ministers (Khrushchev), which is elected by the *Supreme Soviet. Delegates to the Supreme Soviet represent the Supreme Soviets of each of the fifteen Republics, which in turn represent in successive downward steps the regions, districts, and local Soviets in the Republics. The other State offices are under the control of the Council of Ministers, which in effect places them under the control of the Premier, or Chairman. Political administration in the Soviet Union centers in the Presidium, the Central Committee, and the Supreme Soviet. The Presidium is elected by the Supreme Soviet and consists of 32 members. The *Central Committee of the Communist Party was enlarged by the 20th Party Congress, 1956, to 133 full members and 122 candidate members; under Stalin the Central Committee had consisted of 71 full, and 68 candidate members. The Supreme Soviet is elected every four years, meets twice a year, and consists of two parts: the Council of the Union, and the Council of Nationalities. See *Supreme Soviet of the USSR.*

For Khrushchev's relaxation of the iron control exercised by Stalin over both Party and State machinery, without losing altogether his dictatorial control, see Werth.

SOVIETOLOGY. Professor J. M. Bochenski defines Sovietology as "the science concerned with Communism as such" (*Studies,* 1). The Sovietologist is a student of Communism in whatever forms and in whatever countries it manifests itself. "Soviet" in the term does not, therefore, limit its meaning to the Russian form of Communism alone; the study of Chinese Communism, for example, may be called Sinosovietology. Professor Bochenski foresees the development of two branches of Sovietology: (1) General Sovietology, or the study of what is common to Communism wherever it is to be found; and (2) Special Sovietology, or the study of particular national manifestations of Communism. (See Bochenski's essay on "Soviet Studies" in *Studies.*)

SOVKHOZ. State collective farm, situated on land owned by the Soviet government, those who work on it being paid in wages as State employees. In January, 1961, the Soviet Union reported 7,368 such farms in operation. See *Kolkhoz.*

SPARTACUS LEAGUE. German socialist organization formed on January 1, 1916, by a group of Social Democrats led by Karl *Liebknecht, Rosa *Luxemburg, Franz *Mehring, Clara *Zetkin and others. They were also called The International Group because of their support of international rather than exclusively German interests in World War I. The League conducted propaganda against the War, and some of its membership, including Liebknecht and Luxemburg, went to jail, and later these two were murdered by German army officers. Under the pen name of Junius, Rosa Luxemburg wrote from prison an appeal to the German Social Democrats to take united action against the War. *Lenin criticized her failure to see the War as an opportunity for social upheaval in his *On the Pamphlet by Junius.* In April 1917, the Spartacus League joined the Independent Social Democratic Party of Germany, and after the German unrest of 1918 this group formed the Communist Party of Germany.

SPONTANEITY. The name given to the views of those who depreciate the value of *revolutionary theory and wish to depend upon the spur-of-the-moment response to situations as they arise and change. The doctrine that the working class will of itself come to *socialist and revolutionary consciousness without any indoctrination or teaching by the Marxist *Party leadership. *Lenin held that a revolutionary movement depends upon revolutionary theory, and that this theory must be taught the masses by the intellectuals who have fully grasped and worked it out. See his pamphlet *What Is to Be Done?* for a brilliant statement of this position. Lenin: "All worship of spontaneity of the working-class movement, all belittling of the role of 'the conscious element,' of the role of Social-Democracy, *means, quite irrespective of whether the belittler wants it or not,* strengthening the influence of *bourgeois ideology upon the workers" (*Works*, V, 354).

SPONTANEOUS MATERIALISM. See *Materialism, Spontaneous.*

STAKHANOV MOVEMENT. A worker movement in the Soviet Union, organized in 1935, aimed at the voluntary mastery of the latest industrial techniques in order to stimulate economic growth in the most rapid possible manner. It was named after Alexei Stakhanov, a miner who cut 102 tons of coal in one shift, which was fourteen times the standard output. This is one of several psychological devices employed to stimulate the workers to greater effort. See also *Subbotniks; Socialist Emulation.*

STALIN, Joseph Vissarionovich (born Joseph Dzhugashvili) (1879-1953), steel-fisted dictator of Russia for nearly thirty years. Born on December 21, 1879, his father a shoemaker only lately risen from the peasantry, Stalin was educated at Tiflis Seminary. He was expelled from this school in 1899 for radicalism. He then went into underground *revolutionary activity under the name of Koba (The Indomitable) and wrote for the secret press he himself established. He joined the *Bolshevik faction of the *Russian Social Democrats in 1904, and in 1912 he emerged as Editor of *Pravda*, the official organ of the Bolsheviks, writing now under the name of Stalin (Man of Steel). He did not play a dominant role in the *Revolution, but became Secretary of the *Supreme Soviet on April 3, 1922, from which position he could control enough of the selection of delegates to Soviet *Congresses to establish himself as first power in the Government by 1927, when his forces defeated those of *Trotsky and expelled the latter from the *Party, from the *Third International, and from the Soviet Union. Stalin's career from then until his death was on the one hand the careful, merciless acquisition of power, and on the other hand the thorough foundation of the Soviet state and economy and its most rapid possible development by any method. Biographies like those of Trotsky and, better, Deutscher must be consulted for any account of Stalin's years of power in Russia, and of the environment of suspicion and fear which steadily mounted about him as the years passed. He died under what may have been mysterious circumstances in March 1953. *Khrushchev, in his famous *"Secret Speech" to the 20th Congress of the Communist Party (1956), revealed some of the brutality of Stalin's rule, and in so doing turned Communists away from the Party all over the world. Trotsky said of him: "Stalin was a strong, but theoretically and politically primitive, organiser. Stalin was distinguished among the practicals for energy, persistence, and inventiveness in the matter of moves behind the scenes. Stalin, the empiric, was open to alien influences not on the side of the will but on the side of intellect" (*H.R.R.*, III, 289). "To us Russians," wrote V. Petrovich, "Stalin was the man who, in twenty-five years when he was supreme boss, turned over our pretty miserable backward country into the second greatest power in the world, thus paving the way for total Russian supremacy in the world. *Lenin gave the new regime a start, but it was under Stalin that the real job was done" (see Werth, 91ff.). See *Secret Speech on Stalin.*

STALINISM. The term used for the absolute and brutal form of *proletarian dictatorship exercised by *Stalin during his regime in Russia. See also *Cult of the Individual.*

STATE, The. *Marxism always views the state as related to the existence of *classes, and acting always as the instrument for maintaining the dominance of one class over another. *Lenin says, "The state arises when, where, and to the extent that class antagonisms cannot be reconciled" (*Works*, 25, 358). The type of state which arises depends upon the class it serves. There are three main types: Autocracy for slave society; Aristocracy for feudal society; Parliamentary Democracy for *bourgeois society. "But what is the state?" Lenin asks (*P.R.*, 61), and answers, "The state is nothing but a machine for the suppression of one class by another." Therefore it is the task of the *revolutionary proletariat, in respect to the bourgeois

state, "in the words of Marx 'to smash the bourgeois-military state machine' and in this is contained, briefly, the principal lesson of Marxism in regard to the question of the tasks of the *proletariat in relation to the state" (S. & R.). Some Marxists believed that immediately after the *revolution the state would wither away. In defense of the fact that in Russia this was not the case at all, *Stalin told the 18th Party *Congress (and others) that the state remains necessary under Communism so long as *capitalist encirclement prevails. The state passes through two phases after the revolution, said Stalin: (1) it suppresses all remaining opposition, establishes military organization, and begins economic redevelopment; and (2) as the opposition disappears, the state turns more attention to economic organization, to education and culture. In this stage, the state rather than withering away acts to ensure the fullest participation of all in national affairs and progress. *Engels had said, "So long as the proletariat still uses the state, it does not use it in the interests of freedom, but in order to hold down its adversaries; and as soon as it becomes possible to speak of freedom, the state as such ceases to exist" (ltr. to Bebel, March 28, 1875, *S.C.*, 332ff.). See *Withering Away of the State.*

STATE CAPITALISM. Advocated by *Lenin as transitional to *socialism, state capitalism is a combination of private and social enterprise, all under state guidance and so weighted that in the long run the private enterprise will disappear. In Russia it included Soviet joint-stock companies, in which private capital might be invested, in combination with wholly state-owned manufactures. Through the co-operatives controlled by the state, the Soviet Government could control the sale and exchange of all *production. This was a transitional period in Russian economic organization, sometimes called *NEP (New Economic Policy), which was supplanted under the first *Five Year Plan by total state assumption of economic enterprise.

STATE DEFENSE COMMITTEE. A committee headed by *Stalin, appointed by the *Central Committee of the Communist Party, the *Presidium of the Supreme Soviet, and the Council of Peoples' Commissars, on July 30, 1941, with supreme and absolute powers for the conduct of the war (World War II).

STATE MONOPOLY CAPITALISM. This is not to be confused with *State Capitalism, which is *socialist in principle. This term was used by *Lenin to indicate that stage in the history of *capitalism when monopoly capitalism absorbed the state power, making the state the agent of the largest corporations and banks.

In the evolution of capitalism into socialism, Lenin argued, the *state comes to own the non-profit enterprises, which are sustained. It also makes large military expenditures. This stage, which Lenin also called *Imperialism, is, Lenin says,

"a complete *material* preparation for socialism, the *threshold* of socialism, a rung in the ladder of *history between which and the rung called socialism there can be no intermediate rungs" (*Works*, XXV, 333). Lenin argued, following *Marx, that when *production reaches this extreme social character, with the whole nation actually involved in enterprise, then soon or late all political and other relations must come to reflect this basic economic pattern.

STIRNER, Max (1806-1856), pseudonym for J. K. Schmidt, *Left Hegelian and philosophical *anarchist. He was criticized by *Marx and *Engels for his *idealist philosophy, in their book *The German Ideology*, where they call him "Saint Max." His best known work, *Der Einziger und das Eigentum (The Self and Its Own)*, expresses individualistic anarchism, of which this is a sample: "What do I care for right? I have no need of it. I possess and enjoy all I can win by strength. As to that which I cannot obtain possession of, I renounce it, nor do I seek to console myself by boasting of my indefeasible right" (p. 275).

STRATEGY/TACTICS. See *Tactics/Strategy*.

STRAUBINGERS. A term used familiarly by *Marx and *Engels in their correspondence to designate workers whose *class consciousness was undeveloped, or *petty bourgeois.

STRUGGLE. See *Class Struggle*.

STRUVE, Pyotr Bernhardovich (1870-1914), member of the so-called *Legal Marxists, who wished to advocate the views of *Marx in Russia only to the degree that they did not conflict with the established legal processes, and who hoped that by gradual reforms social problems could be solved. Struve joined the *Revisionists in the *Second International, and came to support the Tsarist Government after the *Russian Revolution of 1905. *Lenin subjected his views to extensive and repeated criticism. See also *Legal Marxists.*

SUBBOTNIKS. Voluntary, unpaid workdays, usually Sundays and holidays, and also extra hours after the regular working day, spent to advance the Soviet economy, by workers in industry, transport, on the farms, and in the offices. This type of work was first organized by the workers on the Moscow-Kazan Railroad on April 12, 1919, a Saturday — from which the custom takes its name, the Russian word for Saturday being *Subbota.* On May Day, 1920, the first All-Russian Subbotnik was organized, with about one-half million workers participating in Moscow alone. The effort was led by *Lenin himself, who presented the workers of the Moscow-Kazan Railroad with the Red Board of Honor. See also *Stakhanov Movement,* and *Socialist Emulation.*

SUBJECTIVE/OBJECTIVE. The Marxist uses "objective" to indicate things as they are, whether or not they are consciously known as so. Thus the position of an opponent is called "objectively" thus or so, despite his denials or ignorance of the fact — a useful tool in argument. "Subjective" refers, then, to the human consciousness, the deliberate intent. In Marxist philosophy of *history, the "objectivist" maintains that the determining forces in social development are all external to man, and are basically economic, while the "subjectivist" accords historical initiative to the individual as well as to external economic forces. *Marxism is, it is argued, "objectivist," while *Revisionism is "subjectivist."

SUBJECTIVISM. The term is used by the Communist principally in the realm of the arts, where it means the expression of the artist's own personality or peculiarities in his work in competition with, or to the exclusion of, the exhibition of the goals of the *Party. Compare *Objectivism, Party-mindedness.*

SUN YAT SEN (SUN WEN) (1866-1925), Chinese revolutionary and statesman. Educated as a medical doctor, he formed the radical New China Party in Honolulu, 1894. The next year he tried to lead a revolt in China against the ruling (Manchu) dynasty, but failed. His eleventh attempt at leading a revolt was successful (1911), and in 1912 he was named President of the Republic of China. Ousted by General Yuan Shih-k'ai in 1913, he reorganized with Russian aid the Kuomintang Party, which under Chiang Kai-Shek unified China by 1927.

SUPREME COUNCIL OF NA-TIONAL ECONOMY. Established by the Soviet Government in November 1917, immediately upon the *Bolsheviks' assumption of power as the group responsible for the complete socialization of Russian industry.

SUPREME SOVIET OF THE USSR. The highest organ of state power in the *Soviet Union. It has two chambers: (1) the Soviet of the Union, consisting of deputies elected on the basis of population (one deputy for each 300,000 population); and (2) the Soviet of Nationalities, elected by the member Republics and Regions on this basis: 25 deputies for each Republic, 11 deputies for each Autonomous Republic, 5 deputies for each Autonomous Region, 1 deputy for each National Region (see under *USSR* for the significance of these divisions). The Supreme Soviet elects the *Presidium of the USSR, the Supreme Court of the USSR, and the *Procurator-General of the USSR.

SURPLUS APPROPRIATION (peasant). An element in what was called *War Communism (1918-1919), meaning the obligation laid upon the peasants to deliver to the *state all surplus products, for feeding the industrial cities and the army. This appropriation was carried out in the villages under the *Committees of the Poor Peasants. The program was relaxed under the *New Economic Policy which followed the state of War Communism; under NEP taxes were levied in kind (by tak-

ing produce) but a surplus was left most of the peasants with which they could trade as they wished.

SURPLUS LABOR (or Labor-time). *Marx says, "That part of the working-day in which the workman's labor, being no longer *necessary labor, creates no value for himself, but creates *surplus value for the *capitalist, I name surplus labor-time, and to the labor expended during that time I give the name surplus-labor" (*Cap.*, I, 217).

SURPLUS POPULATION. See *Relative Surplus Population.*

SURPLUS VALUE. This is a key Marxist concept and embodies the heart of Marx's theory of *capitalist *exploitation. A rough equivalent for it is the concept of *profit.* *Marx held that only labor creates value; therefore if capital is to incur interest, that return must come from someone's labor, it must be a *surplus* value, which the capitalist takes through exploitation by paying the worker for less than a full day's work. Or, to put it another way: When the worker hires out, he has become a *commodity on the *market, that is, an object for sale — he sells his labor power to the highest bidder. Now, labor power in the form of the living worker has value as a commodity to the extent of the labor necessary to produce him. This is the *labor theory of value applied to the production of the living worker considered as a commodity. This labor necessary for the production of workers is necessarily equal to the value of the

160

means of his subsistence, and reproduction of further generations of workers by raising children. The labor time necessary to produce value equivalent to the means of subsistence determines the value of labor power at any given moment. The capitalist buys labor power, then, at its value; but in order to find a return on his investment he must require the worker to expend a surplus labor power, more than is met by his wages. This "more" which the worker puts forth Marx calls "surplus value." *Engels says, "The trick has been performed, surplus value has been produced; money has been converted into capital" (*A.-D.*, 283). A number of terms cluster about this concept of surplus value:

(1) *Necessary labor: the labor expended by the worker to produce what is essential to his own maintenance and reproduction.

(2) Necessary labor time: the time during which necessary labor is performed.

(3) *Surplus labor: the value created by the worker over and above the value of his labor power as a commodity, and appropriated by the capitalist.

(4) Surplus labor time: the time during which the worker performs surplus labor.

(5) Capital: the means by which surplus value is extracted from the worker.

(6) Rate of surplus value: the ratio of surplus value to what Marx calls *"variable capital,"

that is, the capital used to pay wages, buy materials.

(7) *Absolute surplus value: greater surplus value obtained by prolonging the working day or intensifying labor.

(8) *Relative surplus value: lesser surplus value obtained by decreasing the necessary labor time through invention, etc.

(9) The stages of productivity, in history, in relation to surplus value:

(a) Simple co-operation: each worker makes some whole product.

(b) Manufacture: each worker makes part of the product (*division of labor).

(c) Large-scale machine industry: each plant makes part of the product (division of manufacture).

(10) Rate of profit: the ratio of surplus value to the total capital invested in the enterprise.

(Summarized from a letter of Marx to Engels, August 2, 1862, in *S.C.*, 129-133; see also *Cap.*, I, on the subjects mentioned.)

Marx based his belief in the necessity of *revolution on his assumption that capital inherently demands surplus value, and that exploitation can therefore only be overcome by the destruction of the capitalist system. Karl *Kautsky earned *Lenin's denunciation by holding otherwise: "The proper method of diverting the surplus value which the capitalist class appropriates, to the service of the community, is that of taxation of large incomes, property, and inheritances" (*L.R.*, 138). And Kautsky could point to the fact that this was the way advocated by Marx and Engels themselves in the *Communist Manifesto*, but he had to ignore their repeated assertions later that the *Manifesto* offered only a temporary and provisional program, not their full-fledged system.

SYNDICALISM, REVOLUTIONARY. A labor movement of the late nineteenth century, stressed in Italy, which took its name from the Italian term for trade unions — syndicates. This was the view that by the general strike the workers could gain control of the state power; and then by organizing the economy into related syndicates, they could bring about social advance. *Lenin: "Syndicalism either repudiates the *revolutionary dictatorship of the proletariat or relegates it, like political power generally, to a very unimportant place. We raise it to first place." In many countries, Lenin pointed out, Syndicalism was "the direct and inevitable result of *opportunism, *reformism, and parliamentary *cretinism," the latter term being used by Lenin for great stupidity.

SYNDICATES, BUSINESS. See *Imperialism*.

SYNTHESIS. See *Thesis-Antithesis-Synthesis*.

SYSTEM OF RELAYS. A plan for employing children in relays, say one group from 5:30 a.m. to 1:30 p.m., and then a second group from 1:30 p.m. to 8:30, etc. This was done by the British *bourgeoisie to limit somewhat children's working hours while retaining the benefits of low-paid child labor. The plan was used in England, as noted in the Royal Report on working conditions dated June 28, 1833 (*Cap.*, I, 279). See also *Relay System*.

TABLEAU ECONOMIQUE. See *Quesnay, François*.

TACTICS / STRATEGY. The Marxist makes the customary distinction between tactics and strategy, namely, that strategy is concerned with the long-range objectives of a movement, while tactics are concerned with the day-to-day operations. It may be, therefore, tactically wise or necessary to backtrack, to contradict or to agree, and the like, all in the interest of final, strategic victory. This accounts for the fact that the *Party Line may seem to waver or even contradict itself from time to time; not that the over-all goal of Communist domination has changed, but that the tactics of the day call for the Line of the moment as the best tactical method of moving ahead toward the ultimate goal.

TALMUDISM. See *Dogmatism*.

TAMMERFORS CONFERENCE. First *Bolshevik Party Conference, held December 12-17, 1905, at Tammerfors, Norway. Here *Stalin and *Lenin met for the first time.

TASS. See *Press, Soviet*.

TECTOLOGY. Another name for *Empirio-Criticism. See also *Bogdanov*.

TESNAYAKS (Tesnayak Socialists). Bulgarian Workers' Party, founded in 1903 by D. *Blagoyev. The Party opposed Bulgarian involvement in World War I, and in 1915 it joined the *Second International and called itself the Communist Party of Bulgaria.

TESTAMENT, LENIN'S. A document left by *Lenin with his wife *Krupskaya, dictated by him to her after his second stroke. It was dated December 1922, with a postscript added in January 1923, and contained Lenin's hopes for the future of the *Party he had founded. At the time the most interesting item was the proposal that *Stalin be removed from his post as General Secretary of the Russian Communist Party on the grounds of his "rudeness" and probable inability to use power "with sufficient caution." Lenin named no successor, though he spoke highly of *Trotsky. The document was known to Trotsky, but suppressed until 1924, when Krupskaya demanded that it be read to a meeting of Party dignitaries. It had no effect upon the fortunes of either Stalin or Trotsky, and the latter's reluctance to reveal it until after Stalin had consolidated his power is a mystery. The full text was published in Russia for the first time in 1956, though it had been leaked abroad and was published in New York in 1924.

TEST-BAN TREATY. See *Nuclear Test-Ban Treaty.*

THEOLOGY, MARXIST. *Marx has been called, by Christopher Dawson, the last of the Hebrew prophets. It is possible to infer a Marxist "theology" which is strikingly parallel to the Christian view. There was, for Marx, an original, *classless society corresponding to the Garden of Eden. There was an act of "original sin" when first man laid claim to *private property in the means of *production. There was, then, consequent evil arising out of the *class struggle which began when private property divided men into opposed classes of owners and non-owners. There is a suffering savior in Marxism, the *proletariat. There comes a day of judgment, the revolution. And there awaits a heaven, the classless society. Of course, though these concepts are authentically Marxist, it must not be supposed that Communism boasts of a "theology"; in fact, it quite expressly denies the existence of God. But the parallel to the Christian doctrines of original sin, depravity, salvation through a Savior, the day of judgment, and heaven is striking.

THEORY OF IMPOVERISHMENT. Marx's theory that *capitalism always tends to the increasing impoverishment of the *proletariat, a theory known also as the Law of Increasing Misery of the Proletariat. This theory was called "of Impoverishment" by *Bernstein, who argued that *Marx meant only relative impoverishment of the workers, whose absolute status may well improve but falls farther behind in ratio to the improvement of the capitalist's status. This *Lenin tended to deny, though he had to admit that in some capitalistic countries it obviously was true that the workers' conditions steadily improved. Marx said: "The accumulation of wealth at one pole is, therefore, at the same time accumulation of toil, slavery, ignorance, brutality, mental degradation at the opposite pole, that is, on the side of the class that produces its product in the form of capital" (*Cap.*, I).

THEORY OF INCREASING MISERY. See *Theory of Impoverishment.*

THEORY OF LABOR VALUE. See *Labor Theory of Value.*

THEORY OF STAGES. The belief of the so-called *Economists that the working class must progress successively through three stages before it is mature enough to consider taking political power: (1) the right to strike, unorganized; (2) the right to form trade unions; and (3) political liberty under parliamentary forms.

THEORY OF THE OFFENSIVE. The revolutionary theory expounded by the Marxist *Bukharin which calls for armed insurrection as the means of seizure of political power. In the attempt to put it into practice in 1921, the German Communist Party was almost destroyed. The question was debated at the Third Conference of the *Third International, and although Bukharin got a majority in the Conference, *Trotsky carried the Russian delegation against him. Finally the views of *Lenin — who believed that no *revolution could be successful unless the *masses were ready for it and gave it support — prevailed.

THERMADOR. A term used for the first stage of the counter-revolution, the first systematic reaction of the dispossessed class. *Trotsky calls it a time for mediocrities whose strength lies in their political blindness, and who therefore suppose that the *revolution can be reversed. This strength does in some instances prove to be sufficient to defeat the revolution. The term is sometimes enlarged to Thermadorian Reaction. (See Trotsky, *M.L.*, 513; and *H.R.R.*, II, 192).

THESES OF APRIL 4. These are the famous "April Theses" which *Lenin drafted on the day following his arrival in St. Petersburg, April 1917, after his trip from Switzerland in the famous closed train. As summarized by *Trotsky, Lenin's theses said: "The republic which has issued from the *February revolution is not our republic, and the war which is now waging is not our war. The task of the *Bolsheviks is to overthrow the *imperialist government. We are in the minority. We must teach the *masses not to trust the compromisers and defeatists. We must patiently explain. The success of this policy is assured, and it will bring us to the dictatorship of the *proletariat. We are beginning the international *revolution, and only its success will confirm our success and guarantee a transition to the *socialist regime" (*H.R.R.*, I, 300). The *April Theses* were published in Lenin's name alone; no one else would sign them.

THESES ON FEUERBACH. Eleven brief statements drafted by *Marx on the thought of Ludwig *Feuerbach, German philosopher and theologian. They were found by *Engels in a notebook left by Marx after his death, approximately forty years after they were written. The eleventh thesis is famous: "The philosophers have only interpreted the world; the point is to *change* it." The Theses are succinct statements of Marx's views on *history, mostly, and repay study. They may be found in *S.W.*, II, 403, and elsewhere.

THESIS-ANTITHESIS-SYNTHESIS (*Dialectic). The three steps in every process of dialectical development, according to the German philosopher *Hegel, a view generally accepted by *Marxism. The first stage is the situation as it is, or object as it is, and the like. Inherent in each situation and object is its opposite. That is, if we call the given moment the *thesis,* then inherent in it is its *antithesis,* developing by a process of *negation, or *contradiction, or *struggle. The antithesis negates — opposes and destroys in part — the thesis, but not without itself being so modified in the struggle that it, too, is negated (*negation of the negation) and the resultant of the struggle is a new situation or object, a new *moment, called the synthesis because it contains the enduring elements of both thesis and antithesis. Thus, as *Marx used the dialectic, there is given the *capitalist system; it is the *thesis.* But capital, in order to draw a return on investment, requires a *proletariat, that is, an exploited class. Thus the thesis — capital — creates by contradiction its own antithesis — a proletariat — which process is accomplished in struggle. In due season, Marx believed, the proletariat will destroy the capitalist, that is, negate capitalism; and in time the proletariat itself will pass into the *classless society, which is the negation of the negation and the new synthesis of the enduring values in both capital and proletariat. The Marxists do not insist that all process occurs in just this triadic form.

THIRD INTERNATIONAL. See *Communist International.*

THREE PILLARS (OR WHALES) OF BOLSHEVISM The name given to three slogans employed by the *Bolsheviks between 1905 and 1917 to gain popular support: (1) a democratic republic, (2) the eight-hour day, and (3) the confiscation of estates for distribution to the peasantry. Within the Bolshevik Party the so-called *Liquidators opposed these slogans with three of their own: (1) the right of labor to organize, (2) free speech, and (3) free press. The former required the overthrow of Tsarism, the latter were possible under Tsarism — and this distinction both sides knew well.

THREE PRINCIPLES. The title of a book (*The Three Principles of the People*) published in 1924 by *Sun Yat-sen, Chinese social-democratic leader and founder of the Kuomintang Party. The principles are: (1) nationality, (2) democracy, and (3) livelihood, or social justice.

TKACHOV, P. N. (1844-1885), follower of Auguste *Blanqui, and theoretician of the revolutionary *Narodniks, a terrorist organization. He advocated that no obedience be made to any law.

TOCSIN, The (*Nabat*). A revolutionary journal edited by *Tkachov, Russian terrorist, from 1875 to 1881, first in Geneva and then in London, which advocated the formation of conspirators' groups within Russia to carry on terrorism.

TRADE UNIONS, Soviet conception of. The trade unions form the "transmission belt" between the *Party and the *masses, according to Marxist theory. They are "organizations of education, organizations which attract and train, they are schools, schools of administration, schools of management, schools of Communism," (Lenin, *Works,* XXXII, 2). The trade unions give practical effect to the *revolutionary dictatorship of the proletariat.

TRAIN, The. The reference is to the military train from which for almost five years *Trotsky directed the rebuilding of the Russian Army and the conduct of the war against external and internal enemies of the Soviet State. A train, hastily placed at Trotsky's disposal as Commissar for War on the night of August 7, 1918, was gradually enlarged until, as Trotsky says, "It was equipped with its own printing plant, telegraph, radio, electric power station, library, garage, and bath." The appearance of "The Train" on any part of the 7,000-mile battlefront which had to be manned against foreign intervention and White Russian counter-revolt renewed confidence in the troops. Confidence was bolstered further by the detachment the Train itself carried, which was often led by Trotsky himself. More than once it was Trotsky and his Train which probably prevented major defeats and inspired attacks and ultimate victories.

TRANSITIONAL PERIOD. The time between the *proletarian revolt and the full Communist society. According to Marxist theory, this period is characterized by three forms of economic structure: (1) *socialism, (2) small *commodity producers, such as farmers and craftsmen, and (3) private *capitalism in small industries and business. The goal of the transitional period, however, is the elimination of these forms in favor of total *Communism.

TREASON TRIALS, RUSSIAN (Stalin's). To secure his own position as head of the Soviet Union, and to secure an absolute unity of effort, *Stalin proceeded in the latter 1930s to eliminate potential and suspected opposition among the top leadership of the Communist Party by four notorious trials, along with the great *purges. The first trial took place in August, 1936, when the old *Bolsheviks, who had assisted Stalin in ousting *Trotsky about a decade before, were tried and executed; principal among them were *Zinoviev and *Kamenev. The second trial occurred in January, 1937, when Yuri Pyatokov, a close associate of Lenin during the *Revolution, and some dozen others were condemned. One of the accused, Karl Radek, escaped with ten years imprisonment. The third trial took place in June, 1937, and saw Marshal Tukhachevsky and seven other leading Army officers secretly tried and executed. And, finally, in March, 1938, the so-called *Right Opposition was liquidated, including Alexei Rykov, *Lenin's own successor as Prime Minister of the Soviet Union, and Nikolai *Bukharin, another close associate of Lenin. One of the striking aspects of the trials was the willingness of the accused to testify against themselves. This willingness has been attributed to prison tortures, serums, or "brain-washing" of some kind. The trials and the purges left Stalin in undisputed control of the state and Party machinery in the Soviet Union. He did not rest, however, until his agents had also penetrated into Mexico, where Trotsky lived in close-guarded exile, to murder him in 1940.

TREATY OF BREST-LITOVSK. See *Brest-Litovsk*.

TREK TO THE PEOPLE. Slogan of the *Narodnik movement, which was the idealization of the village commune as the hope of a democratic Russia. The slogan was common in the third quarter of the last century, but the movement was broken by mass arrests in 1874. Over one thousand of the Narodniks were arrested, many of them deported and some executed.

TRIALS. See *Treason Trials*.

TRIBUNISTS, Party of the. The name used by *Lenin for the Social Democratic Party of the Netherlands, formed in 1909. The name followed from the Party's newspaper, *De Tribune*. In 1918 this Party shared in the formation of the Communist Party of the Netherlands, with *De Tribune* still as its organ. From 1930 until it was suppressed by the outbreak of World War II, the paper was called *The People's Daily*.

TRITE EVOLUTIONISTS. Lenin's term for evolutionists who, like Herbert Spencer, believed in a gradual evolutionary process without *leaps.

TROIKA, The (Three). The word *Troika* is simply Russian for *three,* but its specific reference in Soviet history is to the Committee of Three which controlled the Russian secret police and the administration of justice. This Committee was empowered to hold secret trials after arbitrary arrest, and could condemn the guilty to execution, exile, or imprisonment. The Troika was abolished after the fall of Beria in 1953. (See also *Socialist Legality*.) The word *Troika* was revived by *Khrushchev in 1961 when he sought to have the United Nations headed by a Secretariat of Three, the Troika Plan.

TROTSKY, Lev Davidovich (often, Leon Trotsky; born: Bronstein,

Lev. D.), (1879-1940), one of the shapers of modern Russia, along with *Marx, *Engels, *Lenin, *Stalin. Born in Russia at Kherson, the son of Jewish colonists, Trotsky encountered *socialist ideas at the University of Kiev and was instrumental in forming there the *Southern Russian Workers' Union. For revolutionary activity he was arrested and banished to Siberia in 1898. Escaping to London, he joined Lenin there, writing for *Iskra. When the *Russian Social Democratic Labor Party was split into *Bolsheviks, who followed Lenin, and *Mensheviks, who followed *Plekhanov, Trotsky joined the latter, separating from Lenin until May 1917. After a second capture by the police and exile to Siberia, Trotsky returned to Russia to join in the abortive *Revolution of 1905 there. He then escaped to Vienna and brought out his own newspaper, *Pravda (Truth). This lasted until 1912, when the St. Petersburg *Soviet brought out the Bolshevik Pravda, edited by Stalin, and Trotsky in anger departed for the United States. After the *February Revolution in Russia, Trotsky managed to obtain permission to return to Russia, though the British Government refused for some time to let him leave Halifax by ship. Reaching Russia in May 1917, about one month after Lenin's arrival, he joined forces with Lenin on the basis of the latter's famous *April Theses, which proclaimed Lenin's determination to fight for a *proletarian dictatorship rather than support the revolution under *Kerensky. With Lenin in hiding after July 1917, Trotsky was in actual command of the Bolshevik maneuvers which led to the successful capture of power in October 1917, after which Lenin took the head of government and Trotsky created the Red Army. Meanwhile, Stalin was quietly acquiring a hold on the *Party machinery, and when his differences with Trotsky came to an open struggle in 1926-27, Stalin was able to have Trotsky expelled from the Russian Communist Party and then from the Soviet Union. In exile, which finally brought him to a villa in Mexico, Trotsky wrote voluminously and bitterly attacked Stalin's regime. He was murdered in his villa, by (presumably) an agent of Stalin, on August 21, 1940. The best biography in English of Trotsky is that of Isaac Deutscher, *Leon Trotsky,* of which two of three projected volumes have appeared (fall, 1963); Trotsky writes his own account of his life in his autobiography *My Life,* available in paperback. Trotsky had three principles for revolution, formulated in May 1917, after he arrived in Russia: (1) Do not trust the *bourgeoisie; (2) Control the leadership of the Party; (3) Rely only on your own (workers') force. He was a brilliant writer, powerful orator, and magnetic leader.

TROTSKYISM. The name given to the views attributed to *Trotsky by his opponents in the *Bolshevik Party. After his expulsion in 1927, the name meant forbidden deviation from the *Party Line. Trotsky himself defines what his enemies should have meant: "Trotskyism did not mean the idea that it was impossible to build a *socialist society within the national boundaries of Russia (though *Stalin said it did). Trotskyism meant the idea that the Russian *proletariat might win the power in advance of the Western proletariat, and that in that case it could not confine itself within the limits of a *democratic dictatorship, but would be compelled to undertake the initial socialist measures" (*H.R.R.*, I, 319).

TROTSKYITES. See *Trotskyism, Opposition*.

TRUDOVIKS. The party of *Narodnik intellectuals who favored rights for the peasants but were in general agreement with the *Cadets in favoring constitutional monarchy.

The name was also given to the peasant deputies in the First State *Duma (1905; so-called Bulygin Duma) who represented the peasant hunger for land. The term means: *Group of Toil*. See *Populist Socialists*.

TRUE SOCIALISTS. German *socialist group formed around Grün, Luning, Puttmann, Kühlmann, and *Hess, who adapted the theories of French socialism (*Fourier, largely) to German conditions, and who sought the solution of practical problems in the realm of philosophy. The group was most active in the period 1845-48, just preceding the German Revolution, through a number of periodicals.

It was criticized by *Marx and *Engels in *G.I.*, in *C.M.*, and in periodical articles, for failure to hew to the true *revolutionary conception of the *proletariat.

TRUO. See *Press, Soviet*.

TRUSTS. See *Imperialism*.

TRUTH, Marxist Definition of. The Marxist defines truth simply as the correspondence of human knowledge to its object. *Practice is the only final test of truth. Marx: "The question whether objective truth can be attributed to human thinking is not a question of theory but a *practical* question. In practice man must prove the truth" (*Second Thesis on Feuerbach*). "The criterion of practice distinguishes for every one of us illusion from reality" (Lenin, *M.E.C.*, 137).

TUSSY. The family nickname for Marx's youngest daughter, Eleanor, who married Dr. Edward *Aveling, co-translator of Marx's *Capital* into English.

TWENTY-ONE POINTS, LENIN'S. Twenty-one standards essential to being recognized as a Communist *Party by the *Third International; drafted by *Lenin and adopted by the International in 1921 (see Cole, IV, 1, 335ff.). See *Communist International*.

TWO HUNDRED PERCENT MOVEMENT. A World War II Soviet movement, in the ranks of the *Komsomol (Soviet youth) to stimulate a double stint of labor by each young worker in order to replace one man sent to the front. See also *Socialist Emulation*.

TWO-AND-A-HALF INTERNATIONAL. See *Longuetites*.

ULYANOV, Vladimir Ilych. See *Lenin, V. I.*

UNION OF PUBLIC MEN. See *Private Conference of Public Men.*

UNION OF RUSSIAN FACTORY WORKERS. The organization founded by Father Georg *Gapon, Russian priest, in collaboration with the secret police, as a means of drawing workers out of the more revolutionary labor organizations. Father Gapon organized and led the mass march to the Winter Palace in St. Petersburg on January 9, 1905, which ended in the massacre now known as *Bloody Sunday.

UNION OF RUSSIAN PEOPLE. See *Black Hundreds*.

UNION OF RUSSIAN SOCIAL DEMOCRATS ABROAD. Founded in Geneva in 1894, it was initiated by the *Emancipation of Labor Group and held its first conference in November 1898. Its purpose was to unify the efforts of all *émigré* groups. The *Emancipation of Labor Group, under the leadership of *Plekhanov, accused the Union at once of *opportunist tendencies, and at its Second Conference, April 1900, the Group withdrew to form its own *Sotsial-Demokrat organization, leaving the Union virtually dead.

UNION OF SOVIET SOCIALIST REPUBLICS (USSR). This name for the Soviet Union was advocated by various Communist *Central Committees, especially those of the Ukraine, Belorussia, Azerbaidzhan, Georgia, and Armenia, in a joint meeting, October to December, 1922. At the First *Congress of Soviets of the USSR, opened in Moscow on December 30, 1922, the name was officially adopted and the union of the various member republics declared. A Central Executive Committee was elected, with M. I. *Kalinin as Chairman and V. I. *Lenin as Chairman of the Council of Peoples' Commissars of the USSR. Membership on a voluntary basis was opened to the various nationality groups within Russian borders.

There are fifteen Union Republics: Russian, Ukranian, Belorussian, Uzbek, Kazakh, Georgian, Azerbaidzhan, Lithuanian, Moldavian, Latvian, Kirghiz, Tadzhik, Armenian, Turkmenian, Estonian. There are, in addition, 19 Autonomous Republics, 9 Autonomous Regions, 10 National Regions, 6 Territories, and 117 Districts.

UNION OF UNIONS. During the Russian *Revolution of 1905, unions of professional men — doctors, lawyers, etc. — were established and united under one central organization, the Union of Unions. In 1905 these Unions tended to support liberalization of Tsarist rule. In 1917, however, the Union of Unions led government workers to strike against the Soviet regime in an effort to retard *Bolshevik progress. With the triumph of the Soviets, the Union of Unions went out of business.

UNIONS, TRADE. See *Trade Unions*.

UNITY (AND CONFLICT) OF OPPOSITES. A basic concept in Marxist dialectics which asserts that all things are a unity of opposites. The opposites break out into conflict and thus release the energy which moves *history. See *Dialectics.*

UNITY CONFERENCE. A conference held in Zürich, Switzerland, September 21-22, in an effort to unite all Russian exile organizations on a Marxist platform. Representatives from various journals published abroad — *Iskra, *Zarya, and *Sotsial-Demokrat — attended, but failed to come to agreement. *Lenin was himself present under the name of Frey. See *Borba Group.*

UNITY CONGRESS. See *Congresses* (Fourth).

UNITY OF ACTION. See *Policy of Unity of Action.*

USE VALUE. See *Commodity.*

UTOPIA (*Nowhere*), (Utopianism, Utopian Socialism). In the first instance the title of a book by Sir Thomas More (1478-1535) which represents an imaginary island country where social life is ideally lived. More used his country as a foil to criticize the England of his time, especially to suggest that the root of poverty and social evil lies in private property. In *Utopia* there is socialized property and production. This book was the first attempt to delineate the features of a *socialist country, and it was one of the causes for More's losing his head. Its great weakness, in Marx's view, was that it nowhere showed *how* such a social-

ized state is to be achieved, nor did it relate itself in any way to More's England by some analysis of the epoch in which he lived. For this reason the Marxist dubs as "Utopian" all socialism which is not based upon "scientific" analysis of the present and which lacks clear steps into the future. True socialism, *Marx holds, is "scientific," that is, rests upon ascertained laws of social evolution; all other socialism is "Utopian," dreaming, impractical.

UTOPIANISM, Moral Sources of. *Marx considers the motives of the Utopians to be high and moral, but good motives are not, he thinks, basic historical forces. The Utopian is twice a dreamer: (1) he assumes that his moral standards, by which he formulates his ideal society, are self-evident and universal; and (2) he assumes that these standards will of themselves exert force upon *history. See Engels's discussion of Utopianism in Marx, *P.P.* (Introduction), p. 11. See *Utopia*, above.

VALUE, LABOR THEORY OF. *Engels writes: "The two propositions which *Ricardo proclaimed in 1817 right at the beginning of his *Principles [of Political Economy]*, (1) that the value of any *commodity is purely and solely determined by the quantity of *labor required for its *production, and (2) that the product of the entire social labor is divided among three classes: landowners (rent), *capitalists (profit) and workers (*wages), had ever since 1821 been utilized in England for *socialist

conclusions" (Marx, *P.P.*, Preface).
See, *Labor Theory of Value* for
complete discussion.

VALUE, LAW OF. See *Law of
Value.*

VALUE, SURPLUS. See *Surplus
Value.*

VARIABLE CAPITAL. "That part
of *capital represented by *labor
power does, in the process of *production, undergo an alteration of
value. It both reproduces the
equivalent of its own value, and
also produces an excess, a *surplus
value, which may itself vary, may
be more or less according to the
circumstances. This part of capital
is continually being transformed
from a constant to a variable magnitude. I therefore call it the
variable part of capital, or, shortly,
variable capital" (Marx, *Cap.*, I,
209). *Marx goes on to say, "Surplus value is purely the result of
a variation in the value of variable
capital, of that portion of the
capital which is transformed into
labor-power . . . . [But] in order
that variable capital may perform
its function, *constant capital must
be advanced in proper proportion,
a proportion given by the special
technological conditions of each
labor process" (*Cap.*, I, 214-15).
Once more: "Surplus value bears
the same ratio to variable capital
that *surplus labor does to *necessary labor" (*Cap.*, I, 218).

VARLIN, Louis Eugene (1839-
1871), French bookbinder who was
a member of the *First International, and was killed fighting for
the *Paris Commune in 1871.

VERIFICATION FROM BELOW.
See *Workers' and Peasants Inspectorate.*

VILLAGE COMMUNE, Russian
(*Obshchina,* or *Mir*). The communal form of peasant use of the
land, dating back to ancient times,
and characterized by crop rotation,
undivided woods and pastures, collective responsibility, periodical
compulsory redistribution of the
land, prohibited purchase or sale
of alloted land. *Lenin: the village
commune "serves as medieval bar-
rier dividing the peasants, who are
as if chained to small associations."
The *Narodniks saw the village
commune as the first step to *socialism, and the hope of the future
for Russia. In 1906 the peasants
were permitted by law to leave the
commune, and in the next nine
years over two million families
did so.

VILNO ECONOMISM. The view
of A. Kremer, organizer of the
*Bund, and Y. O. Tsederbaum
(better known as *Martov), drafted by them in Vilno, in 1894, and
printed in Geneva in 1897. This
view advocated mass agitation
among the workers, but on the
basis of *Economism. It was criticized by both *Plekhanov and
*Axelrod.

VLASSOVITES. The members of
an all-Russian brigade organized
by, and fighting for, the Germans
in World War II.

VOGT, Karl (1817-1895), professor
at Giessen (Germany), dismissed
as a revolutionist in 1847, who
turned into a secret agent of the

German police and is exposed as such in Marx's pamphlet, *Herr Vogt*. In philosophy, Vogt was the exponent of what *Marx called vulgar *materialism, that is, mechanism.

VOICE, The (*Golas*). A Russian revolutionary newspaper, issued in Paris, edited by *Martov. *Lenin called it "the best *socialist paper in Europe." In January 1915 it was succeeded by *Our Word* (*Nashe Slovo*), which began on January 29 and was edited by Antonov-Ovsenko, a Russian Marxist who had the distinction of arresting the Ministry of the *Kerensky Government when the *Bolsheviks took power in the *October Revolution, 1917.

VOICE OF THE PEOPLE (*La Voix du Peuple*). A journal published by the French socialist *Proudhon, begun in Paris in 1849. It was critical of *Marxism.

VOICE OF THE SOCIAL-DEMO-CRAT (*Golos Sotsial-Demokrata*). A *Menshevik paper, published outside Russia by Dan and *Martov in 1908 to attack the views of Lenin.

VOLUNTARISM. The assumption that the human will is free and decisive in the making of choices. To this assumption the Marxist opposes his conviction that the will of man is governed by the laws of matter as they come to expression in the sciences and the relations of *production. See *Materialism, Dialectical; Historical Materialism*.

VOPROSY FILOSOFI. Russian philosophical journal which began publication in 1947 under the editorship of Professor B. M. Kedrov. It is the focal point for philosophical discussion in the Soviet Union, and in it were published between 1947 and 1956 some 1,000 articles by some 800 different writers. In 1958 another philosophical journal, *Filosofskie Nauki* also began publication, as an additional outlet for public discussion.

VORBOTE (*Herald*). A German magazine published by the *Zimmerwold Left, a group favorable to the views of *Lenin, 1915. A magazine of the same title was published in the 1860s by the German section of the *First International; see *Becker, Johann P.*

VORWARTS (*Forward*). The daily newspaper of the German Social Democratic Party, begun in 1876 with Wilhelm *Liebknecht as Editor. *Engels was a contributor in the 1880s; but in the 1890s, under the editorship of *Kautsky, the paper turned toward *Revisionism and became the organ of the *Second International in its Revisionist emphasis. The paper remained in publication until the advent of Hitler in 1933, when it was suspended. It reappeared in April 1946 as the organ of the Socialist Unity Party, and so it continues.

VULGAR MATERIALISM. See *Materialism, Vulgar; Materialism, Mechanistic.*

173

WAGES, IRON LAW OF. See *Iron Law of Wages.*

WAGES, Marxist View of. "Taking them as a whole, the general movements of wages are exclusively regulated by the expansion and contraction of the industrial reserve army [the unemployed], and these again correspond to the periodic changes of the industrial cycle" (Marx, *Cap.,* I, 637). *Marx took the position that wages tend to remain at the level of bare subsistence, governed by the demand for ever greater return on *capital. German Bishop *Ketteler, who also took a keen interest in economic affairs, wrote: "At the present day *labor is become a ware, subject to the laws that govern all *commodities. Wages, which are the price of labor, are consequently regulated as the price of other wares, by supply and demand" (*Die Arbeitsfrage,* 17). Marx calls wages the price of labor power, saying that labor itself has no *value — it is the source, creator, substance of value itself. "Wages are not what they appear to be, namely, the *value* or *price* of *labor,* but only a masked form for the *value,* or *price,* of *labor-power*" (*S.W.,* 29). The magnitude, or amount, of wages is governed by two factors: (1) the value of the absolute necessities of life for the worker and his family, and (2) the cultural requirements of the epoch as the worker must share in them. Marx adds that "it is the laborer's labor of last week, or of last year, that pays for his labor-power this week or this year. . . . The *capitalist class is constantly giving to the laboring class order-notes (wages) in the form of money, on a portion of the commodities produced by the latter and appropriated by the former. The laborers give these order-notes back just as constantly to the capitalist class, and in this way get their share of their share of their own product" (*Cap.,* I, 568).

WAR COMMUNISM. Complete centralization of production, distribution, and every economic function associated with these, to mobilize the total resources of a country for best use in its defense and the building up of *socialism within it. War Communism is considered an emergency rather than a necessary step in the development of socialist society, but it was practiced in Russia from the summer of 1918 to the spring of 1919, in the face of the counter-revolution and foreign intervention. *Lenin: "We were forced to 'War Communism' by war and ruin. It was not, nor could it be, a policy that corresponded to the economic tasks of the *proletariat. It was a temporary measure" (*Works* XXXII, 321). War Communism was followed by the *New Economic Policy (NEP). While in effect, War Communism consisted of: (1) prohibition of all free trade, (2) rationing according to *class principles, (3) appropriation of farm produce, (4) centralization of industry and control of it, (5) assignment of raw materials to manufacturers, (6) relative uselessness of common currency. It is also called Military Communism.

WEDEMEYER, Georg (d. 1866), supporter of *Marx and *Engels in numerous meetings and committees. He copied out the *German Ideology* for Marx in 1845-46 and collaborated with him on the *Neue Rheinische Zeitung*. After the collapse of this paper he went to America, where he fought in the Civil War on the side of the North.

WEITLING, Wilhelm (1808-1871), German tailor who fled the German police because of his revolutionary views and action. He joined the Paris *League of the Just in 1838 and for it wrote a pamphlet, *Humanity, As It Is and Should Be.* In it he demands equality for all men, but hopes to achieve it through peaceful parliamentary methods. He was active in the *First International.

WESTPHALEN, Jenny von (1814-1881), born on February 12, 1814, a neighbor to the family in which, in 1818, was born a son, Karl, with whom she became a childhood friend. When Karl *Marx left for the University of Berlin, his letters home were full of the name Jenny, and finally in 1843 they were married, even as Karl was on his way into exile in Paris. Jenny's elder brother was Prussian Minister of the Interior, 1850-58. She lived a life of dire poverty at Karl's side, pawning her heirlooms as they were received, selling her beds on occasion to buy food, losing three of her children to diseases perhaps curable had there been funds, and yet remaining loyal to

Karl to her last heart beat, on December 2, 1881, when she succumbed to cancer. There were six Marx children: Jenny (1844-1883, married Charles *Longuet; Laura (1845-1911), married Paul *Lafargue, and died by her own hand in a mutual suicide pact with her husband; Edgar, nicknamed Mush (1847-1855); Heinrich, nicknamed Fawkes (1849-1851); Franzisca (1851-1852); Eleanor (1855-1898), married Edward *Aveling.

WHISTLE, The (*Svistok*). Satirical supplement to the Russian liberal magazine *Contemporary*.

WHITE GUARDS. Volunteers from among the *bourgeois anti-Bolsheviks who sought to defend private property against the Soviets in the last stages of the 1917 *Revolution. In general, the Whites were those Russians who opposed the *Reds — the old versus the new order.

WHITE LININGS. A label for Russian university students who came from wealthy and noble families, and who supported the *Tsarist regime against students of revolutionary temper. The name derives from the white silk linings of the wealthy students' uniforms.

WILLICH, August (1810-1878), Prussian military officer who was active on the side of the German Revolution of 1848. With *Schapper, Willich was a leader of the "Left" faction of the *Communist League, in exile in London. In 1853 he came to America, where he worked as a carpenter until the outbreak of the Civil War.

He joined the Northern forces and became a general.

WITHERING AWAY OF THE STATE. "Marx's book against *Proudhon [The Poverty of Philosophy]* and later the *Communist Manifesto* directly declare that with the introduction of the *socialist order of society the *state will dissolve of itself and disappear. . . . Therefore, the state is only a transitory institution which is used in the struggle, in the *revolution, in order to hold down one's adversaries by force" (Engels, letter to Bebel, March 18, 1875, *S.C.*, 377ff.). *Lenin calls this "probably the most striking and certainly the sharpest passage *against* the state, so to speak, in *Marx and *Engels." Inasmuch as the state shows no sign of withering away in Communist Russia, various explanations have been devised to account for its longevity. For these, see *State*.

WOLFF, Ferdinard, nicknamed the Red Wolf for his beard and for his radical views, was close to *Marx, on the editorial staff of the *Neue Rheinische Zeitung* with him, and like him a German exile in London much of his life. He is not to be confused with Wilhelm Wolff — see below.

WOLFF, Wilhelm (1809-1864), close friend of *Marx and *Engels, called by them *Lupus* (Latin for wolf), to whom the first volume of *Capital* is dedicated.

WORKER (*Rabochy*). First Social Democratic workers' paper issued in Russia itself. It appeared in two numbers only (1885), and was secretly printed and circulated by the *Blagoyev Group, known as the *Party of the Russian Social Democrats.

WORKERS' CAUSE (*Rabocheye Dyelo*). A journal on the side of the *Economists, published by the *Union of Russian Social Democrats Abroad, in Geneva, from April 1899 to February 1902. It appeared in nine issues comprising twelve numbers. *Lenin was critical of it in his *What Is To Be Done?*, for its economism.

WORKERS' OPPOSITION. A group headed by Alexander G. Shlyapnikov, in 1917 Labor Commissar in the Soviet Government, which in 1920 advocated the administration of the national economy by the *trade unions, in opposition to *Lenin's plan of *democratic centralism. In a form parallel to that of *Syndicalism, the Workers' Opposition conception of the role of the trade unions was that of organizing and operating the industrial and transport enterprises. The Opposition made no progress, and disbanded.

WORKERS' PRESS DAY. The day celebrated in Russia (May 5) as the anniversary of the first issue of the *Bolshevik newspaper *Pravda* (*Truth*) in St. Petersburg, in 1912, under the editorship of Joseph *Stalin.

WORKERS' THOUGHT (*Rabochaya Mysl*). An *Economist newspaper published by the *Russian Social Democrats Abroad, from October 1897 to December 1902, in a total of sixteen issues. *Lenin criticizes it as *opportunist in outlook, in his *What Is To Be Done?*

WORKERS' AND PEASANTS' INSPECTORATE (*Rabkin*). A device established by *Lenin in 1919 for "verification from below," that is, a separate "people's" organization organized to keep watch over the administrative machinery of the *Soviets, up to the highest echelons, to point out inefficiency and corruption. The Inspectorate itself, however, had no watchmen, and has in some ways acted accordingly. See *Criticism and Self-Criticism*.

WORKING CLASS. See *Proletariat*.

WORKING PEASANT PARTY. One of several internal anti-*Bolshevik groups exposed in Russia in 1930-31, and broken up by trial and executions. It had its center within the Peoples' Commissariat for Agriculture, in the Soviet Government, and represented the interests of the *kulaks.

WORKSHOPS REGULATION ACT, British. See *Factory Acts, British, Early*.

YEDISSTVO GROUP. An organization of *Mensheviks formed in March 1917 and led by *Plekhanov. It supported the Provisional Government of *Kerensky against *Lenin and *Trotsky.

YEZHOVSHCHINA. Name given to the great Russian *purges of 1936-38, derived from N. I. Yezhov, Commissar for Internal Affairs (in-cluding the secret police) during that period. See *Purges; Treason Trials*.

YOFFEE. See *Deborin, Abraham M.*

YOUNG HEGELIANS. See *Hegel* and *Left Hegelians*.

YOUNG PIONEERS. See *Pioneers*.

YOUNG SOCIALISTS. A group formed within the German Social Democratic Party in 1890, composed chiefly of university students and young writers. *Engels called them the "heroes of the revolutionary phrase," afraid of taking any practical action. They were expelled from the Party at its Erfurt Congress in 1891.

YOUTH SHOCK BRIGADES. See *Socialist Emulation*.

YOUTH SUNDAYS. *Komsomol (Soviet youth) programs for collecting scrap metal for the Soviet war effort. The labor was voluntary, and other goods, including money, were also accepted. During World War II there were five such Sundays; forty-three million persons took part, and four hundred sixty million rubles worth of material was gathered for defense.

ZASULICH, Vera J. (1851-1919), Russian revolutionist who first joined the *Narodniks, then emigrated in 1880 and joined *Plekhanov to form the first Russian Marxist organization, the *Emancipation of Labor Group. She returned to Russia and attempted the assassination of General Trapov, but escaped imprisonment when the jury freed her. Fleeing abroad once again, she joined *Lenin and Plekhanov on the staff of *Iskra. When the split came between Lenin and Plekhanov, in 1903, she remained on the side of Plekhanov and the *Mensheviks, and played no active role in the *Revolution of 1917.

ZEDERBAUM, Y. O. See *Martov.*

ZEMLYA I VOLYA. See *Land and Freedom (Liberty) Group.*

ZEMSTVO (Zemstvo Campaigns). The name employed from early Russian history for councils, that is, local planning units established among the peasants and agricultural communities to plan the best use of land and facilities. The Zemstvo was, in form, the forerunner of the modern Russian *Soviets, also meaning councils, but more generally associated in practice with those elected in industries. Also provincial or county councils, elected by property owners and limited to economic and cultural activities, first established by the *Tsarist government in 1864. The Zemstvo Campaigns, August 1904 to January 1905, consisted of conferences, public meetings, and banquets arranged by Zemstvo leaders to press their demands upon the Tsar for constitutional reforms.

ZETKIN, Clara (1857-1933), German socialist leader who opposed German entry into World War I, and agitated for mass strikes to prevent it. She was active in the *Spartacus League, and helped organize the German Communist Party in 1918. She lived her last years in the Soviet Union.

ZHELYABOV, A. I. (1851-1881), founder of the Russian terrorist organization, *Narodnaya Volya (*People's Will, or Freedom*). He planned the assassination of Tsar Alexander II, which happened on March 1, 1881. Arrested two days before the attempt, Zhelyabov was in prison when the Tsar was killed, but he wrote a full account of his implication in the plans and was tried and executed. At his trial he said: "I solemnly acknowledge that faith without works is dead, and that every genuine Christian should fight for justice, for the rights of the oppressed and the weak, and if need be, should also suffer for them. That is my faith."

ZIMMERWOLD CONFERENCE. An international socialist conference held at Zimmerwold, near Berne, in Switzerland, in August 1915. There were thirty-eight delegates from eleven countries in attendance, most of them *Centrists — those midway between the extremes in the *Second International, that is, between *Lenin and *Revisionism. The Conference advocated peace, but did not adopt the theses offered by Lenin which called upon *socialists everywhere to seize the opportunity to turn the world war into civil wars, working if need be for the defeat of their own nations. When the Conference rejected Lenin's theses, he organized another Conference of eight delegates — called the Zimmerwold Left, or Internationalists — which met September 5 to 18, 1915, and adopted his theses. This latter Conference also decided to publish a magazine in German, *Vorbote* (*Herald*). The Left held another conference, at Kienthat, on April 24, 1916.

ZIMMERWOLD LEFT. See *Zimmerwold Conference.*

ZIMMERWOLDISTS. The label given those who attended the *Zimmerwold Conference.

ZINOVIEV, Gregory E. (Radomylski) (1883-1936), Russian revolutionary who took the side of the *Bolsheviks in 1905 and was active in the St. Petersburg revolt of that year. He worked with *Lenin during World War I, but in 1917 joined *Kamenev and others in opposing Lenin's drive to seize power by *revolution. He was leader of the Petrograd *Soviet after the *October Revolution, and head of the *Third International. With Kamenev he became involved in the *Stalin-*Trotsky feud, and like Kamenev he allowed himself to be used by Stalin to get a majority in the *Central Committee against Trotsky. In 1925, Zinoviev broke with Stalin to join the *Opposition, but returned to him when Trotsky and the Oppositionists were expelled from the *Party in 1927. In 1932 he was again expelled, and again re-admitted, on questions of state policy. In 1935 he was implicated in the assassination of S. M. *Kirov, a liberal who had opposed Stalin, and was sentenced to prison; in the purge trial of 1936 he was once again charged and this time sentenced to execution.

SECTION II

The Classics of Marxism

The Classics of Marxism

No amount of reading about a great writer is equivalent to reading him. It may well be that reading about him is a useful or even indispensable prerequisite to reading him with understanding, but it is no substitute.

Eventually, then, the student of Marxism must read Marx and Engels — and Lenin and Trotsky — if it is genuine understanding he is after. And without such understanding, criticism is not likely to be meaningful. In short, the better you understand, the better you are able to attack — and the better to build. And if you think that your faith in democracy will be toppled by some acquaintance with Marxism at the sources — why, then you have not troubled to understand democracy very well either. Be of good cheer, it is not so. The more you understand of Marxism, the better the democratic way as the West understands it will look to you.

Fortunately, the classics of Marxism are relatively few; which may surprise you, considering the impact of Marxism upon the world and the avalanche of literature on Marxism which these classics have caused. But all together, the "great books" which have molded Western history may total something just more or less than one hundred. To this lasting one hundred Karl Marx contributed one — *Capital*. This is the mountain peak of Marxism you are after, and should you scale it — Volume I alone, for Volumes II and III are not only compilations made after Marx's death, but are for specialists in economics — should you scale the heights of Volume I of *Capital*, all the rest of Marxist economics will fall into place.

If *Capital* is the mountain peak, there are also the foothills. Moreover, one reader gets at his author's ideas best by one route, while another reader takes quite a different path. And still more, Marxism has been developed on a broader base than the economic one Marx devised. So there are good reasons enough for speaking of Marxist classics in the plural, and for listing more than that massive Volume I of *Capital*. There are those, indeed, who maintain that Communism would have arisen without Marx's studies in economics; which may be so, but then it would not have been Marxism, and might not have been carried into history with such passionate devotion. Read and judge for yourself.

In this reading process, it is very useful to separate Marxism into two strands, roughly associated with the names of Marx and Engels. This separation is in part artificial, and only for purposes of study; for Marx and Engels worked in closest harmony, with one goal in mind, namely, the revolutionary overthrow of the capitalistic system. But to make apprehension come the more readily, consider Marxism, first, as a study in *economics* — called in Marx's day *political economy,* a term which well symbolizes the close relation between economic and political, that is, all of social, life. This was Marx's specialty. And consider, second, Marxism as *philosophy*. Within the philosophy, two strands may be discerned: dialectical materialism, and historical materialism, terms for which you should consult the *Vocabulary*. To these — and other matters — Engels addressed himself. Marxism economics, and Marxist philosophy divided into dialectical and historical materialism — how shall we get at these, remembering all the while that they are but three facets of one comprehensive and sophisticated system developed for explaining life, history, the past, present, and the future?

The best, and most difficult, source for Marxist economics is *Capital* itself. Terms like *commodity, labor value, price, surplus value, wages, capital, alienation, exploitation,* and the like, each finely chiseled, may here be seen in their respective places in the mosaic of Marx's carefully developed system. Little has been added by the later Marxists to the master's analysis, except for Lenin's development of the concepts of the state and imperialism — and this Lenin construed as no more than a consistent expansion of Marx's premises.

From the earliest of his works, the *Economic and Philosophic Manuscripts of 1844,* to the only volume of *Capital* which *Marx* lived to see published, almost all of his published work develops these same concepts, of which two are fundamental — labor value and surplus value. You may find, therefore, that some of the earlier writings lead you more easily into the pages of *Capital* than a direct assault upon it does, and for this purpose some of Marx's earlier works are listed below.

You may prefer to begin with summaries of Marx's economic views by later Marxists, and for this purpose the best of these are also suggested.

Marx's discussion of economics is never, you will notice, far removed from his consciousness of history. He wrote economics with an eye on revolution. We study history, he said, in order to change it. Theory, even economic theory, as an end in itself was never enough for him. So, even in *Capital,* the environment — and you feel it — is dynamic, and this dynamic belongs to Marxist philosophy, with which Engels came more and more to deal, though Marx wrote most of their first joint works on the subject, while Engels's first two works dealt wholly with economics.

Lenin, like Marx, was an activist, and saw little sense in studying anything as an end in itself. In fact, "art for art's sake" is taboo among the Marxists, an inheritance from the masters. So Lenin's pamphlet on Marxism also sets you on the philosophical and historical path.

Dialectical materialism gets its classic exposition in Engels's *Feuerbach* and, still more so, in his *Anti-Dühring* and *Dialectics of Nature.* Lenin added the capstone with his *Materialism and Empirio-Criticism.*

Now, of course, dialectical and historical materialism complement each other, but if the stress is on the dialectic in the books just mentioned, then the stress may be said to be on the historical in those first joint works of Marx and Engels: *The Holy Family,* and *The German Ideology.* In fact, the section on Feuerbach in the latter of these books is, I think, the simplest exposition of historical materialism which Marx and Engels ever made. The *Communist Manifesto* encompasses in rhetorical form all of the basic ideas of Marxism, but probably belongs here in its essential thrust. The Russian Plekhanov educated a whole generation of Russian Marxists, said Lenin, and his *Development of the Monist View of History* may well be the simplest initiation for non-Russian anti-Marxists, too, into the mysteries of historical materialism. Lenin also spent himself in expositing this side of Marxism, particularly as it involved revolution and the dictatorship of the proletariat, most systematically in his *State and Revolution.*

The Vocabulary of Communism

And, in a way, Trotsky drew all of these strands together — the economic, the dialetical, and the historical — in his story and interpretation of *The History of the Russian Revolution,* a revolution which was the first massive application of Marxism to history.

Here follow, then, the classics of Marxism with some brief suggestion of their contents. There is no prescribed order for reading them; one may speak to you more clearly than it does to someone else. Come to mastery by any route you please; and after mastery, spend yourself in refutation, for refutable these classics are, and refuted they must be — in our generation.

Despite the fact that the list gets a little long, it is only a selection — the current Moscow edition of Lenin's works in English is scheduled, like the Russian edition, to run to forty volumes; Trotsky wrote at the drop of a pen; and the collected works of Marx and Engels threaten to exceed Lenin's output.

The general plan of selection is as follows: to give the basic works of Marx and Engels first, starting with economic theory and going to philosophy, including not only the classics but also the introductions and summaries from the hand of the masters and their followers. Then follows a section on the attempts made by both Marx and Engels to apply their ideas to actual history by their study of revolutionary movements, of science, and of the past; so, too, with certain works of Lenin and Trotsky. After this some good books of personal sketches are suggested. Concluding the list are selected titles from the Russian revolutionary writers who preceded Marxism in the nineteenth century, the works of the first Russian Marxist, Plekhanov, and a suggestion for getting into Chinese Communism.

The editions mentioned are those I have used. Many of them are published by the Foreign Languages Publishing House in Moscow (F.L.P.H.), which the Soviet Union subsidizes. The reader will usually find the same titles published by International Publishers in the United States and Lawrence and Wishart in England, if he is squeamish about Russian-made products. One must always reckon with the fact, especially with Russian-produced books dated prior to 1956, that under Stalin the Russians had a penchant for rewriting history; this could, though I have no instance in mind, extend to editing texts. The Russian-produced *History of the Communist Party,* for example, manages to recount the tale of the revolution of 1917 with hardly the mention of Trotsky, and gets Lenin solidly on the side of "revolution in one country" which is the issue on which Stalin and Trotsky took opposite sides, and on which Trotsky supposed Lenin stood with him. Editions of Marx and Engels, however, are less easily tampered with, and usually there is no good motive for so doing. The reader may therefore study the Moscow text with reasonable assurance. On questions which rouse his suspicions he may wish to consult editions published in other lands.

In 1961 the Foreign Languages Publishing House issued a second edition of its *Fundamentals of Marxism-Leninism,* a manual of 890 pages which, bearing in mind the bias which animates its source, is a very useful summation of Marxism as viewed currently by the official spokesmen of the system. It is by no means written with cool objective judgment, and it is better studied after some critical apprehension of Marxism is obtained. But on this condition it is probably the best one-volume summary of the subject.

Lenin advised against "dabbling in revolution." So it is, too, with dabbling in Marxism or any other area of research. The books listed here were written to move the minds of men and to upset the social and economic system which is the common possession of the Western world. Give them the respect their success demands, but read them with the skepticism *our* success entitles us to have. Marx and Engels and their followers were by no means infallible. Meet them with the best that is in you; and after you have paid them the effort of study, and given your democratic way of life the attention and devotion it, too, deserves, prepare to answer them in words of deep devotion to liberty and in deeds of courage and love.

If you wish to set these Marxist works in their place in the whole movement of socialist thought, there is no better way than to study G. D. H. Cole's monumental four-volume (in seven parts) *History of Socialist Thought.*

MARXIST ECONOMICS

Basic Works:

(1) Karl Marx, **Capital** (1867 —). 3 volumes. Moscow, F.L.P.H., 1957-1961. Here in three weighty tomes is the distillation of the lifework of a genius; and despite the heavy going, it is one of the epoch-making books of the Western world. The pace is slow, but infinitely systematic, and after study, the way through at least the first volume (which is enough for the layman) becomes reasonably clear. It is pure economics, passionately written; and if not always

persuasive, it is always impressive. Volume I is all Marx lived to publish; Volumes II (1885) and III (1894) were edited by Engels from the manuscripts Marx left behind him. A collection of miscellaneous manuscripts later produced by Kautsky is sometimes included as Volume IV. Volume I covers the basic economics of Marxism; Volume II deals principally with the circulation of capital; and Volume III analyzes profit and surplus value. Volume IV is titled *Theories of Surplus Value.*

Useful Introductions:

(2) Karl Marx, **Economic and Philosophic Manuscripts of 1844** (1932). Moscow, F.L.P.H., 1961. These unfinished manuscripts, unpublished until their appearance in MEGA in 1932, contain the first fruits of Marx's systematic investigation of political economy. As a result of his experience on the *Rheinische Zeitung,* Marx thought himself to be a dunce in economics; and after his expulsion from Germany, he seized upon an enforced leisure in Paris to plunge day and night with characteristic feverish zeal into economics. These manuscripts summarize the views at which he arrived on wages, profit, rent, estrangement or alienation, Communism, and bourgeois society, with all the advantages of brevity and the disadvantage of first and unfinished efforts. Included also in this Moscow edition is Engels's early "Outlines of a Critique of Political Economy," the piece which first attracted Marx to him; in itself a brief introduction to the views which they jointly gave their lives to developing.

(3) Karl Marx, **The Poverty of Philosophy** (1847). Moscow, F.L.P.H., n.d. Marx chose this title to mock the French socialist Proudhon, whose book entitled the *Philosophy of Poverty* he here attacks. In many respects this book puts flesh on a brief outline of Marxist economics. The reader who can disentangle the positive views of Marx from his often detailed and tedious criticism of Proudhon will be rewarded a rather complete outline of Marxist political economy. The edition here cited includes two long letters in which Marx sums up his criticisms of Proudhon, as well as relevant selections from Marx's *Political Economy* (item 5 below) and a speech he delivered on the subject of free trade. It may be noted in passing that Engels paid his critical respects to Proudhon in three articles first published in a Leipzig newspaper (*Volksstaat*) in 1872, and republished as a pamphlet under the title *The Housing Question.*

(4) Karl Marx, **Wage Labor and Capital.** In *Selected Works,* item 26 below. Under this title Marx published a selection of the articles he contributed to the *Neue Rheinische Zeitung* from January 4 to May 19, 1849, during which time he was its editor. The articles in turn were based on lectures he had given in 1847 to a German Workers' Society in Brussels, and constitute therefore a relatively popular exposition of "Marxism" as its originator understood it at the time. Engels points out in his introduction to the booklet that after the publication of these lectures Marx came to one significant change of view — "one of the most important points in the whole of political economy" — in that he saw the distinction between *labor* and *labor power,* and came to understand that capital purchases not labor but labor power (see item 5, below). This collection of articles should, then, be studied in conjunction with Engels's brief introduction, which appears in the *Selected Works* edition. Marx deals here with the fundamental categories of analysis of capitalism, though his exposition was interrupted by the suspension of the *Neue Rheinische Zeitung* and never taken up again, the lectures themselves being presumably lost.

(5) Karl Marx, **A Contribution to the Critique of Political Economy** (1859). This preliminary study to *Capital* was published in Germany in 1859. In his preface to *Capital,* Marx says that the ideas contained in the book are now summarized in the first three chapters of *Capital* itself; the reader had best, therefore, get them there. Copies of this 1859 volume are not common, and it is listed here only because occasional reference to it is made in Marxist literature. Engels says that in writing this book Marx came fully to understand and use the distinction between *labor* and *labor power.*

Useful Summations:

(6) V. I. Lenin, **The Teachings of Karl Marx.** New York, International, 1930. Lenin made various summaries of the teaching of Marx. This is one; another appears as an essay in item 27, below; a third has been published as a brief biography of Marx. Each is a clear, concise, and informative exposition of Marxism, based on Lenin's well-known contention that Marx summed up and drew together three streams of Western thought: French socialism, German philosophy, and British economics. The booklet listed here ends with a bibliography of Marx's works, of Marxist literature, and of anti-Marxist literature, drawn up by Lenin in 1913.

(7) Leon Trotsky, **The Living Thoughts of Karl Marx.** Long-mans, 1939. Trotsky, who was himself hardly less able than Marx, gives here in Marx's words, with necessary comment, the substance of *Capital,* prefaced by a clear introduction to the whole of Marx's thought. Having Trotsky's sturdy hand on a tour of rough Marxist terrain is an opportunity not to be scorned, and this may for many students be the best introduction to Marxist economics. Other sum-maries of Marx's views abound in texts on economics, in histories of social thought, and the like. No doubt the best history of socialism in English is *History of Socialist Thought* by G. D. H. Cole, where the reader will find a very extensive discussion of Marx's views.

Continuation of Marx's work:

(8) V. I. Lenin, **Imperialism, the Highest Stage of Capitalism.** Lenin used the term imperialism to mean not only the extension of political domination by a stronger nation over a colonial people, but also, specifically, to mean "monopoly capitalism," which, Lenin teaches, is the real motivation in the international competition for colonies. This competition leads, Lenin argued, to world war, and he based his analysis of the causes for World War I on his theory of imperialism. This theory, he insists, is no deviation from Marx and Engels, but only the logical extension of their thought, as is the discussion on revolution with which this booklet ends.

MARXIST DIALECTICAL MATERIALISM

Basic Works:

(9) Friedrich Engels, **Anti-Dühring** (1878). Moscow, F.L.P.H., 1959. This is Engels's most systematic exposition of dialectical ma-terialism, and it has become the source book on the subject for later Marxists — though Lenin's own work on materialism (item 15 below) joins it in that category. Once more the reader must sift out the positive structure of the writer's ideas from an orientation to criticism. Here Engels is attacking the system of Eugen Dühring, whose pre-tensions to constructing a system of universal knowledge Engels delights in pricking. Engels subsequently published as a separate work the Intro-duction and Part Three of this book under the title *Socialism: Utopian and Scientific,* which contains the substance of the larger book, and presents in Engels's usually clear and concise style a summation of the "scientific" basis of Marxist philosophy, namely, dialectical materialism, as Marx and Engels understood it.

(10) Friedrich Engels, **Dialectics of Nature** (1925). Moscow, F.L. P.H., 1954. This is a collection of materials which Engels had begun assembling no later than 1873 — some twenty years before his death — with the aim of showing the dialectic at work in the processes of nature. He intended to demonstrate three basic facts: (1) matter is motion, or, motion is the mode of the existence of matter; (2) the separate sciences differ because they investigate matter in different kinds of motion; (3) the sciences, or forms of motion which they investigate, are dialectically — thesis, antithesis, synthesis — related. When Marx died without completing the publication of *Capital,* Engels laid aside his work on this book and spent the rest of his life editing Marx's manuscripts for publication as Volumes II and III of *Capital.* The notes for this book, found in four folders and 181 separate parts, were published for the first time in 1935 in MEGA.

Marxist Historical Materialism

Basic Works:

(11) Engels and Marx, **The Communist Manifesto** (1848). New York, Appleton-Century-Crofts, 1955. (Crofts Classics). This edition of the *Manifesto* — and there are many — includes a good introduction, useful annotations, and selections from Marx's *Eighteenth Brumaire* (item 18, below). While Engels's Preface to the English edition of the *Manifesto* first published in 1888 is given here, the reader might like to use the edition in *Selected Works* (item 26, below) to read Engels's other prefaces — to the German edition, 1872; the Russian, 1882; the German of 1883, and again of 1890 — each of which adds a little light of its own. The *Manifesto* was composed for publicity and as a rallying platform for a specific organization, The Young Communist League of London, for whom it was written. It expresses the basic ideas which Marx and Engels were to give their lives to working out, but this fact is more clearly discernible when you return to the *Manifesto* after studying Marxism more carefully. At first reading, the *Manifesto* probably strikes one as bombastic, passionate, rhetorical, broadly generalized — and so it is; but in it is the essence of Marxism.

(12) Engels and Marx, **The Holy Family, or Critique of Critical Critique** (1845). Moscow, F.L.P.H., 1956. This first joint production constitutes not only Marx and Engels's attack upon the so-called Left Hegelianism with which they had once been associated, but

also their most systematic formulation of historical materialism. Lenin says that parts of the work consist of "incredibly captious criticisms and mockery," and in this the reader will find him correct (Lenin, *Works,* V, 38, p. 46). But if one picks his way carefully, there is discernible a clear path through the intricacies of historical materialism. In addition, Chapter 6 provides a brief history of French materialism which Lenin considered so valuable as to be worth learning in its entirety. There is some humor, too, especially in the description of how the idealist arrives at the "idea" of fruit, and then tries to return to "real pears."

(13) Engels and Marx, **The German Ideology** (written 1845-46; publ. 1932). New York, International, 1960 (1947). Together with *The Holy Family*, this volume presents the most systematic statement the authors made of historical materialism. The exposition given in the first section of this volume (Part II of the original German edition is not here translated) is probably the simplest statement of historical materialism Marx and Engels ever made. The book was written in Brussels when the authors had some leisure and had come to know each other well. Part I is entitled A Criticism of Feuerbach, but it is in fact a statement of the authors' own views on history. Part II, omitted in this edition, consists of a minute critique of Left Hegelianism, varying from *The Holy Family* only in perspective and by inclusion of a minute examination of the work of Marx Stirner, radical Left Hegelian. Part III, which is included in this edition, is a criticism of the movement in Germany called "True Socialism."

(14) Engels and Marx, **On Religion.** Moscow, F.L.P.H., n.d. Marx and Engels themselves wrote no book under this title. This is a compilation, selected from the various works of the authors, all exhibiting the general theme set by Marx's Introduction to his doctoral thesis, in which he quotes the Greek poet Aeschylus: "In short, all gods I hate." This volume opens with that Introduction and ranges far over all the works of the two friends to illustrate the role of "opiate of the people" which historical materialism assigns to the religions of man.

Continuation of Marx and Engels's Work:

(15) V. I. Lenin, **Materialism and Empirio-Criticism** (1908). Moscow, F.L.P.H., n.d. This is the one Marxist work which is generally acknowledged to carry forward the views of Marx and Engels on both dialectical and historical materialism. Lenin read

philosophy with characteristic avidity, and he read it widely; his critics have sneered at his competence in the field, especially at his insistence that the only alternatives in philosophy are idealism or materialism, each pushed to its extreme. The substance of his attack upon Mach and Avenarius, and their Russian adherents, which forms the essence of this book, is their attempt to find a position midway between the extremes. Empirio-Criticism came to expression also as Positivism, and Lenin's criticism is of interest in this connection. The book may in fact lack philosophical acumen — this the reader had best judge for himself — but it breathes the passionate spirit of its author on every page.

(16) V. I. Lenin, **The State and Revolution** (1917). Moscow, F.L.P.H., n.d. The author's subject in this small volume is in the field of historical materialism, and is best summarized by the subtitle of the booklet: "The Marxist Teaching on the State and the Tasks of the Proletariat in the Revolution." Written in hiding, during the progress of the great revolution he came to direct, this is Lenin's justification of the absolute dictatorship of the proletariat during the "transitional period" between capitalism and classless society. Lenin is bent on rationalizing out of the work of Marx and Engels his own conception of "democratic centralism," by which he meant in practice a dictatorship (centralism) exercised in the name of the great majority of the people (democratic). He quotes extensively from the masters, and sharply attacks Karl Kautsky whose views on this matter were more genuine democratic, as we in the West understand the term. His attack on Kautsky's views was more completely spelled out in his pamphlet *The Proletarian Revolution and the Renegade Kautsky*.

PRACTICAL APPLICATION

Basic Works:

(17) Karl Marx, **Class Struggles in France, 1848-1850.** In *Selected Works,* item 26, below. Marx's intentions with, and the considerable theoretical interest of, this small work are best set forth by Engels: "Marx's first attempt to explain a section of contemporary history by means of his materialist conception, on the basis of the given economic situation. . . . to demonstrate the inner causal connection in the course of a development which extended over some years." Originally published as newspaper articles, in the *Neue Rheinische Zeitung,* the booklet aims to extract maxims for the guidance of

future revolutionaries from the failures of those of the French unrest of 1848-50.

(18) Karl Marx, **The Eighteenth Brumaire of Louis Bonaparte.** In *Selected Works,* item 26, below. Marx wrote the articles here compiled for a New York magazine, *Die Revolution,* in 1852, as an analysis of the historical process which brought Louis Napoleon to absolute sway after France's revolutionary struggles of 1848-50. He argues that the *coup d'état* of Napoleon can be understood only as the logical consequence of a class struggle won by the bourgeoisie. Engels in his preface to the third printing of the articles in pamphlet form (1885) argues that Marx demonstrates here again his "discovery" of the "great law of motion of history," namely, that history is "the struggle of social classes," a struggle "conditioned by the degree of development of their economic position, by the mode of production and of exchange determined by it."

(19) Friedrich Engels, **The Condition of the Working Class in England in 1844.** (1845) In *Marx and Engels on Britain.* Moscow, F.L.P.H., 1953. In this edition Engels's book occupies the greater part of the volume cited, which also contains articles and letters by both men on the working class in Britain. This book was Engels's first, and grew out of investigations he made after being sent from his home in Barmen, Germany, to work in his father's mills at Manchester. His description of poverty and exploitation reads grimly still, and it did not in fact find an English publisher until 1892, some forty-seven years after its appearance in Germany. This kind of documentation of their charges against capitalism both Marx and Engels systematically hunted out.

(20) Friedrich Engels, **Germany: Revolution and Counter-Revolution.** New York, International, 1933. As Marx applied himself to a study of the revolution in France, so Engels drew from events in Germany what lessons he found. This volume is a compilation of a series of articles written from Germany by Engels and edited by Marx for the *New York Daily Tribune,* 1851. The articles interpret events in the German revolution in terms of historical materialism. Added are Engels's "History of the Young Communist League," the London organization for whom Marx and Engels composed *The Communist Manifesto,* and two articles on its counterpart in Germany.

(21) Friedrich Engels, **The Origin of the Family, Private Property, and the State.** In *Selected Works*, item 26, below. Engels's intention, in his own words, is to show how "the determining factor in history,

194

the production and reproduction of immediate life," forms the basis of the first social unit, the family; and how, as "productivity of labor develops more and more, the old society based on ties of sex burst asunder . . . and . . . in its place a new society appears, constituted in the state . . . and . . . in which class antagonisms and class struggles now freely develop."

(22) Friedrich Engels, **The Peasant War in Germany** (1850). Moscow, F.L.P.H., 1956. Here Engels compares the peasant wars of the early Reformation with the German Revolution of 1848. He seeks to draw parallels between the early revolts, which Marx called "the most radical fact of German history," with the movement in which he was himself involved in 1848, keeping always before his readers the changes imposed by different historical and economic circumstances. Engels, said Lenin, "laid particular stress on the lessons of experience." Letters and short articles by both Marx and Engels on this same matter are included in this volume.

Continuation of Marx and Engels:

(23) Leon Trotsky, **The History of the Russian Revolution.** 3 volumes. New York, Simon & Schuster, 1932-34. The tremendous upheaval in Russia of 1917 here comes to vivid portrayal by one of the key participants. Trotsky not only writes with a brilliance which seems little dimmed by translation, but he so interfuses theory and interpretation with the stuff of history that Marxism comes here as if to the test. No doubt the perspective on the whole complex of events is colored by the role of the writer, but this is history which grips, moves, and affords a fascinating insight into the mind and deeds of Marxism.

(24) V. I. Lenin, **What Is to Be Done?** (1902). New York, International, 1929. Among the many articles Lenin devoted to practical revolution this occupies first rank. It was composed shortly after the writer returned to Europe from Siberian exile, and is the fruit of long brooding and discussion over the direction and the methods the Russian revolutionist must pursue. Determined and intransigent, Lenin forced the Russian Social Democratic Party to confront the views of this pamphlet, and drove that Party to a split over them in 1903, from which was born the two wings, Bolshevik (majority, Leninist) and Menshevik (minority). On these same issues he drove himself to a break with the old Russian Marxist, Plekhanov, and with Trotsky. The pamphlet, therefore, is worth study. It calls for a revo-

lutionary organization, a newspaper, resistance to compromise, study of Marxism, indomitable will to action.

(25) V. I. Lenin, **Against Revisionism.** Moscow, F.L.P.H., 1959. Lenin himself published no book under this title, but did all his life combat any tendency to soften Marxism in the direction of parliamentary means or association with non-revolutionary groups. Most of the significant articles which he wrote in this vein are here collected, principally those against Bernstein, and later, Kautsky — the theme of all being undeviating resistance to any "revision" of Marxism as Lenin understood Marx, rejection of all "compromise" with capitalism, with democracy, and with existing order generally, except for such tactical reasons as might arise in maneuvers which in the long run benefited the revolution. The powerful invective, intemperate scorn, complete self-confidence, and often brilliant clarity of vision, characteristic of Lenin, are nowhere better revealed.

Selections and Compilations

(26) Marx and Engels, **Selected Works.** 2 volumes. Moscow, F.L.P.H., 1958. This is the best and most comprehensive selection to be had of the major short works of the authors, with annotations and notes, and introductory materials. It is to this edition of some of the shorter works that reference is made above. There are many others.

(27) Max Eastman, ed., **Capital, The Communist Manifesto, and Other Writings by Karl Marx.** New York, Random House (Modern Library). A very useful and easily obtainable compilation of significant works, not including all of *Capital* as the title may suggest, but selections from it. Included also is Lenin's essay on Marxism and a good introduction by Eastman.

(28) Marx and Engels, **Selected Correspondence, 1846-1895.** New York, International, 1942. Various selections of the letters are available, including one of Marx's interesting correspondence with Dr. Kugelmann. MEGA contains more than 1,500 letters exchanged between Marx and Engels (also published in German in six volumes), plus hundreds more written to other correspondents. This edition contains 234 letters, annotated and with added notes and index. Some of the letters have achieved a status of their own, like Engels to J. Bloch, in which he modifies the excessive emphasis sometimes placed on historical determinism, and Marx's letters on Proudhon,

to Annerkov and to Schweitzer. Letters are always glimpses into personal lives and they often illuminate abstruse problems.

(29) **Reminiscences of Marx and Engels,** Moscow, F.L.P.H., n.d. A compilation of short articles by many hands, including members of the Marx family, telling about the daily lives and habits of the founders of Marxism. For a glimpse of "the human side" of a system far from humane in its consequences, there is nothing superior to this.

(30) Biographies. Both Trotsky and Lenin can be gotten at biographically, Trotsky in his autobiography entitled *My Life* (Grosset & Dunlap), and Lenin in several volumes of reminiscences, the best written by his wife Krupskaya (Moscow, F.L.P.H., 1959). The best biography of Trotsky is undoubtedly that of Isaac Deutscher, to be completed in three volumes, two of which have appeared (fall of 1963). David Shub on Lenin is useful. The best biography of Marx is generally thought to be that of Franz Mehring, in German and English, though August Cornu has one on Marx and Engels, of which the third volume has now appeared, in French, which will perhaps take top rank.

THE RUSSIAN PRE-MARXISTS

(31) Vissarion Grigoryevich Belinsky, **Selected Philosophical Works.** Moscow, F.L.P.H., 1956. With Alexander Herzen, whose name appears below, Belinsky was the initiator of the pre-Marxist Russian materialism. Beginning his career in journalism as a literary critic, Belinsky used the medium of literary critique for the dissemination of anti-tsarist ideas. Some typical quotations: "And there will come a time — I fervently believe this — when no one will be burnt, no one will be decapitated, when there will be no senseless forms and rites, no contracts and stipulations on feeling, no debt and obligation, and we will not yield to will, but to love alone. . . . There will be neither rich nor poor, neither kings nor subjects, there will be brethren, there will be men. . . ." "It is absurd to imagine that this could happen by itself, with time, without upheavals, without bloodshed."

(32) Nikolai Gavrilovich Chernyshevsky, **Selected Philosophical Essays.** Moscow, F. L. P. H., 1953. Chernyshevsky was the central figure among the pre-Marxist revolutionary writers who dominated Russian radicalism in the seething 60's of the last century. He took special concern for the plight of the peasantry. His medium, too,

was literary criticism, and his mentors were Herzen and Belinsky. "Oh, gentlemen, gentlemen, you think it is a matter of having a republic in name and of your being in power. But it is not so. It is a matter of freeing the lower class from slavery, not only in law, but in fact . . . so that they may eat, drink, marry, bring up their children, maintain their parents, and receive education." "The sphere of art embraces everything in reality (in nature and in life) that is of interest to man not as a scholar, but as an ordinary man; that which is of common interest — such is the content of art."

(33) Nikolai Alexandrovich Dobrolyubov, **Selected Philosophical Essays.** Moscow, F.L.P.H., 1956. Influenced by Belinsky and Herzen, and follower as well as associate of Chernyshevsky, Dobrolyubov attacked the Russian autocracy through literary criticism and satire. In his brief lifetime of twenty-five years, he advocated materialism in philosophy, democracy in politics, and equality in economics. "Better to suffer shipwreck than to sink in the mire." "My ideal does not yet exist on earth, except, perhaps the democratic society. . . ." "Given a certain degree of development of the people, literature will become one of the motive forces of society."

(34) Alexander Herzen, **Selected Philosophical Works.** Moscow F.L.P.H., 1956. Lenin paid Herzen the tribute of memorializing the centenary of his birth, and said that "he rose to a height that placed him on a level with the greatest thinkers of his time." He is the founder of the Russian socialist school which took the form of Narodnism; and he created what Lenin called the first free Russian journalism, by writing and publishing abroad. From Herzen arose the stream of pre-Marxist Russian revolutionary materialism of which the five names here discussed formed the leaders. His writing is solid but clear. "We live on the borderland of two worlds; hence the contrast and uneasiness which weigh upon thinking peoples. The old convictions and former conceptions are shaken, but still dear to our hearts. The new ideas, great and all-embracing as they may be, have not yet born fruit."

(35) Dmitry Pisarov, **Selected Philosophical, Social, and Political Essays.** Moscow, F.L.P.H. 1958. Most of Pisarov's work was done behind bars because he early advocated revolutionary overthrow of the Tsarist regime, and was apprehended and jailed. Like the Marxists generally, who came after him, Pisarov exhibited uncommon faith in the "masses" and in their ability to conduct their own affairs. The channel for his views was often literary criticism. "We cannot

draw closer to the people through the medium of journals. This can only be achieved by those who live among the people." "Man is a kindly creature by nature." "Abstractions can provide interest and be understood only by the abnormally developed and insignificant minority."

EARLY RUSSIAN MARXISM

(36) Georgy Valentinovich Plekhanov, **The Development of the Monist View of History** (1895). Moscow, F.L.P.H., 1956. This is a highly readable exposition of the general philosophy of Marxism, with clear-cut emphasis on dialectical and historical materialism woven into a survey of French materialism, French historians, Utopian Socialism, and German idealism. This book, said Lenin, "helped to educate a whole generation of Russian Marxists" — including, he might have added, himself. It is still a very understandable introduction to Marxism.

(37) Georgy Valentinovich Plekhanov, **Selected Philosophical Works.** 5 volumes. Moscow, F.L.P.H., n.d. Because Plekhanov was not only the first important Russian Marxist, but also the founder of the Bolshevik Party in its early form, he is the bridge from Marx and Engels on the one hand, and from Herzen, Belinsky and the others listed above on the other, to the modern Bolshevik Party which took power in Russia in 1917 — not the less so despite the break between him and Lenin in 1903 (Lenin tells the story in "How the Spark [*Iskra*] was Nearly Extinguished" — Vol. IV, *Collected Works*), which continued into the Revolution of 1917. Plekhanov writes clearly, with enthusiasm, and on a wide range of subjects.

CHINESE COMMUNISM

(38) Mao Tse Tung, **An Anthology of His Writings.** New York, New American Library, 1962 (International, 1954). This selection, edited with an introduction by Anne Freemantle, offers an insight into the theorist and guiding genius of the Chinese Revolution. Various separate works of Mao, *On Contradiction, On Art,* and the like; selected works in four volumes; and a continuing complete edition of his works can be had in English; but for the student this selection may be enough to catch the shades of emphasis which the Chinese have introduced into Marxism.

SECTION III

Anti-Marxist Classics

Anti - Marxist Classics

ARE THERE ANTI-MARXIST *classics*? YES . . . AND NO.

No in the sense that "anti" books of any variety rarely, if ever, attain the status of classics. A classic is a book which has molded history by taking positive possession of the minds of men; it has blazed new paths in intellectual wildernesses or illumined hidden recesses of the soul. "Anti" books do not accomplish these things, perhaps for no other reason than that they are not intended to. The books written to confute Marx, however important and useful such books are, do not rank with the classics.

Yes, however, in the sense that those affirmations of other, opposite views, which also contest the teachings of Marx, may well be classics. As I have suggested in the Introduction, the *Declaration of Independence* wrestles, in fact, with the *Communist Manifesto,* though neither mentions the other. The student does well, then, to find his anti-Marxist *classics* among the other great works in the same fields which Marx and Engels explored, whether or not these other works came before or after Marx in time, and whether or not they mention him or his doctrines by name.

Listed below are both deliberately anti-Marxist works, and classics which hold title to respect in their own strength quite independently of Marxism. I have called them all "classics" for convenience' sake, but the reader will remember that true classics are rare. Only one of Marx's works commonly appears on lists of the "One Hundred Great Books" and that is *Capital.* Similarly, only two of the following titles are generally acclaimed among the "One Hundred" and they are Adam Smith's *Wealth of Nations,* and *The Federalist.* This means that while there is general agreement on the importance to history of *Capital* and of the *Wealth of Nations,* say, there is no such consensus regarding the worth of many of the other entries I have made. You might wish, in fact, to compose your own list of "classics" on both sides, but the following books seem highly significant to me in the critique of Marxism, just as the titles in the foregoing list have been instrumental in apprehending it.

ANTI-MARXIST MARXISTS

Like all active movements, Marxism has been full of intra-family quarrels and fallings-out. Assuming that the best criticism can be made on the basis of the best comprehension, we can be instructed by what Marxists criticize in each other. The bad boy of Marxism, who probably aroused more violent antipathy than any other internal critic, was Eduard Bernstein, acquaintance of Marx, friend of Engels, and originator of the reformist trend called Revisionism. He thought Marx guilty of gross mistakes, and made little bones of it both in periodical articles and in the following book:

(1) Eduard Bernstein, **Evolutionary Socialism** (1899). New York, Schocken Books, 1961. "The further development and elaboration of Marxist doctrine," Bernstein wrote, "must begin with a criticism of it" (p. 25). And criticize he did. Marx was wrong in believing that the class struggle would grow more acute; it has not. He was wrong, too, in supposing that capitalist society would divide neatly into two major classes; it has not. He was wrong, too, in supposing that excessive concentration of productive industry in a few hands would rapidly occur; it has not. On the contrary, Bernstein writes, capitalism by and large is becoming more amenable to social pressures and legislative control. If socialism is to be attained, it must be by way of democratic, "evolutionary" means, not by violent revolution. Moreover, Marx conceived of labor value too narrowly, and used the concept too rigidly in his explanation of exploitation. Bernstein employs pages of statistics to demonstrate the inapplicability of Marx's "law of the increasing misery of the proletariat" in his theory of economic crises. All this he does in the name of Marx, saying, "It is Marx finally who carries the point against Marx" (p. 27). Bernstein favors co-operatives, the development of trade unions, and the interpretation of Marx's *Capital* that it is not a blueprint for Communism, but a massive rationalization of views which Marx harbored long before the book was written. The violent reaction from Lenin and the Bolsheviks to Bernstein's work is some measure of how deeply it struck home. (See Lenin's collected in *Against Revisionism,* item 25 in the previous list). For an interesting discussion, see Peter Gay, *The Di-*

lemma of Democratic Socialism; Eduard Bernstein's Challenge to Marx (Collier Books).

(2) Karl Kautsky, **Bolshevism at a Deadlock.** London, Allen & Unwin, 1931. If Bernstein was close to Marx and Engels, Kautsky was far closer. Though Marx thought little of him, judging from references in his letters, Engels accepted Kautsky as collaborator in editing the manuscripts left by Marx at his death for Volumes II and III of *Capital,* and Kautsky alone edited Volume IV after Engels's death. Moreover, Kautsky was one of those who attacked Bernstein and Revisionism, and it was not until Marxism in theory had become Russian Communism in revolution and practice that Kautsky became its open critic.

This book is not his first attack. There had been an exchange in 1918 between Kautsky and Lenin on *The Dictatorship of the Proletariat,* the title of a pamphlet in which Kautsky warned of the dangers of dictatorship, not *of* but *against* the proletariat, to which Lenin contemptuously replied. In 1919, Kautsky responded with a book, *Terrorism and Communism.* Trotsky answered with a pamphlet under the same title — Kautsky warning against, and Trotsky justifying, terrorism in the revolutionary period. To this Kautsky responded with another pamphlet in 1921, *From Democracy to State-Slavery,* an analysis of Bolshevism in action which Trotsky was later (see next item) to echo.

In *Bolshevism at a Deadlock* Kautsky analyzes the economic failures of the Soviet regime, and ventures the prediction of its imminent collapse. He was a better analyst than prophet. Kautsky's argument runs thus: Marx and Engels had insisted that a fully developed industrial base was indispensable to the achievement of Communism. So had Lenin, Kautsky says, until the "unexpected happened." In 1917, "at one stroke, unforeseen circumstances delivered the complete control of the State into the hands of Lenin. . . . This dazzling turn of fortune went to his head and made him reverse his former theoretical convictions. He suddenly became of the opinion that the extremely small, backward stratum of the industrial workers of Russia was capable of plunging at once into Socialism and organising a Socialist State" p. 17) . This error was paid for by the proletariat, for the Bolsheviks were obliged to make the dictatorship a weapon of tyranny, not only against the old regime but against the proletariat itself. The Five Year Plans were forced upon industry, and collectivization was bloodily imposed upon kulak and peasant in a frantic effort to provide the missing economic base upon which alone Socialism could be achieved. A steadily growing, parasitic bureaucracy had to be created to enforce the Plans, resting upon naked force and brutal terror.

The only hope Kautsky saw was the true "democratisation of the Soviets," leading to free elections. In lieu of this, Kautsky supposes that a revolt against Stalin is inevitable, and he speculates upon its probable course and success. The book is an attack upon Marxism in action, written from the inside by one of the old hands who hoped still that the dreams of a true proletarian state might be realized by democratic means.

(3) Leon Trotsky, **The Revolution Betrayed; What is the Soviet Union? Where is it going?** New York, Pioneer Publishers, 1945 (1937). With Lenin, one of the two ablest Marxists of this century, Trotsky could turn not only intimate and firsthand knowledge against Stalinism, but also a rapier wit and mordant pen. This book is a sharp attack upon the direction which Bolshevism took under the leadership of Stalin. It is all the more useful a critique of Marxism itself if one takes what I think is the logical position that Stalinism is the inevitable outcome of any dictatorship of the proletariat.

"If you remember that the task of socialism," Trotsky says, "is to create a classless society based upon solidarity and the harmonious satisfaction of all needs, there is not yet, in this fundamental sense, a hint of socialism in the Soviet Union" (p. 3). Despite massive strides in industrialization, the Soviet is still far behind its capitalist competitors, and the State, far from withering away, "has grown into a hitherto unheard of apparatus of compulsion" (p. 51), creating a new and affluent bureaucracy intent only upon a self-perpetuation for which it is willing to employ the tyrannies of Stalinism. All this is, says Trotsky, quite the opposite of Lenin's envisioned "democratic centralism." Economic inequalities, social antagonisms, and political favoritism flourish; the roles of women and children and the family are reduced once more to pre-revolutionary reaction; state capitalism has been substituted for true socialism; the dictatorship flaunts the "freedoms" guaranteed by the Constitution; and no degree or amount of praise of the progress of the Soviet Union by its professional lackeys and "friends" like Sidney and Beatrice Webb (whom Trotsky singles out for special depreciation) can obscure its essential betrayal of the ideals for which, Trotsky says, Lenin fought. Probably no more stinging indictment of Stalinism has appeared; and, again, if one takes

Stalinism to be a logical development of Marxism, this is a critique worthy of study.

(4) Leon Trotsky, **Stalin's Frame-Up System and the Moscow Trials.** New York, Pioneer Publishers, 1939. During the infamous Treason Trials staged in Moscow, 1936-38, prosecutor Andrei Vyshinsky repeatedly accused the victims of having been misled by Trotsky and/or his son Leon Sedov. Though both were in forced exile, Trotsky and Sedov were charged with treasonable acts against the Soviet Union. Trotsky, who at the opening of the first Trial was in Finland, from which he was expelled by the power of the Soviet Union and obliged to seek refuge in Mexico, responded with a pamphlet, *I Stake My Life.* This pamphlet was an address, prepared for delivery from Mexico via radio-telephone connection to a New York rally in Trotsky's support on February 9, 1937. Trotsky challenged Stalin to place him on public trial in Moscow, and offered to place himself in the hands of the G. P.U. (Soviet secret police) if any of the charges made against him in the Moscow Trials were found to be true by an impartial commission. Such a commission was formed, chairmanned by the American philosopher, John Dewey, with nine other members, and legal counsel. It began hearings on April 10, 1937, and rendered its verdict on September 7, finding both Trotsky and Sedov "not guilty of the charges made against them in the Mass Trials of August 1936 and January 1937."

The Commission published its proceedings under the title *The Case of Leon Trotsky,* and its conclusions under the title *Not Guilty,* both by Harper, 1937. The booklet under review here consists of Trotsky's closing address to the Dewey Commission, plus excerpts from the Proceedings. It is not only a defense of "Trotskyism," but also a scathing indictment of Stalin's terrorism and tyranny. The booklet includes the Commission's findings in brief summary, and brief biographical sketches of the Commissioners and of the chief defendants in the first two Treason Trials.

*   *   *   *

It must be remembered, of course, that Bernstein, Kautsky, and Trotsky were what I have called Anti-Marxist *Marxists.* All pledged inviolable allegiance to Marx; all quote copiously from him; all wrap his mantle about their shoulders. They attack, therefore, what they consider to be aberrations from true Marxism, and they preach what they hold to be genuine Marxism with the fervor of the missionary. But, read in this context, it will be seen that they not only call into question a wide range of doctrines traditionally associated with Marx, but together mount as powerful a critique of the tyranny of the "dictatorship" as the reader is likely to find. It may also be observed in passing that a careful reading of, say, Lenin's polemics — and he was almost always in heavy controversy — affords one some insight into the criticisms of Bolshevism from the beginning, for one can infer the doctrines which Lenin attacks from what he says against them. Read thus, even the ablest Marxist of our time witnesses against Marxism at precisely those points he considers most significant, though (and in this Trotsky was the more honest) Lenin did not always put the best construction upon the views he had under fire. Nevertheless, the whole range of intra-party controversy is instructive toward a critique of Communism.

CRITIQUE OF MARXIST ECONOMICS

There is really no end of treatises on economics, and the minute examination of all the perspectives raised by Marx is no doubt the work of a lifetime. The following books, however, either attack Marxist economics directly or espouse theories directly at variance with salient features of Marxist doctrine.

(5) Adam Smith, **The Wealth of Nations** (1776). The full title of this book, which the English historian Buckle is supposed to have called "the most important book ever written," is *An Inquiry into the Nature and Causes of the Wealth of Nations*. Smith believed that mankind was on the verge of universal prosperity, with productive forces coming into being which could provide a steadily rising standard of living for all men. His book is an examination of the ways in which such a millennium could be brought about. It became the classic statement of the so-called *laissez faire* (or Manchester) school of economic philosophy, namely, the position that an absolutely free market system abounds to the most efficient production and fairest distribution of goods.

Smith came to economic theory by way of moral philosophy — he was Professor of Moral Philosophy at Glasgow University, and published his first book on the *Theory of the Moral Sentiments*. He held the view that man is essentially perfectible, and that his natural instincts lead in that direction. Therefore he maintained in the *Wealth of Nations* that each man's pursuit of his own "enlightened self-interest" without interference by government or any other coercive power would in the long run make for the greatest good of the whole. An "invisible hand" so harmonizes the apparently conflicting and competitive self-interests, that the result of universal "selfishness" is universal benefit, for as each serves himself he is instrumental to the production of the most goods, by the most efficient means — one of which is the increasing division of labor. Moreover, Smith held, as more and better goods are produced, expanding markets for them must arise as the needs and wants of the producers grow apace. The free market is the key, in Smith's eyes, to the most production and the widest distribution of the best products. His views have been, therefore, the staple fare of all "non-interventionist" economists since the publication of the *Wealth of Nations*.

If, as Mortimer Adler says, the reader fully grasps the teaching of this book, and that of Marx's *Capital,* "he would be well on the way toward seeing the relation between two of the most influential books in modern times" (*How to Read a Book,* p. 169). Smith ranges over both national and international economic policies in developing his thesis, and the book explores a wide range of related subjects and interests. Like *Capital,* it is ponderous, and, sometimes, arid. It is, however, one of the refutations of Marx, though written long before Marx produced his major work. Marx was, of course, thoroughly acquainted with it, and drew from Smith support for his theory of labor value.

(6) David Ricardo, **Principles of Economics** (1823). Next to Adam Smith, Ricardo was probably the most influential British political economist, one to whom Marx accorded the accolade of "honest man." Ricardo was a stockbroker by profession, engaged, unlike Smith, in the hurly-burly of the competitive system which Smith adored. Perhaps for this reason Ricardo tended to take a less optimistic view of universal competition than did Smith. He saw that not all were winners.

Influenced by the studies of Thomas Malthus, published in his *Essay on the Principle of Population* (1798), to the effect that a population always tends to outgrow its food supply, Ricardo held that the free-trade system advocated by Smith was indeed the best market system, although not everyone was blessed by it. In the competitive struggle there was no "invisible hand" which protected all from pauperism: on the contrary, the propensity of the laboring classes to produce more offspring than the labor market could absorb or support always forced some to the edge — and over the edge — of want.

Lassalle, the German socialist, formulated Ricardo's position into the slogan, "The Iron Law of Wages" and employed it against the free market system. Ricardo's analysis furnished Marx with support for both his theories of labor, and of surplus, value; but it ranks as one of the fundamental expositions of the *laissez faire* position and is generally regarded as a classic of its kind. The reader may wish to peruse Malthus's *Essay* in connection with his study of Ricardo, for the belief — which Marx vigorously denied, incidentally — that a population does in fact naturally outgrow its food supply was unquestionably a factor in Ricardo's development of his own views; and the idea of a "population explosion" is once more in the news.

(7) Ludwig Von Mises, **Human Action; A Treatise on Economics.** New Haven, Yale University Press, 1949. I choose Professor Von Mises as representative of the "non-interventionist" economists who today defend the free market against government intervention and other forms of "interference." The reader may prefer the work of Friedrich A. Hayek (*The Road to Serfdom*), or that of any number of critics of the "welfare state," but no doubt Von Mises is both typical and scholarly.

Von Mises casts his defense of the free market system into a study of Praxeology, "the general theory of human action" (p. 3). "The goal of an action," Von Mises holds, "is to remove a certain uneasiness" (p. 15), or "the satisfaction of some desires" (p. 18). Economics deals with the "order of preference and sequence" in human desires, and the values which satisfy them. The satisfaction of desire, in the economic realm, proceeds best in the free market. The author is therefore highly critical of any "planning" imposed on the market system by government or other external factor. Unemployment need not occur, he holds, in the truly free market; and when it does occur, it is always the result of a refusal to accept, not an inability to find, employment: "unemployment in the unhampered market is always voluntary" (p. 596). Praxeology concerns itself with the production of satisfactions, not with their distribution; and therefore poor relief, just return, and the like, are outside its scope (p. 600).

Von Mises concludes that "what makes the existence and the evolution of society possible is precisely the fact that peaceful cooperation under the social division of labor in the long run best serves the selfish concerns of all individuals" (pp. 841-2), and that "interventionism has exhausted all its potentialities and must disappear" (p. 851). The author's argument is learned and involved, and the treatise is massive. A shorter exposition of the same position may be found in Von Mises's *The Anti-Capitalistic Mentality* (Van Nostrand, 1956). Both are rugged vindications of rugged individualism, which Professor Von Mises prefers to call everyone's "freedom of choice."

(8) Guido De Ruggiero, **The History of European Liberalism.** Boston, Beacon Press, 1959. This and the next entry offer succinct and brilliant historical sketches of the philosophy underlying modern democratic liberties as Americans understand them. Professor De Ruggiero's work is a translation from the Italian. He understands Liberalism as that philosophy which begins with the recognition of human freedom, a philosophy opposed, therefore, from the outset to Marxist materialist determinism. The book scans the doctrines of this philosophy of human liberty as they have been developed in the past two centuries in England, France, Germany, and Italy; and the author counters the challenges to freedom by both right and left totalitarianisms. Within the matrix of freedom, *laissez faire* economics are not the only alternative, the author finds, but Marxism is rejected.

(9) Elie Halevy, **The Growth of Philosophic Radicalism.** Boston, Beacon Press, 1955. Dealing more specifically with economics than does De Ruggiero, Halevy surveys the views of the *laissez faire* economists, dealing particularly with Bentham, Smith, Burke, Godwin, Ricardo, and Mill. From the influential work of Bentham on the calculus of pleasure and pain as it governs human conduct to the sophisticated logical work of the Mills (father and son), Halevy develops the fundamental principles of the free economy as its most distinguished expositors understand them. A fine survey for the student.

CRITIQUE OF HISTORICAL AND DIALECTICAL MATERIALISM

It would be convenient if there were some succinct criticism of Marxist materialism and its Hegelian dialectical roots. There may well be, but it is unknown to me. Let us begin with Hegel. He was under attack during his lifetime by his contemporaries. Nietzsche was critical, and realist philosophy in general attacked him. Kierkegaard mounted existentialist weapons against him, and the reader may find F. H. Heinemann's *Existentialism and the Modern Predicament* as useful as any volume in setting this critique in perspective (Harper Torchbook, 1958). For the criticism of certain aspects of Marxist philosophy, the following may be useful.

(10) Isaiah Berlin, **Historical Inevitability.** London, Oxford University Press, 1954. In this relatively brief lecture, Professor Berlin (himself the author of a competent biography of Marx) attacks the view that "nations or cultures or civilizations . . . are more 'real' and

more 'concrete' than the individuals who compose them," a view he attributes to Fichte, Hegel, Spengler, and "somewhat hesitantly" to Arnold Toynbee (p. 8). This view, Berlin says, comes to take on the form of an "objective march of history" which denies absolutes and objective standards, equates historical understanding with the perception of patterns in events, and reduces the individual to the victim or illustration of the trend. The patterns may be thought to reflect a transcendental, permanent, unchanging reality above or beyond history, or they may be conceived simply as the results of scientific investigation. In either case, "the individual's freedom of choice (at any rate here, below) is ultimately an illusion" (p. 20). For Marx, as for Hegel, freedom meant only recognition of, and identification with, the pattern, or direction, of history. This conception, Berlin insists, in fact destroys personal responsibility, negates morality, and makes man the victim of his times; while at the same time neither Marx nor Hegel nor anybody else really lives as if "you ought" were meaningless, or blame were ineffective. Though, he continues, those who, like Tolstoy, flee determinism into blind mystery, holding that man is so encompassed with the inexplicable that judgment is impossible, really leave him no more scope of freedom than do the necessitarians.

Man as we know him, Berlin concludes, neither lives nor ought to live as if blind materialist (say, Marxist) necessity controlled his will. Let him rather assume full responsibility for his own doing, and not-doing; and let each expect the same of everyone else; for in the words of Justice Brandeis, "The irresistible is often only that which is not resisted." Marxism, therefore, is by no means guaranteed by an inexorable history, as the Communist believes; and the call to heroic opposition is not without hope of success.

(11) Albert Camus, **The Rebel**. Vintage Books, 1956. "One might think," Camus begins, "that a period which, in a space of fifty years, uproots, enslaves, or kills seventy million human beings should be condemned out of hand. But its culpability must still be understood" (p. 3). To understand why murder has become legalized and "innocence called upon to justify itself" is the problem which this brilliant French novelist set himself. Murder as a weapon of policy is the ultimate climax of rebellion; and rebellion began in man's determination to secure justice among men by his own efforts. "Only two possible worlds can exist for the human mind," Camus argues, "the sacred (or, to speak in Christian terms, the world of grace) and the world of rebellion" (p. 21). Modern man chose the way of rebellion,

declaring openly the death of God; and came in due course to Auschwitz, Belsen, Siberia.

The roots of modern rebellion do not go too far back. It began with what Camus calls "Metaphysical Rebellion." He finds it in the Marquis de Sade, who demands freedom, but "not of principles, but of instincts" (p. 38). The Russian Dostoyevsky understood the principle of rebellion, and in his novel *The Brothers Karamazov* he has Ivan delineate "the essential undertaking of rebellion, which is that of replacing the reign of grace by the reign of justice" (p. 56), an undertaking which leads inevitably to the "law of murder" (p. 58). For, Camus says, "from the moment that man submits God to moral judgment — and this is what the rebel does — he kills Him in his own heart. . . . God is denied in the name of justice, but can the idea of justice be understood without the idea of God?" (p. 62).

His answer to this crucial question is No — as history, he says, demonstrates. Justice has become in practice the will of the strong, wherever rebellion has usurped power. When Nietzsche's Zarathustra proclaimed that "God is dead," he added the inescapable consequence, "All is allowed!" And with this assertion, "contemporary nihilism really begins" (p. 57). But it must not be forgotten that "Nietzsche did not form a project to kill God. He found Him dead in the souls of his contemporaries" (p. 68). Now followed Max Stirner, who professed "the most acute manifestation of nihilism's conscience," and the poet Lautreamont, "who makes us understand that rebellion is adolescent," even as he extols it (pp. 77, 82). Rimbaud, with his *Season in Hell*, "gives the most peculiarly appropriate expression to rebellion that it has ever received," epitomizing that surrealism generally which is "absolute rebellion, total insubordination, sabotage on principle, the humor and the cult of the absurd" (p. 91).

Metaphysical rebellion has its consequence in "Historical Rebellion." Camus finds such rebellion in the French Revolution. He finds it in the work of Hegel, too, whose "undeniable originality lies in his definitive destruction of all vertical transcendence — particularly the transcendence of principles." Hegel "sought to destroy, more and more thoroughly, all idea of transcendence and any nostalgia for transcendence" (p. 136). Following Hegel is Marx, whose "originality lies in affirming that history is simultaneously dialectic and economic." But Marx's hope of a classless and perfect society, though in fact the only possible justification for the sacrifices Communism demands and imposes, makes of history only a "desperate dream," unrelated to reality. From Hegel, too, follows Russian nihilism, Fascism, and Nazism.

What is modern history, Camus concludes, but "a prolonged endeavor to give order, by human forces and simply by force, to a history no longer endowed with order" (p. 221). Having shorn history of meaning, having cut it adrift from superior authority, man has made of it a monster which devours its own offspring. Rebellion, in Marx, in Hegel, and in all the others, begins with the determination to establish human justice by human hands; it ends by sacramentalizing terror, tyranny, and death to the gods of negation and nothingness. What is the answer? "Grace," is Camus' answer. Sins are to be forgiven, not expunged; God is to be judge, not his creature. "Restraint" is imposed upon man by the command of his Maker. Not quietism, not rebellion, but obedience, discipline, faith — this is the way of grace, and the only alternative to rebellion.

This book merits careful perusal and intense study, as a profound analysis of Marxism at its point of fundamental dynamic and weakness.

THE AMERICAN ALTERNATIVE

How shall one catch the essential spirit of America, and oppose that to Communism in theory and in practice? I have already suggested that the best way is to meditate on, and to apply in practice, the immortal affirmations of the *Declaration of Independence* (see Introduction). Of histories of the United States each reader may have his own choice, be it the Beards' *Rise of American Civilization* or another; of analyses of American institutions, he may prefer Lord Bryce's *American Commonwealth* or De Tocqueville's *Democracy in America* (adapted in one volume as *American Institutions*, 1855), or others. Besides these, the following titles have been useful to me.

(12) **The Federalist Papers** (1787-88). Written by Alexander Hamilton, James Madison, and John Jay, and first published as a series of letters "to the people" over the pseudonym of *Publius* in the New York press, the *Federalist Papers* (often simply *The Federalist*) as they came to be known, were produced to persuade the citizens of America that a federal union was the best form of government for them. Collected into two small volumes in 1788, and republished countless times since, the *Papers* remain the most important discussion of federalism ever written, and hold first rank among discussions of representative government. They have been called (by Brander Matthews) "the

ablest political essays in the English language . . . a perpetual store-house of political wisdom." To catch and to keep the spirit of American institutions, no better source than this can be found. Steeped in the spirit of *The Federalist,* an American is more than a match for the Marxist; and never was the spirit of these American writers more critically to be desired than today, and not in America only — though no less urgently, surely, at home than abroad. A glance at the table of contents will indicate the subjects discussed: the relations between the states safeguarded by union; foreign affairs buttressed by union; taxation and revenue rationalized; the common defense enhanced; the powers of the Union defined and explained; the checks and balances doctrine; the congress and the executive and the judiciary defined. The handbook of democracy, this; no better source of Americanism.

(13) Henry Steel Commager, **The American Mind.** New Haven, Yale University Press, 1950. This arresting volume is subtitled *An Interpretation of American Thought and Character Since the 1880's.* The author holds that "there is a distinctively American way of thought, character, and conduct. I have tried," he says, "to discover and to interpret this American way in some of its most revealing manifestations" (p. vii). The book ranges over American literature, American pragmatism, religious thought and practice, American sociology and economics, politics, law, and architecture. The style is lively — perhaps too uninterruptedly lively sometimes — and the insights are deep, suggestive, and often rounded into delightful turns of phrase. There are no dull moments in Professor Commager's book, and the reader comes away with a deepened appreciation of his heritage, and an enriched re-dedication to its principles.

(14) Vernon L. Parrington, **Main Currents in American Thought.** New York, Harcourt, Brace, 1927-30. Subtitled *An Interpretation of American Literature from the Beginnings to 1920,* Professor Parrington's work is obviously of wider range, though narrower scope, than that of Commager — though the author interprets "literature" in a very broad sense, and includes in his purview writing in the professions as well as *belles-lettres.* The book first appeared in three volumes, each with a separate and indicative title: I. *The Colonial Mind.* II. *The Romantic Revolution in America, 1800-1860.* III. *The Beginnings of Critical Realism in America, 1860-1920.* He is attempting, Professor Parrington says, "to give some account of the genesis and development in American letters of certain germinal ideas that have come

to be reckoned traditionally American" (p. iii). In Volume I, the ideas are those of the Liberal doctrine of natural rights, blended with the conservative Puritan theology. In Volume II, the ideas are those of French romanticism and revolution; and in Volume III, the ideas are those arising out of the critique of American middle-class democracy. The author frankly admits to tastes and preferences of his own, largely those of the Liberal mind, and the reader will expect to see these emerge in this stout volume. Parrington's style is not light, his learning is extensive, and the book must be studied; but it is commonly accepted as one of the best of its kind.

For easier reading one might prefer Ralph H. Gabriels's *Course of American Democratic Thought,* another fine study of the American mind. Studies in our own heritage are, happily, increasing. Professor Perry Miller has explored the Puritan background in his *New England Mind* (available in a two-volume Beacon Press paperback), and the papers of Jefferson, John Adams, and Franklin are all being re-edited and re-published. Perhaps, too, the student will wish to push his own reading back into the sources of American political thought — for example, Locke's *Second Treatise on Civil Government,* Rousseau's *Social Contract,* Hooker's *Ecclesiastical Polity.* There is no dearth of materials for the American who becomes seriously interested in what it means to be himself.

THE CHRISTIAN CRITIQUE

Marxism not only has its own doctrines of man and social salvation, but it expressly rejects Christian interpretations. It has, in turn, been subjected to searching Christian analysis. Following are some titles written from this perspective, and statements of the social philosophy of the main branches of Christendom.

(15) Jacques Maritain, **True Humanism.** London, Bles, 1938. "Let us say that humanism . . . essentially tends to render man more truly human and to make his original greatness manifest by causing him to participate in all that can enrich him in nature and in history" (p. xii). Professor Maritain distinguishes two kinds of humanism: (1) that which "recognizes that the center for man is God," and (2) that which "believes that man is his own center" (p. 19). Illustrative of the first is the Christian humanism which Professor Maritain finds best taught by Thomas Aquinas; illustrative of the second is Marxist humanism, "a religion of atheism . . . which

arose chiefly through the fault of a Christian world unfaithful to its own principles" in the face of a dominant materialism.

Marxism forgets that the root of evil is *in* man, and that therefore no rearrangement of the socio-economic structure can escape the infection of evil. Marx's criticism of the faults of capitalism and the threat of industrialism to personality are often well taken, Professor Maritain holds; but Marx's alternative has become, in practice, far starker a brutality than the one he condemned. Marxism is not the way out of the labyrinth of modern problems; rather, the true hope of mankind lies in a reappreciation of "the humanism of the Incarnation," that is, the due respect of man *"in* his connection with God and *because* he is totally dependent upon Him," a humanism whose type and ideal is heroic sainthood (p. 65). It was, indeed, Marx's ardent desire "to find a way out of that despair and decomposition of human personality in which anthropocentric humanism ends" (p. 73). It was this desire that motivated his essentially noble aspirations; but his answers fell tragically short of eliciting the deepest, the highest, and the richest potential of man. These can be developed only in communion with God and loving service of one's fellow man.

Such a Christian humanism, however, is duly admonished by Marxism that "it is vain to assert the dignity and vocation of human personality if we do not strive to transform the conditions that oppress these; strive to deal so that men can live worthily and gain their bread in honor" (p. 87). A Christian humanism implies, that is, a Christian social philosophy cognizant of the Marxist indictment of evils of uncontrolled greed. From the Christian perspective, the temporal cultural order finds its ends in the promotion of the spiritual ends of man. But this temporal order is "the kingdom at once of man, of God, and of the devil," a situation which makes it "the task of the Christian in this world to dispute his domain with the devil and wrench it from him" (p. 101), knowing the while that he does so in the strength of God.

Maritain then proceeds to a detailed discussion of the role of the Christian in contemporary history, a role destined to bring in, so far as he is able, "Christendom," which is "a *temporal* regime whose formation, in very varying degrees and in very varying ways, bears the stamp of the Christian conception of life" (p. 126). This temporal regime would be pluralist in character rather than wholly and indubitably Christian, but "man would represent the standard of the terms of reference of all the things of this world" (p. 185).

This is the challenge of "true humanism," and challenge it is, for "in terms of an effective realization or refraction of the Gospel in the socio-temporal sphere, we are still truly in a pre-historic age!" (p. 237). Maritain's contrast of Marxist humanism with Christian humanism is full of suggestive insights and profound alternatives, based upon an uncommon appreciation of what Marx was attempting to accomplish and of what St. Thomas has to say to the modern world.

(16) Ernst Troeltsch, **The Social Teaching of the Christian Churches and Sects.** London, Macmillan. This massive work is a systematic examination and exposition of the doctrines of the Christian Church in its Catholic and Protestant manifestations, as well as of the major Christian sects, concerning the socio-economic problems involving the state, the family, business and industry.

Troeltsch begins with the social ethic of Jesus, which is that men are called to love one another in all walks of life; and living thus out of love, they share in the coming of the Kingdom of God. On the one hand, Troeltsch says, this is pure individualism, because *each* is called as an individual to *personal* sanctity; on the other hand, Jesus' ethic is truly communal because love itself is reciprocal and can be realized only in community. The Kingdom is not *of* this world, but is *in* it, and consists essentially in subjecting worldly institutions to the dominion of Christian principles. Asceticism is not Christ's ideal; it is essentially an evasion of the Christian task of winning the world for the King. How the Catholic Church developed its massive "medieval synthesis"; how Luther and Calvin elaborated the doctrines of the "calling" and of "stewardship"; how the Anabaptists and the Mystics conceived of the Kingdom as already achieved in reality, or by faith glimpsed in the heart: all this constitutes the body of this learned work.

Throughout history, Troeltsch finds three motifs at work in Christian solutions of "the social problem": (1) that which is associated with Catholicism, the Church-dominated society in which all other institutions and all individuals are subordinate to the magisterial authority of the Church; (2) the radical individualism of the Sectarians, who conceive of the Christian as an atom of holiness amidst the Babylon of a world dominated by the Devil; and (3) the tradition associated with Protestantism, in which the Christian task is understood to be the infiltration of all existing institutions with an eye to transforming these into citadels of the Kingdom by means of loving service within them. Troeltsch's masterful summation of the history of Christian social thought can well be an anti-Marxist arsenal, and a thorough, historical exposition of the Christian approach to many of the problems on which Marx expressed his own views.

(17) **The Papal Encyclicals.** Catholic social philosophy, which is addressed to the same issues that concerned Marx, comes to official expression in Papal Encyclicals. On socio-economic questions, three are rightly famous:

(A) **Rerum Novarum,** Pope Leo XIII (1878-1903). Keenly aware of what one of his successors (Pius XI) was to call the "great scandal of the nineteenth century, that the Church lost the working class," Pope Leo XIII issued in 1891 his Encyclical on "The Condition of the Working Class," commonly called *Rerum Novarum* from, as is customary, its opening words.

"All agree," Leo says, "and there can be no question whatever, that some remedy must be found, and quickly found, for the misery and wretchedness which press so heavily at this moment on the large majority of the poor." The remedy, he goes on, is not Socialism (Communism), because the right to private property, which Socialism destroys, must be maintained as in accord with natural reason, natural law, and for the preservation of the Family. Human inequality cannot be wholly ignored or overcome, but co-operation between persons and among classes is both possible and essential, on a basis of mutual respect for the common dignity of man. Neither riches nor poverty is of eternal consequence in itself; but the right use of wealth and the chastened endurance of poverty point to eternal weal, while the abuse of wealth or disdain of poverty point to eternal woe. "Man should not," the Pope quotes approvingly from Thomas Aquinas, "consider his outward possessions as his own, but as common to all, so as to spare them without difficulty when others are in need." Labor is commended by God; poverty is no disgrace; but the state is enjoined by God through the Church to obtain economic justice for labor, and to watch that "the poorer population" may themselves "share in the benefits they create — that being housed, clothed, and enabled to support life, they may find their existence less hard and more endurable."

All conditions of life and of employment which endanger morals or the practice of religion are to be controlled by the state, which is ordained by God to administer the "common good" and to preserve "the community" by positive aid to the weak and by restraint of the greedy, the lawless, the revolutionary. The Pope demands reasonable hours of labor, restraint upon the kind and quantity of work exacted from women and children, "just wages" based upon the working man's "right to procure what is required in order to live." He stresses again the need of all men to possess private property, and recommends the development of workmen's "associations" for mutual aid, strength, and progress.

(B) **Quadragesimo Anno,** Pius XI (1922-39). On May 15, 1931, on the fortieth anniversary of Leo's *Rerum Novarum,* Pope Pius XI issued a re-affirmation of Leo's teaching, entitled "On Reconstructing the Social Order." Pius reviews the social progress inspired by Leo's teaching, and the objections made to that teaching by Liberalism and by some Catholics. He re-emphasizes the natural right to private property, coupled with the social responsibility such ownership entails. He stresses the natural dignity of labor and the right of all men, *as men,* to recognition based upon "the respective social functions each performs." He maintains that "free competition . . . clearly cannot direct economic life," nor can "economic dictatorship." "Justice" must pervade economic relations.

To this end the Pope proposes the creation of "syndicates" of workers, including employers, based on Christian principles and sponsored by the state, to control "three kinds of conflict: (1) the struggle for economic supremacy itself; (2) the bitter fight to gain supremacy over the state . . .; (3) the conflict between states themthemselves." Pius insists that industrial peace and progress will best be enhanced if the workers come to share in the ownership of the industrial enterprises they man.

(C) **Mater et Magistra,** Pope John XXIII (1958-63). On May 15, 1961, Pope John XXIII issued an Encyclical on "Christianity and Social Progress" and deliberately re-emphasized once more the teachings of his predecessors. The Church, John says, is called to be the Teacher of mankind, and as such has spoken clearly on economic matters in the *Rerum Novarum* and *Quadragesimo Anno,* both of which he carefully summarizes. He sums up, too, the Pentecostal broadcast of Pope Pius XII, spoken in 1941, which stressed "the indisputable competence" of the Church "to decide whether the bases of a given social system are in accord with the unchangeable order which God our Creator and Redeemer has fixed both in natural law and revelation."

The state, John goes on, must maintain justice, must defend the poor, must establish human liberty, taking care all the while not to absorb the person in the growing complex of social relationships. The

Pope laments the fact that "great masses of workers . . . in not a few nations, and even in whole continents, receive too small a return for their labor," while "in some of these nations . . . the wealth and conspicuous consumption of a few stand out." To the contrary, the Pope says, the "demand of social justice" is that "all classes of citizens will benefit equitably from an increase in national wealth." The level of economic prosperity in a nation is to be assessed from "the distribution of goods according to the norms of justice," a distribution more likely to be achieved if "workers gradually acquire some share in the enterprise" in which they labor.

Not only the distribution, but also the conditions of the production, of goods must conform to the demands of human dignity; employees must be treated as persons, not merely as "hired servants," and must be allowed certain rights of judgment and of choice, guaranteed if need be by unionization and association.

The Pope reaffirms the natural right to private property and its corollary rejection of Socialism, though not of social responsibility. He seconds Pius XI's teaching that productive properties which confer upon their owners "power too great to be left in private hands" should be state-owned. John supplements his predecessors by stressing the needs of agriculture, the desirability of a harmonious development of both the agricultural and the industrial segments of the economy of nations. He argues that taxation must be based upon "the ability to pay," that the state must ensure adequate farm financing and also such price support of agricultural goods as is required by the "general welfare."

Wealthy nations owe assistance to underdeveloped countries by means of financial loans, gifts of foodstuffs, "scientific, technical and financial cooperation" — all in the interests of the recipient, and not as covert protection of the wealthy nation's own ends.

The Pope rejects birth-control as the solution to population growth around the world, and proposes instead the spread of education, international co-operation in solving economic problems, and enunciation of the natural moral order as the proper approach. Stress upon morality is an international need, and the founding of moral order upon the truths of God is indispensable to its vitality — a task not only for the priesthood but also for the laity all over the world, a task to be assumed in the faith and upon the strength of participation in the universal Body of Christ.

The Vocabulary of Communism

THE DOCTRINE OF ELITES

(18) Gaetano, Mosca, **The Ruling Class.** In express rejection of Marx's doctrine of the rulership role of the proletariat, a number of thinkers have elaborated the doctrine of "elites." This is the contention that mankind is in fact always ruled by a relatively small number of leaders, and that shifts in control of political power are merely the "circulation of elites." In some sense this view is as old as the Greeks, especially Plato and Aristotle, but the work of Mosca opened its modern perspectives, though Henri de Saint Simon, the French aristocrat, had proclaimed the so-called law of the two "elites," one in charge of the values a society accepts, the other in charge of its material assets.

Mosca was followed by another Italian thinker, Vilfredo Pareto, whose four volume *The Mind and Society* expanded the path Mosca had blazed. Echoes of Mosca's work are also to be found in books as diverse as James Burnham's *Managerial Revolution* and Milovan Djlas's *The New Class,* both of which stress the emergence of elites to take positions of dominance, Burnham's "managers" in the democratic world and Djilas's "new class" in the Communist world. A good study of Mosca's work is James Meisel's *The Myth of the Ruling Class; Gaetano Mosca and the Elite.*

ANTI-COMMUNISM

The books listed above not only oppose Marxism but also advocate positive positions of their own on the problems with which Marx and Engels wrestled. The reader may be wondering, however, whether there are no titles to be recommended which deliberately meet Communism head-on. There are, of course. The problem is one of choice and discrimination, which a reader who has made some study of his own American institutions, and of the Marxist challenge to them, can best perform for himself. Let him be steeped first in the basic documents of our own heritage; let him also have come to some basic understanding of what Marxism is all about — and then any bookstore, any library, any paperbook stand will have titles more than enough of "anti-Communist" books of all varieties. The following, then, are only typical of anti-Communism, and are, I think, competently and fairly done.

(19) J. Edgar Hoover, **A Study of Communism.** New York, Holt, 1962. The Director of the FBI has written his second study of Communism — the first was entitled *Masters of Deceit* — to compare and

contrast Communism and Democracy. The presentation of the Marxist position is thorough and competent; the challenge which Democracy presents to this totalitarianism is equally trenchantly proposed. The style is concise, the material easily managed. I choose this book as illustrative of a clear, scholarly, and unequivocal confrontation of Communism with Democracy. There are others, but the student can make no mistake in mastering this; and he is not likely to find another book which does the job Mr. Hoover set out to do better than it is done here.

(20) Richard H. Crossman, ed., **The God that Failed.** New York, Harper, 1953. This, and the next, volume present the reaction to some experience within the Communist fold by a group of talented writers who found that the Marxist "god" who held out such enticing prospects of temporal blessing, in fact "failed" to keep his promises, turned out to be, indeed, a monster. Here, then, men sensitive to man, aware of shades and nuances of feeling and value, submit Marxism in practice to searching analysis and evaluation. The writers are Arthur Koestler, Richard Wright, Louis Fischer, and Stephen Spender, with a contribution edited from Andre Gide. The result is a telling and memorable critique of the pretensions of Marxism to saving mankind from its miseries.

(21) Howard Fast, **The Naked God; the Writer and the Communist Party.** New York, Praeger, 1957. All of the passion and power which the reader expects from this American writer come into play here as he dissects his own experience within and withdrawing from the Communist circle. As high as were his hopes, so profound and violent are his disillusionments; and the reader once again finds Communism exposed from within by one who by vocation and aptitude is equipped to seek and to share insights and perspectives which illumine the tyranny of body and mind which Communism imposes.

(22) Arthur Koestler, **Darkness at Noon.** New York, Macmillan, 1941. For some readers the path of truth is best walked by way of fiction, a fiction which reveals much that is non-fictional about life. This novel, and another by the same author entitled *The Yogi and the Commissar*, is a critique of Communism in brutal action, based on documentary evidence on the Stalin regime and the famous Treason Trials. It is Koestler's penetrating insight that when the Marxist sun is seemingly at its zenith, then there is in fact "darkness at noon."

The Vocabulary of Communism

*   *   *   *   *   *

There is no good reason why the list of anti-Marxist books should end here. Already, perhaps, you think of titles which should have been included. Good. Include them in your own list. In a way, if you and I are alertly anti-Communist, and devoutly (and I use the word deliberately) democratic-American, almost all that we read will provide grist for our thinking. It will speak *for* the rights of man, or *against* the usurpation of them.

A